DEEDS
AND MISDEEDS

IN

CLASSICAL ART AND
ANTIQUITIES

by
Arvid Andrén

© Arvid Andrén 1986
Printed in Sweden
ISBN 91 86098 31 4
Goterna, Kungälv 1986

Contents

Preface   4
Plunder for Gain and Glory   5
Plunder for Cultural Benefit   32
Stealing from Dead and Living   40
Imitation and Deception   51
Notes   98
Illustrations   127
Index   148

Preface

This is a freely revised and enlarged version of a recent book of mine, written in Swedish and published in 1983, as Number 19 in the present pocket-book series of Studies in Mediterranean Archaeology. My aim has been to give a concise and readable description, with bibliographical notes for detailed information, of how art and craft products of the ancient Greek and Roman world have been dispersed, disfigured, destroyed, and treated or imitated for fraud, throughout the ages and to such an extent that our knowledge of this marvellous artistic production, in spite of constantly improved methods of research, is and will remain defective, conjectural, disputable, and liable to error.

I am greatly indebted to the late Professor Christian Callmer, and seriously grieved that my thanks can no longer reach him, for his constant help in drawing my attention to, and carrying to my writing desk, several publications relevant to my theme.

I render my sincere thanks to Dr. Sylvia Törnkvist for similar assistance in the final stage of my work.

Mr. Brian Whitney has read the major part of my manuscript, helping me frequently in the difficult choice of *le mot juste;* and for this I thank him most heartily.

Lund, May 1985,

A.A.

Plunder for Gain and Glory

Innumerable works of ancient art, Greek, Etruscan and Roman, have been lost for ever in consequence of plunder and robbery, perpetrated in war and peace, in antiquity as well as in medieval and modern times, by rulers, governors, military commanders, and tribal chieftains, by soldiers and civilians, seldom for love of beauty, but generally in order to get hold of objects which could be turned to practical use, or sold at high prices, or exhibited for display of power and magnificence. The list of recorded activities of this kind can be made very extensive.

Herodotus narrates (VIII, 27 ff.) how Xerxes in 480 B.C., having forced his way through the pass of Thermopylae, sent some of his invading troops to Phocis in order to seize the splendid gold and silver treasures presented to Apollo at Delphi by Croesus, king of Lydia, and how the god himself saved his property by letting thunderbolts and boulders fall upon the Persians. Meanwhile, marching south with the main body of his army, Xerxes arrived at Athens, plundered and burnt the temples of the Acropolis and devastated the deserted city. It is significant that while he let his soldiers mutilate the fine archaic marble statues of the citadel (which were discovered some twenty-three centuries later), he ordered Antenor's bronze statues of Harmodios and Aristogeiton, the men who slew the tyrant Hipparchus in 514 B.C., to be carried off to Susa as war trophies.

Xerxes thus emulated his father Darius, who, in 494 B.C., sacked Miletus and burnt the temple of Apollo Philesios at Didyma, despoiling it of the treasures presented to the shrine by Croesus (Herod. I, 90 f., VI, 19), and carrying away Kanachos' bronze statue of the god to Ecbatana. After Alexander's conquest of Persia, however, the Apollo was restored to the Milesians and the group of Tyrannicides to Athens, where it was placed in the Agora beside the two bronze statues of the heroes made by Kritios and Nesiotes after the retreat of the defeated Persians. Pausanias, travelling during the reigns of Hadrian and Antoninus Pius, saw the two groups and told their history in his invaluable guide book to the marvels of Greece (I, 8, 5). Hadrian himself must have studied them with interest during his stay in Athens in 128 A.D., to judge from the fact that two marble statues found in the Emperor's magnificent villa at Tibur, now Tivoli, and long known as the Roman Gladiators of the Farnese collection, have been identified since 1859, thanks to the German archaeologist Carl Friederichs, as copies of Kritios' and Nesiotes' Tyrannicides, probably made by order of Hadrian himself.

Another example of art treasures carried far away as war trophies is given by Curtius Rufus in his description of Alexander's capture of Tyre in 332 B.C. (*Hist. Alex.*, IV, 3, 22), where the author speaks of a statue of Hercules which the Carthaginians had carried away from Syracuse and set up in the city of their forefathers, together with spoils from other cities. The statue was probably taken in the years when the Carthaginians occupied large quarters of Syracuse, until they were driven off and vanquished by Timoleon, in 341 B.C.

With the Romans coming upon the scene of history, the examples of rich booty taken from defeated enemies increase in number enormously. During the centuries in which the Romans were extending their dominion over the Apennine peninsula and Sicily, over Macedonia and Greece, and over the Hellenistic kingdoms in the East, they established a practice of robbing conquered cities of their art treasures, which were sold by auction or, more often, carried off to Rome, to be displayed in triumphal processions and set up in memory of victors and victories.

This practice was initiated in Etruria, where immigrant Greek artists and imported Greek art wares had been incentive to a rich artistic production, mainly in terracotta, bronze, and gold. Livy relates (V, 22, 3–7) how the Romans after the capture of Veii in 396 B.C. carried off votive offerings and images of deities from the temples of the city, acting, however, *colentium magis quam rapientium modo*, "more like worshippers than robbers", by handling the statue of Juno with ceremonial veneration, asking the goddess if she wished to go to Rome, and seeing her image nod assent to the question. The statue was placed in a new temple on the Aventine, dedicated by the conqueror of Veii, the dictator Marcus Furius Camillus.

Later on, the Romans plundered cities and sanctuaries without ceremony; but they elaborated a formula, named *evocatio*, by which the protective deity of an enemy city was invited to abandon it for equal or ampler cult in Rome.

The acquisition of art treasures by the sword so often practised by the Romans seems to have given them a bad reputation among the Greeks. Metrodorus of Scepsis, a Greek historiographer born about 145 B.C., and known as *Misoromaios*, 'Roman-Hater', is referred to in Pliny's *Naturalis Historia*, XXXIV, 34, as having asserted that the Romans captured the Etruscan city of Volsinii for the sake of its 2000 bronze statues. The assertion has been accepted by some scholars as testimony of the wealth of Volsinii and of the real cause of the Roman aggression, but it is obviously a piece of malicious propaganda. The true history of the fall of Volsinii is to be gathered from a tradition partly retold by many authors and in full detail by the Byzantine historiographer Zonaras (*Epitome*, VIII, 7), describing how the citizens of Volsinii appealed to Rome for aid against their slaves, who had usurped all power in the state, whereupon a Roman army vanquished the slaves, captured and destroyed the strongly fortified city, and resettled its surviving inhabitants in another place. The Romans obviously seized the opportunity of intervention in the strife between the Volsinian citizens and their slaves, or serfs, in order to weaken an inveterate enemy before entering upon what was to be called the First Punic War. A similar policy is not unheard of in later times.

The victorious consul, Marcus Fulvius Flaccus, was granted a triumph *de Volsiniensibus* in 265 B.C., according to the list of Roman triumphs known as *Fasti triumphales.* In Festus' epitome of Verrius Flaccus' work on the significance of words, s.v. *Picta (toga),* the same consul is said to be portrayed in the garb of triumph in the temple of Vertumnus. He evidently followed the example set by Camillus, by bringing the cult statue of the Etruscan god Vertumnus from Volsinii to Rome and erecting a new temple for it on the Aventine.

The conqueror, of course, also carried off a great quantity of bronze statues from the vanquished city, which induced Metrodorus to make his absurd statement about their vast number enticing the Romans to wage a difficult war. Some of these statues were placed in front of the twin temples of Fortuna and Mater Matuta near the Forum Boarium, where the excavations at the church of Sant' Omobono, begun in 1937, brought to light two fragmentary stone bases with marks of the feet of statues and clamps for fastening, and with two Latin inscriptions of identical wording and archaic spelling:

M. FOLVIO Q. F. COSOL D(edet) VOLSINIO CAPTO.

Another bronze statue taken from Volsinii, probably at the time of its capture and destruction, was the Vertumnus set up in the Vicus Tuscus, the ancient Etruscan quarter near the Forum Romanum. The statue is mentioned in Varro's *De lingua Latina* (V, 46) and described in one of Propertius' elegies (IV, 2), in which the god presents himself as "Etruscan originating from Etruria, but feeling no grief for having abandoned the hearths of Volsinii in time of warfare":

> Tuscus ego Tuscis orior, nec poenitet inter
> proelia Volsinios deseruisse focos.

Taken as booty of war from Etruria was probably also the famous Lupa Capitolina, the bronze she-wolf which now stands in the Palazzo dei Conservatori, presenting us with problems not yet definitely solved. If the large fissures in its hind legs are really caused by lightning, as stated by two independent experts, the statue is reasonably identified as the one mentioned by Cicero (*De div.,* I, 20; *Or. in Cat.,* III, 19) as having been hit by a stroke of lightning in 65 B.C., together with two figures representing the suckling twins, Romulus and Remus. And if this is true, there is reason to suppose, with J. Carcopino, that the damaged statue was removed to the *favisae,* the subterranean rooms of the Capitoline hill, in which, according to Gellius, *Noctes Atticae,* II, 10, votive offerings and figures fallen from the roof of the temple of Jupiter were stored. This would also explain how the statue survived the plunders of the Dark Ages, until it reappears in the tenth century, to be used as a symbol of Roman jurisdiction in the place of executions at the Lateran (pp. 22, 31).

During the Second Punic War, and in the wars fought by the Romans in the East, enormous quantities of statues, paintings, gold and silver vessels and other fine products of Greek art and craft were carried off to Rome as booty. The first rich spoils were taken by M. Claudius Marcellus after the capture of Syracuse in 211 and by Q. Fabius Maximus from Tarentum in 209 B.C. Other rich spoils arrived after the victories won by T. Quinctius Flamininus over Philip V of Macedonia in 197 and by L. Cornelius Scipio over Antiochus III of Syria in 189 B.C. Livy, XXXVI, 59, comparing Lucius Scipio's triumph with the one celebrated by his brother Africanus over Hannibal, transcribes a list of booty carried in the former's procession, including 134 statues representing conquered cities, 1231 elephant tusks, 234 gold crowns, 1423 pounds of chased silver vases, 1023 pounds of gold vessels, and hundreds of thousands of gold and silver coins (cf. Pliny, N.H. XXXIII, 148). Rich booty was also won through M. Fulvius Nobilior's subjugation of the Aetolians in 189 and L. Aemilius Paullus' victory over Perseus of Macedonia in 186 B.C., likewise after the conquest and destruction of Corinth by L. Mummius in 146 and L. Licinius Lucullus' victory over Mithridates of Pontus in 71 B.C.; Mummius, says Pliny (N.H. XXXIV, 36), filled Rome with statues, and Lucullus and his brother Marcus also brought a great many to the city.

Stern conservative Romans with Marcus Porcius Cato as spokesman regarded this inflow of costly works of art with disapproval, as a threat against the simple customs and praiseworthy virtues of old. Cato, however, had greater success with his stubborn demand for the destruction of Carthage than with his warnings against the greed for gain and luxury which the sight of those foreign art treasures was generating among his fellow citizens. In a speech delivered in 195 B.C. he complains, according to Livy (XXXIV, 4), of hearing too many praising the beautiful things from Athens and Corinth, and deriding the clay figures of the ancient temples of Rome.

All in vain. The old statues and temple ornaments of painted terracotta from the age of the Etruscan kings and the early Republic were soon outshone by the growing mass of captured Greek masterpieces in painting, sculpture, and chased metal, exhibited in temples, porticos, basilicas, and other public buildings of the city.

The last great spoils of war, during the Republic, were taken by Octavian in Alexandria after his victory over Mark Antony and Cleopatra in the naval battle off Actium in 31 B.C. At that time, however, a growing number of Romans had learnt to covet Greek works of art for their own, especially, according to Pliny (N.H. XXXIII, 148–149), after Attalus III of Pergamum had bequeathed his kingdom to Rome: for on his death in 133 B.C. all scruples disappeared in buying at auctions of the king's treasures, so that this bequest did more damage to Roman morals than Lucius Scipio's lucrative victory over Antiochus of Syria.

The desire thus born eventually developed into a collecting mania that did not hesitate, even in peace, to violate the property of the living, the tombs of the dead, and the sanctuaries of the gods.

Suetonius relates (*Divus Iulius*, 81) how the colonists settled in Capua by Julius Caesar demolished some tombs of great antiquity to make room for country houses, doing their work with greater eagerness because they found a quantity of vases of ancient workmanship together with the remains of the dead. Strabo narrates (VIII, 6, 23) how Caesar's veterans in Corinth destroyed the ancient tombs of the devastated city to get hold of their clay and bronze vases, which were sold as *necrocorinthia*, 'Corinthian death-vessels', in the antiquarian market established in Rome, where they fetched such high prices that Tiberius, according to Suetonius (*Tib.*, 34), proposed a regulation of this commerce.

Roman magistrates on duty in the provinces often used their power for personal enrichment, regarding the provincials as a source of gain. One of these magistrates, Gaius Verres, became notorious by being prosecuted by Cicero, who, in publishing his *Actiones in Verrem*, presented to posterity a detailed list of the crimes committed by the accused. Verres had first made profitable use of his office in Cilicia, where he colluded with the governor of that province, Gnaeus Cornelius Dolabella (who was prosecuted and banished, while Verres saved himself by giving evidence against him). Later on, in the years 73–70 B.C., he was a dreaded governor of Sicilia, where be collected precious works of art by theft and extortion. The evidence collected against him by Cicero was of so damning effect that his counsel Quintus Hortensius abandoned his defence and the accused himself went into exile to Massilia. He was eventually proscribed by Mark Antony, according to Pliny (N.H. XXXIV, 6), because he had refused to give up to him his Corinthian bronzes.

Pliny, writing about the different kinds of bronze used by ancient masters (N.H. XXXIV, 1, 6–8, 48, 82), gives much information – to be taken *cum grano salis* – on the origin, composition and value of the compound called Corinthian. It was said to have been produced by accident when Corinth was captured and burnt, in 146 B.C. There were three varieties of it: a white one, shining almost like silver, because the copper was mainly alloyed with that metal; a yellow one, in which the blending with gold prevailed; and a third, in which the three metals were mixed in equal proportions. The bronze thus composed was valued above silver and almost even above gold, and figures made of it were often so much loved by their owners that they carried them about with them. The orator Hortensius, for instance, never parted from a sphinx which he had got from his client Verres; the ex-consul Gaius Cestius took a statuette with him even on the battle-field; and the emperor Nero brought with him on his journeys an Amazon made by Strongylion, and surnamed *Eucnemon* because of her beautiful legs.

Augustus, too, figures in connection with this famous bronze. Suetonius states (*Aug., 70*) that the Emperor was assailed with satire for being over fond of costly table services and Corinthian bronzes, and that he was even said to have caused some men to be proscribed for the sake of their Corinthian vases. This, however, reeks of slander and is in contrast to Suetonius' own statements (*Aug., 73, 76, 77*) about the Emperor's simple furniture and household goods, his plain food, and his moderate use of wine. And it does not accord with Pliny's information (N.H. XXXIV, 58) that Augustus, warned by a dream, returned Myron's bronze statue of Apollo, which Mark Antony had taken from the Ephesians.

A bronze statue of peculiar attraction was the Apollo Temenites at Syracuse, celebrated for its size and beauty. It is described by Cicero, *Actio Secunda in Verrem,* IV, 53 (119), as *signum pulcherrimum et maximum,* which Verres would have stolen, had he been able to do so. Tiberius did what Verres had to relinquish, by removing the statue to Rome, where it was to be set up, says Suetonius (*Tib., 74*), in the library of the new temple dedicated to the deified Augustus by Tiberius and his mother, Livia Augusta. It was undoubtedly identical with the Apollo Tuscanicus described by Pliny (N.H. XXXIV, 43) as a colossus to be seen just in the same library, measuring 50 feet from its toe, and leaving the spectator in doubt as to whether it was more remarkable for the quality of the bronze or for the beauty of the execution. If Pliny is right in calling the statue Etruscan, there is some reason to suppose that it had been taken as booty by Dionysius I, tyrant of Syracuse, who ravaged the cities and sanctuaries of Magna Graecia and in 385/84 B.C., according to Aelian (*Varia Hist.,* I, 20), raided the coast of Etruria and carried away the treasures of the temples of Apollo and Leucothea at Pyrgi. Tiberius perhaps felt himself to be in the right by bringing the statue back to Italy.

The practice of collecting Greek art through force was pursued on a large scale by two successive emperors. Josephus in his *History of the Jews* (19) and Suetonius in his biography of Caligula (*Gaius,* 22 and 57) narrate how this emperor adorned his palace and parks in Rome with works of art which he had taken from Greek temples, and how he gave orders that

Pheidias' chryselephantine statue of Zeus at Olympia and other famous statues of Greek gods should be brought to Rome, where he intended to substitute their heads with portraits of himself. He was informed by a technician that the removal of the colossal gold-and-ivory statue of Zeus was impossible (as is easily understood from Lucian's description of such statues in the dialogue *Gallus,* 24); but persisting in his intention, he ordered that the statue should be taken to pieces for transport to Rome. Before this work was begun, however, the colossus suddenly emitted such a laugh that the scaffolds erected for the purpose collapsed and the workmen ran away in terror; and this prodigy was taken as an omen foretelling the approaching murder of the emperor.

Nero pursued the same kind of robbery with the same ruthlessness as Caligula. Tacitus relates in his *Annals* (XV, 45; XVI, 23) how Nero sent two emissaries to Greece, authorized to procure statues and paintings for his Domus Aurea. The shrine of Apollo at Delphi, crowded with anathemata presented to the god by states and monarchs in the course of six centuries, saved from the Persians in 480 B.C. and but little damaged by plundering Gauls in 279 B.C., is said by Pausanias (X, 7, 1) to have been deprived of 500 bronze statues by Nero.

After Nero's death, says Pliny (N.H. XXXIV, 84), the most celebrated of the works thus taken were dedicated by Vespasian in the Templum Pacis and his other buildings in Rome. In this Temple of Peace, according to Josephus' *History of the Jewish War* (VII, 5), were also preserved the seven-branched golden candlestick and other treasures which were taken from the Temple of Jerusalem in 70 A.D. and carried in the procession of the triumph celebrated by Vespasian and his two sons, as shown in the reliefs of the Arch of Titus.

The sections of Pliny's encyclopaedic *Naturalis Historia* which deal with art and artists give invaluable insight into the prodigious wealth of Greek masterpieces which could be seen in Rome in the first century A.D., owing to the activities of victorious generals, splendour-loving emperors, and rich collectors.

This insight, however, is limited by the learned author's attitude to art. His commentaries on this subject, based on excerpts gathered in a long life of assiduous reading, and his method of inserting them as complement to the chapters dedicated to the nature and use of gold and silver, copper and bronze, pigments, clay, and marble, reveal him as a man well versed in matters of practical use but very little in aesthetics. As to art, he was evidently interested in high prices, technical skill, likeness to nature, dramatic representations, and anecdotes about artists and art collectors, while relying on authors more competent than himself, mainly Greek, for judgement upon the aesthetic qualities of the works and the importance of the different artists. But he was also ready to believe unbelievable tales told in Rome about certain works set up there.

He was chiefly concerned with works made by the famous artists of what we call the Classical Age of Greece: statuary by Myron, Pheidias, Polykleitos, Skopas, Praxiteles, Leochares, Euphranor, and Lysippos, paintings by Zeuxis, Parrhasios, Aristeides, Nikias, and Apelles. He was, as a rule, less interested in works of later artists and sometimes ascribed to a famous earlier master a work which was probably made by a later artist of the same name. And he naturally left many important paintings and sculptures unmentioned, even of those preserved in Rome. For in Rome, he explains (N.H. XXXVI, 27), the quantity of such works was so great that you could not remember them all, and because of manifold claims of duty and business, you could not find leisure and quiet enough to admire them properly.

His approach to art is well illustrated by his comments upon some works which he has seen, or could have seen, in Rome. He seems to have been ignorant of Pheidias' role in the erection of the marble temples on the Acropolis of Athens after Xerxes' ravages, stating (N.H. XXXVI, 15) that Pheidias was said to have also worked in marble, and that a marble Aphrodite "of surpassing beauty" made by him was in the Porticus Octaviae. Among the works of Polykleitos he records (N.H. XXXIV, 55) a bronze group in the Hall of the emperor Titus, representing two nude boys playing with knucklebones, which was "considered by most spectators to be the most perfect work of art in existence". The genre character of this work suggests, however, that it may have been made by Polykleitos the Younger. Among bronze works ascribed to Praxiteles, our author mentions (N.H. XXXIV, 69) an Aphrodite which rivalled the master's world-famous marble statue of the goddess in Cnidos and was destroyed when the temple of Felicitas was burnt down in the reign of Claudius. He defines (N.H. XXXVI, 26) a nude marble Aphrodite by Skopas, in the temple built by Brutus Callaecus at the Circus Flaminius, as a work "surpassing even the famous Praxitelean goddess, and suited to make any other place renowned". But the most highly esteemed of all the works of Skopas was, he asserts (N.H. XXXVI, 26), a marble group in the temple erected by Gnaeus Domitius at the same circus, showing Poseidon with Thetis and Achilles, Nereids riding on dolphins, sea monsters or sea horses, Tritons and other creatures of the deep, "the whole made by one man's hand, a splendid work, even were it that of a life-time". Among the works of Lysippos he records (N.H. XXXIV, 64) the bronze statues of Alexander and his bodyguard, brought from Macedonia to Rome by Q. Caecilius Metellus (in 148 B.C.), and remarkable because "all the King's friends are portrayed quite lifelike". But he mentions Lysippos' Apoxyomenos (N.H. XXXIV, 62), the bronze statue of an athlete scraping himself, dedicated by Marcus Agrippa in front of his bath, only to tell the anecdote of how Tiberius removed it to his bedroom but put it back because of the outcry of the Roman populace.

Among the paintings of old masters brought to Rome, Pliny seems to have been particularly impressed by Pausias' large picture of a sacrifice of oxen in the Porticus Pompei (N.H. XXXV, 126–127), a work in which the length and bulk of an ox was indicated by showing a front and not a side view of the animal, and by painting it entirely in various tones of black, so that it appeared to stand out in relief from the flat surface. About Apelles' Anadyomene, the picture of Aphrodite emerging from the sea, which was dedicated by Augustus in the temple of Caesar, Pliny declares (N.H. XXXV, 91) that it was surpassed by the Greek verses singing its praise, and that the glory of the artist was increased by the fact that nobody was able to restore the picture, which was so damaged by age and rot that Nero substituted another for it, made by a certain Dorotheos.

Enumerating works of later sculptors, Pliny records (N.H. XXXVI, 33–34) some marbles in Asinius Pollio's famous gallery in Rome, dwelling on a group representing the heroes Amphion and Zetos in the act of tying Dirke on to the horns of a bull, as she had intended doing to their mother Antiope. The group, says Pliny, was a joint work of Apollonios and Tauriskos of Tralles and brought to Rome from Rhodes; and it was remarkable also by being carved (as our author was made to believe) out of a single block! A gigantic marble group representing the Punishment of Dirke was discovered in 1546 in the Thermae of Caracalla and acquired for the Farnese collection, hence it is known as the Toro Farnese. It is now one of the most conspicuous exhibits of the Museo Archeologico Nazionale of Naples and traditionally regarded as a copy (exact or diversified?) of the work described by Pliny.

The collaboration of different sculptors, however, is censured by Pliny (N.H. XXXVI, 37) as being an obstacle to their individual fame, This was the case, says he, with the Laokoon in the palace of Titus, a group which was carved out of a single block of marble by the sculptors Hagesander, Polydoros, and Athanadoros of Rhodes. It is valued by Pliny as a work "superior to all the paintings and bronze statues of the world"; and this eulogy was echoed and amplified by Michelangelo and many others, ever since 1506, when the group reappeared, showing the Trojan priest and his two sons in death-agony from the venomous bites of sea serpents, a vengeance of the Gods for his warning against the Wooden Horse. The group, as already seen by Michelangelo, is constructed of several pieces, which is necessary in all large and composite works in marble. Pliny evidently had a poor knowledge of sculptural technique.

The wars fought by the Romans in Hellenic and Hellenized countries provided them not only with innumerable works of famous Greek artists, but also with countless Greek prisoners of war, who were sold as slaves. Many of these slaves were more skilled and educated than their Roman masters and devoted themselves to different cultural activities in their new home: teaching Greek language and literature, rendering Greek epics and plays into Latin, as did L. Livius Andronicus of Tarentum in the third century B.C., or taking up work as artists and artisans, as did C. Avianius Evander, a Greek sculptor who, according to Porphyrio's commentary to Horace (*Sat.* I, 3, 90 f.), was brought from Athens to Alexandria by Mark Antony and later on to Rome, where he made "many remarkable works". He was one of the numberless Greek artists who, by compulsion or of their own will, gathered in Rome to earn a living from the growing demand for lifelike portraits of prominent Romans and for copies of famous Greek statues. Captured Greek art treasures and captive Greek artists were initial agents in the development of what we call Roman art.

The enormous accumulation in Rome of precious works of Greek art was fatal, however, both for the works themselves and, in the course of time, for the city. The paintings, statues and other costly things destined for Rome often ended on the bottom of the sea, as shown by many wrecked ships and lost shiploads discovered in Mediterranean waters in modern times. And the works which arrived in Rome were probably often damaged through faulty stowage or rough sailing, and some of them also met with harsh treatment in Rome, being 'restored', 'embellished' or 'modernized' by order of despots more interested in the subject-matter of a work of art than in its aesthetical merit and historical importance.

Pliny relates (N.H. XXXIV, 63) that the emperor Nero was so fascinated by a bronze statue of Alexander the Great, made by Lysippos, that he ordered it to be gilded; but as its artistic merit was spoiled by this increase of its monetary value, the gold was removed, and the statue was considered even more valuable, though retaining scars from the removing tools and incisions in which the gold foils had been fastened. The same author records (N.H. XXXV, 93–94) that the emperor Claudius thought it more suitable to have the face of Alexander cut out from two paintings by Apelles in the Forum Augusti and substituted with portraits of Augustus. Pliny also records (N.H. XXXVI, 32) that in the temple of Apollo on the Palatine stood a marble Artemis by Timotheos, the head of which was made by Avianius Evander; whether the original head was lost or damaged or displeasing is left unsaid. Suetonius relates (*Divus Iulius*, 61) that Caesar's horse, remarkable for having hoofs cloven as to look like toes, was immortalized by a bronze statue dedicated before the temple of Venus Genetrix; but if Statius is right in saying (*Silvae*, I, 1) that the equestrian statue of Caesar in the same place was originally a work by Lysippos representing Alexander on Bucephalus, the statue must have suffered substantial changes.

A constant menace to all works of art gathered in Rome was, moreover, the fact that the capital was a densely built city liable to be ravaged by fire.

Pliny informs us of some very famous works which were destroyed when the buildings housing them were burnt down. The old temple of Ceres, dedicated in 493 B.C., and remarkable for its painted terracotta decoration executed by two Greek artists, Damophilos and Gorgasos, was destroyed by fire in 31 B.C., together with Aristeides' painting of Dionysus and Ariadne, which Lucius Mummius had withdrawn from the auction of booty from Corinth and placed in this temple (N.H. XXXV, 24, 99, 154; cfr. Strabo, VIII, 6, 23). The temple of Felicitas was burnt down in the reign of Claudius, and the fire also destroyed Praxiteles' bronze statue of Aphrodite, said to rival his marble Aphrodite in Cnidos (N.H. XXXIV, 69). The most famous of the many marble works of Praxiteles to be seen in Rome (N.H. XXXVI, 22–23) was the Eros of Thespiae, of which we are also informed by Cicero, Strabo, Pausanias and other authors: it was said to be the only reason for visiting Thespiae, was brought to Rome by Caligula, restored to the Thespians by Claudius, and brought back to Rome by Nero, where it stood in the Scholae Octaviae, until it was destroyed by fire in the reign of Titus.

Pliny also relates (N.H. XXXIV, 38), with an undertone of regret, that before the Capitoline temple was burnt down by the soldiers of Vitellius (in 69 A.D.), people of his generation could see, in the cella of Juno, a bronze figure of a bitch licking its wound: a work of such miraculous excellence, and of such deceptive resemblance to nature, that the temple custodians were answerable for its safety with their lives, since no sum of money seemed equal to its value. The figure deserved its praise, to judge from what is probably a remarkably fine marble copy of it in the Museo Barracco in Rome.

An untold number of statues, paintings and works in precious metal must also have been destroyed in the many violent conflagrations which consumed large quarters of Rome, in the reign of Nero in 64, in that of Titus in 80, and in the years 191, 237 and 283 A.D. But in spite of all this, if we believe the fourth-century catalogues of the city's monuments known as *Notitia* and *Curiosum,* Rome in late Imperial times boasted of having 2 colossi, 22 equestrian statues, 80 gold statues, 73 chryselephantine statues, and no less than 3785 bronze statues.

In this multitude was of course included a very great number of statues made in Rome at different times, especially in honour of a long series of emperors. Conspicuous among these statues was Zenodorus' bronze colossus of Nero, of which we are exceptionally well informed. Pliny (N.H. XXXIV, 45–46) describes its clay model, which he admired in the artist's workshop, adding, however, that the finished statue proved "that skill in bronze-founding had perished, since Nero had been ready to lavish gold and silver, and Zenodorus was counted inferior to none of the artists of old in his knowledge of modelling and chasing". The further story of the colossus is told by Suetonius (*Nero*, 31, 1; *Vesp.*, 18), Dio Cassius (66, 15) and other authors. Nero placed it in the vestibule of his Domus Aurea; Vespasian changed it into a statue of the Sun, and Hadrian moved it closer to the Flavian amphitheatre, with the help of twenty-four elephants. Commodus provided it with the attributes of Hercules and replaced its head with a portrait of himself; but after the death of this emperor it was changed back into its earlier shape of the Sun, and as such it stod on its base at the Colosseum as late as 354 A.D., when it is referred to in a calendar mentioning its being crowned with flowers at a spring festival. It was probably destroyed by the barbarians who plundered Rome in the following century, indifferent to the fact that this mass of useful bronze was not of Corinthian quality.

A designed reduction of the accumulated art treasures of Rome was initiated, however, already in 330 A.D., when Constantine the Great transferred the seat of government to Byzantium, renamed the new capital after himself, and adorned it with a host of statues taken from Rome and, preferably, from less distant cities and sanctuaries in Greece. By this traffic, Constantine emulated the plunders perpetrated by earlier Roman emperors, and set an example for his successors.

A more violent reduction of Rome's art treasures set in with the storm of Germanic invasions, when migrating tribes hunting for objects of precious and useful metals turned their gaze on the old capital of the world. In 410 Alaric the Visigoth sacked Rome, and this chock was followed by others. In 452 the threat from Attila the Hun was averted, but three years later the city was raided and plundered by Gaeseric the Vandal, and in 472 by the troops of Ricimer the Goth.

It has been maintained that the barbarians raiding Rome only seized objects of gold and silver, but did not delay their migration by detaching and carrying away statues. This is probably true as regards marble statues, heavy and of no practical use to migrant robbers; but statues of bronze, and many other objects of this metal were certainly taken in great quantities, to be melted and converted into articles useful in war and peace. The Byzantine historiographer Procopius, who was secretary to Justinian's famous general Belisarius during his wars against the Vandals in Africa and the Ostrogoths in Italy, states (*Bellum Vand.*, I, 5) that Gaeseric's ships, freighting the gold and silver treasures taken from the Imperial Palace and the gold-covered bronze tiles torn off from half the roof of the Capitoline temple, all safely arrived at Carthage, except one vessel, which was wrecked with its cargo of bronze statues.

From Procopius (*Bellum Vand.*, II, 9), supplemented by Josephus, Dio Cassius and other authors, we also learn what happened to the seven-branched candlestick and the other sacred gold utensils of the Temple of Jerusalem which were taken by Titus and deposited by Vespasian in his

Temple of Peace. Having been rescued from the fire which destroyed this temple and most of its art treasures in 191, shortly before the death of Commodus, they were carried off to Carthage by Gaeseric in 455. Belisarius took them back from the defeated Vandals in 533 and brought them to Justinian, who returned the candlestick to Jerusalem, as a gift to the churches of the Holy City. Few precious artefacts, if any, are known to have made so many long peregrinations, in Antiquity, as the venerated treasures of the Jews, before they were destroyed by vandals unknown.

In spite of the repeated ravages by fire and foe, Rome in the early sixth century was still a city of magnificent monuments. Theodoric, king of the Ostrogoths, who ruled Italy from Ravenna in the years 489–526, acting in the name of the Byzantine emperor, was so impressed by these monuments that he took measures to protect them. Cassiodorus, the king's chancellor, carried out his master's policy by repairing the ancient buildings of the city and appointing guardians for protection of its statues. The learned man evidently looked at these statues with amazement, as marvellous things that no artist of his own age was able to emulate. In his *Variae,* VII, 15, he describes them rhetorically as "a population almost equal to the one given by Nature to the City: statues of men showing veins marked in the bronze, muscles swelling with effort, sinews strained in moving, so that the different figures look as if they had grown rather than been cast; and statues of horses full of fire, with flaring nostrils, well-knit limbs and ears laid back, as if the animals were longing for the race, although the metal cannot move".

This mute and motionless population, however, was repeatedly reduced by conquests, reconquests and plunders of the City during the years (535–554) when Belisarius and after him Narses were fighting against the Ostrogoths commanded by Vittiges and Totila. Procopius, describing the victories and defeats of this long and devastating war, narrates (*Bellum Goth.,* I, 22) how Hadrian's mausoleum, made into a fortress, was defended by Belisarius' men in 537 by breaking its big marble statues into adequate pieces, which were thrown down upon the heads of the assailing Goths.

Nevertheless, according to the same author (*ibid.,* IV, 21), there were still many fine statues to be seen in Rome as the Gothic war drew towards its end. At the Forum Pacis, belonging to Vespasian's fire-ravaged Temple of Peace, he saw a bronze bull which he held to be a work of Pheidias or Lysippos, since many other statues made by these artists stood in the same place, one of which was inscribed with the name of Pheidias; and among these statues he also records the bronze heifer by Myron. This was a work praised by a host of poets; but Procopius' reason for attributing the bull to one of the two artists mentioned opens the door to doubt as to whether the bronze heifer he saw was really the famous one made by Myron.

The next barbaric plunder of Rome was not perpetrated by barbarians. Paulus Diaconus narrates, in his *Historia Langobardorum,* V, 11–13, how the Byzantine emperor Constans II, visiting Rome in 663, seized the opportunity to carry away a lot of bronze statues and the bronze tiles from the dome of the Pantheon, although this temple was consecrated in 609 as the church of Sancta Maria ad Martyres. But the sacrilege was avenged: for returning home with his booty, the emperor was slain at Syracuse, and the spoils carried off to Alexandria by Saracen pirates.

From now on, the Saracens became a millennial threat to the countries along the northern coasts of the Mediterranean and their shipping. Using Agropoli and Civitavecchia as bases for their raids against Rome, they succeeded in 846 in sacking the basilicas of St. Peter and St. Paul. Two centuries later, Robert Guiscard and his Normans showed as little respect for Christian churches as did the Islamic Saracens, by subjecting Rome in 1084 to ruthless plundering and carnage, and leaving San Clemente, San Lorenzo in Lucina and many other churches in smoking ruins.

And between the catastrophies, and throughout the later Middle Ages, ancient Rome was slowly but incessantly destroyed by her own citizens, who built new houses and churches into and upon the old monuments, ruining their walls in search of building materials, carrying away their columns for indiscriminate use in churches, making lime for mortar from marble sculptures and revetments, and procuring metal from what bronzes could be stolen and from the iron clamps set in lead which secured ashlars of marble or travertine. The Forum Romanum, once the Centre of the World, crowded with temples, basilicas, triumphal arches and statues, was thus gradually tranformed into a field of ruins, where carved and polished marble was hewn into pieces suited for lime-kilns scattered all over the place. In the course of time, this sort of destruction was even more effective than the devastation caused by wars, plunder, conflagrations, lightning, and earthquakes.

And this destruction, of course, was not limited to Rome. Everywhere else ancient walls were razed and ancient sculptures broken into pieces, in the need for metal and building material, or from the widespread belief that pagan images were the haunt of dangerous demons. Owing to this belief, for instance, the large marble groups representing adventures of the Odyssey, signed by the masters of the Laokoon group, and placed in the cave at Sperlonga, were broken into hundreds of fragments, probably by the monks who had established themselves in the Roman villa named Spelunca which was built just outside the cave, and where Tiberius was said to have had a narrow escape from some huge blocks falling from the mouth or ceiling of the cavern.

The statues carried off to Constantinople from Rome and Greece by

Constantine the Great and his successors met with the same deplorable fate as those left behind in the old capital. Byzantine historiographers narrate how remarkable works of Greek art were destroyed through disasters happening to their city.

Giorgios Kedrenos, describing the conflagration which devastated large quarters of the city in 475, states that the fire consumed the palace and art collection of the patrician Lausos, which contained Pheidias' Zeus from Olympia, of ivory, Praxiteles' Aphrodite from Cnidos, of marble, and Lysippos' Kairos, the personified Opportunity, from Sicyon. There is reason to doubt, however, that these works of unrivalled fame could have been acquired for a private collection, and that the colossal chryselephantine statue of Zeus, with its gold and ivory mounted on a wooden form supported by an inner framework of beams, could have been taken to pieces and correctly rebuilt (cf. p. 11). The Aphrodite was probably a marble copy in the size of the original; the Zeus, which is said to be "of ivory", was probably a reduced copy carved in that material.

Niketas Choniates, who was an eyewitness to the terrible bloodshed and devastation perpetrated in Constantinople by the brutal knights of the Fourth Crusade, both before and after their conquest of the city in 1204, narrates how "those barbarians, devoid of all sense of beauty", broke all bronze statues within reach into pieces to obtain metal for coinage. One of the statues thus destroyed was a colossal Athena, which may have been Pheidias' Athena Promachos, originally erected on the Acropolis of Athens. Another was the Seated Hercules by Lysippos, which was brought from Tarentum to the Capitol in Rome during the Second Punic War and from there to Constantinople, where it was placed in the Hippodrome, together with many other bronze statues. Among these were two quadrigae, one of which was said to have been taken from Chios by Theodosius II, the other to have been set up, or only supplied with a Victory on the charioteer's hand, by Constantine the Great. Enrico Dandolo, Doge of Venice, preserved the four horses of the last-mentioned team by adding them to the enormous spoils which he brought home from this expedition. Fifty years later, they were elevated to form a strange adornment to the façade of the glorious church of San Marco.

Of the many bronzes assembled by force to adorn the Hippodrome, only one mutilated monument was left behind by the robbing Crusaders, who probably had no idea of its significance. It is the sad remnant of the memorial dedicated to Apollo in Delphi by the Greek cities whose soldiers conquered the Persians at Plataea in 479 B.C.: the lower part of a bronze pillar formed of three intertwined snakes, the lost heads of which carried a golden tripod, also lost. The identification of the monument is secured through Herodotus' description (IX, 81) and the fact that the names of the victorious cities are engraved on the coils.

The practice of destroying ancient edifices and sculptures in order to obtain stone, lime and metal for new buildings and decorations was pursued everywhere in the countries which once belonged to the vanished Roman Empire, throughout the Middle Ages and for many centuries afterwards; in the East by the Muslim Turks, who had no regard for buildings and idols of heathen and unbelieving peoples; in the West even by antique-loving popes, cardinals, and noblemen of the Renaissance.

Least damage was done to those ancient buildings, sacred or profane, which were converted into churches or mosques, or were maintained and strengthened for reasons of defence and traffic. On the Acropolis of Athens the small temple of Athena Nike and the columns of the Propylaea were incorporated into the walls protecting the entrance to the citadel, and the Parthenon, used as a church from the fifth century on, was transformed into a mosque by the Turks. Other Greek temples are also tolerably well preserved thanks to their having been converted into churches, as were, for instance, the so-called Theseum in Athens, the temple of Athena in Syracuse, still incorporated into the cathedral of the city, the so-called Temple of Concord at Agrigento, and that of Athena at Paestum.

In Rome, the Tiber bridges and the Aurelian Wall were kept in repair, and the Mausoleum of Hadrian was made into a fortress, named Castel Sant' Angelo. Other ancient buildings survived in the shape of churches, as did, for instance, the Curia Senatus, the temple of Antoninus and Faustina, that of Venus and Roma, and many other edifices in the Forum Romanum, the Pantheon in the Campus Martius, and the small temples in the Forum Boarium and the Forum Holitorium. But most ancient buildings in Rome were continually used as quarries. The great architects of the Renaissance and the Baroque studied the rules laid down in Vitruvius' *De Architectura,* made measured drawings of much-admired old monuments, and erected magnificent new ones with stone taken from the ruins which served them as models. The Colosseum, whose southwest side of outer arcades was reduced by earthquakes into a mountain of fallen travertine blocks, furnished building material for the Palazzo Venezia, the Palazzo della Cancelleria, the Palazzo Barberini, and many other constructions. The columned Septizodium, erected by Septimius Severus to screen the substructures of his palace on the south corner of the Palatine, was completely demolished by order of Pope Sixtus V in 1588–1589, to be used for adornment of the new gigantic church of St. Peter.

The same method of procuring building materials continued to be in use for centuries, as is shown, for instance, by what was undertaken on the soil of Veii. During the pontificate of Alexander VII (1655–1667), according to a contemporary account, a Cardinal Chigi, conducting excavations on the steep hill called Piazza d'Armi, which was the citadel of the

Etruscan city, discovered "a beautiful temple with fluted columns of the Ionic order", together with a carved marble frieze and pedimental marble reliefs representing an emperor sacrificing a ram and a sow. All this was bought by a Cardinal Falconieri to be used for the building and adornment of a chapel in the church of San Giovanni de' Fiorentini in Rome. The temple was probably erected for the cult of Juno by the inhabitants of the Roman town which occupied a small part of the vast area of the Etruscan metropolis. During the pontificate of Pius VII (1800–1823) the site of this Roman community was also excavated by antique-hunters, who unearthed a considerable quantity of marbles, conspicuous among which are two colossal portrait heads of Augustus and Tiberius, now in the Vatican, and twelve Ionic columns, which were used to sustain the portico of the papal post office, now Palazzo Wedekind, in the Piazza Colonna, where they are still to be seen.

About the same time the ruins of the many magnificent villas built by Augustus and Tiberius on the island of Capri were utterly destroyed by Norbert Hadrawa, an official of the Austrian embassy at the court of King Ferdinand in Naples. With the King's gracious permission, Hadrawa in 1786–1804 carried out a series of devastating excavations in the Imperial villas, discovering marble sculptures, which were sold to foreign collectors, and despoiling the ruins of their columns and variegated marble floors, which were used for the adornment of churches and palaces in Naples, Portici, and Caserta. Hadrawa pursued his search and sale of antiquities in the unembarrassed manner of the time and described his exploits with naive complacency in a series of letters published in Italian and German.

Owing to the building and destruction which has gone on for three millennia on the soil of Rome, under the rule of Kings, Consuls, Emperors, and Popes, students of the topography and architecture of this ancient capital of the world are confronted with problems probably more numerous and intricate than those offered by any other old city. Problems to be tackled by endless research into an enormous conglomerate of buildings, intact or reduced to ruins and debris, with such help as can be obtained from literary and epigraphical sources, from the fragmentary third-century marble plan known as the Forma Urbis, and from Baldassare Peruzzi, Marten van Heemskerck, G.A. Dosio, A. Lafréry, Étienne Dupérac and many other artists, whose drawings and engravings show us Roman monuments which since their time have been further reduced, or completely destroyed.

While the destruction of ancient buildings was going on, however, in Rome and everywhere else in Italy, many popes, cardinals, noblemen, and other persons of wealth and power, concurring with the great sculptors and painters of the age in their praise of Greek and Roman figurative art, began eagerly to adorn private and public buildings with such pieces of ancient sculpture as were discovered among the ruins. Thanks to this ambition, many important works of Greek, Etruscan and Roman plastic art were saved and eventually formed the nuclei of great and famous collections.

Specimens of ancient sculpture were collected already in the thirteenth century, as booty of war. Giorgio Vasari, in his biographies of eminent painters, sculptors, and architects, tells us about figured Roman sarcophagi and other ancient sculptures in marble which the Pisans had brought home after their victories and set up at the Duomo and in the Campo Santo, where the sculptors Nicola Pisano and Andrea Pisano studied them with great profit to their own art.

The most important collections of antiques, however, were those brought together by the cardinals and popes in Rome. During the pontificate of Martin V (1417–1431), his kinsman Cardinal Prospero Colonna assembled a considerable number of ancient marble sculptures in the family palace on the western slope of the Quirinal. This collection contained the marble group of the Three Graces, now in Siena, and the huge marble torso signed by Apollonios, son of Nestor, of Athens, which stood in the Palazzo Colonna as early as the 1430's, when its inscription was copied by the travelling antiquary Cyriac of Ancona. The sculptures of the Colonna collection, or most of them, were probably discovered either among the ruins of what was presumably Caracalla's gigantic Temple of Serapis, an enormous cornice fragment of which still remains in the garden of the Palazzo Colonna, or in the nearby ruins of the Thermae of Constantine, where many other ancient statues have been found, including the two colossal marble statues of the Dioscuri, which were set up in the Piazza del Quirinale by Pope Sixtus V (1585–1590), and the bronze statues of a Boxer and a Hellenistic Ruler, which are now in the Museo Nazionale delle Terme.

In 1471 Pope Sixtus IV founded the first municipal museum of Rome by assembling in the Palazzo dei Conservatori some ancient bronzes, among which were the Etruscan she-wolf, which for some six centuries or more had kept guard over the place of executions at the Lateran (p. 31), and the highly praised Spinario, the figure of a boy extracting a thorn from his foot, which had perhaps survived unburied; it is first mentioned in Master Gregory's *De mirabilibus urbis Romae,* written in the twelfth century.

When Cardinal Giuliano Della Rovere had been elected Pope in 1503, taking the name of Julius II, he moved his Apollo and other ancient marbles from his palace at San Pietro in Vincoli to the Belvedere of the Vatican. Three years later, this papal collection was enriched by the acquisition of the Laokoon, discovered in 1506 and immediately recognized from Pliny's description of the group (p. 13). Another important acquisition was made during the pontificate of Clement VII (1523–1534), when Apollonios' marble torso passed from the Palazzo Colonna to the Belvedere. With the Apollo Belvedere, the Laokoon, and the Belvedere Torso, the Vatican had acquired what was to remain the élite of its ever-growing collections of antiques and a source of inspiration for admiring sculptors and painters of many countries.

The largest sixteenth-century collection of ancient marbles in Rome was the one assembled by Cardinal Alessando Farnese, Pope Paul III, in the magnificent family palace built by Antonio Sangallo the Younger and Michelangelo. It contained a great number of sculptures discovered in the 1540's in the Thermae of Caracalla, including the gigantic Toro Farnese (p. 13) and the colossal Hercules signed by Glykon of Athens. To these marbles were added those collected by Cardinal Giovanni de' Medici, Pope Leo X, among which were the copies of the Tyrannicides, found in Hadrian's villa at Tivoli (p. 5).

Important collections of ancient marbles were also assembled in Rome by the cardinals Andrea Della Valle, Ippolito d' Este, Domenico Grimani, Girolamo Capodiferro, Rodolfo Pio di Carpi and Federico Cesi, by the banker Bindo Altoviti and by members of the families Galli, Sassi, Maffei, Porcari, Ciampolini and many others. Among the collectors was also the painter Giulio Romano, who bought the Ciampolini collection and sold part of it to Pope Clement VII; later on, says Vasari, he went into the service of Federico Gonzaga, Duke of Mantua, built himself a magnificent house in that city, and adorned it with many antiques acquired in Rome.

This is one example of many others of how the collections of ancient sculptures found in Rome and its neighbourhood were reduced, dispersed or removed from the city. The Grimani collection was transferred to Venice in 1523, where it was enriched, in 1586, with some specimens of ancient sculpture acquired in Greece and Asia Minor by Giovanni Grimani, Patriarch of Aquileia. The Medici collection was reduced when taken over by the Farnese family who, says Vasari, presented Francis I, king of France, with a rare Jupiter and other ancient statues which adorned the villa built for Cardinal Giulio de' Medici at the foot of Monte Mario (now Villa Madama). The antiques of the Della Valle family in the Palazzo Valle-Capranica were incorporated with the Medici collections in Florence which, according to Vasari, were restored and arranged by Donatello and enriched, in the sixteenth century, with a number of ancient bronzes, including the so-called Idolino, found at Pesaro, the famous Chimaera and a Minerva, both found at Arezzo, and the Arringatore, discovered at the Lago di Trasimeno.

In the war between Charles V, Holy Roman Emperor, and Francis I of France, both of whom claimed Italian states as inheritance, the mercenary troops of the former captured Rome in 1527 and subjected it to the abominable plunder and massacre known as the *Sacco di Roma*. The Roman collections of antiques, however, suffered no substantial harm, since the looting soldiers were merely intent on money and jewellery, and the commanders apparently had no interest in carrying away old statues.

With the diffusion of Renaissance ideas, however, rulers and magnates of many realms also had the ambition to enrich their art galleries and curiosity cabinets with specimens of ancient sculpture. These were mostly acquired from dealers and collectors in Rome, through special emissaries or by agents stationed in different European cities. Vasari narrates that Francis I in 1540 sent the painter Primaticcio as his agent to Rome, where he purchased no less than 125 ancient marble sculptures and moulds for making bronze copies for the château of Fontainebleau, of the Laokoon and other famous statues in the Vatican, and of the equestrian statue of Marcus Aurelius, recently moved to the Capitol. In 1649 Philip IV of Spain sent his court painter Velazquez to Rome with a similar commission. Other august collectors of antiques, mostly acquired in Rome, were Charles I of England, Thomas Howard Earl of Arundel, Cardinal Richelieu, Louis XIV, Cardinal Mazarin, and the prince of painters, Peter Paul Rubens. Rembrandt also, according to an inventory of 1656, had a collection of ancient marbles and casts, including several busts of Roman emperors.

Owing to the removal and dispersion of the early Roman collections of antiques in the sixteenth and seventeenth centuries, the appearance of these collections, well arranged in stately palaces or confusedly displayed in yards and gardens, is known to us only through drawings and engravings made by Marten van Heemskerck, Hieronymus Cock and other Renaissance artists, through Johann Fichard's travel book Italia, written in 1536, and particularly through Ulisse Aldrovandi's records of ancient sculptures to be seen about the same period in some hundred houses, palaces, churches and gardens in Rome.

In the seventeenth century, however, several new antique collections were formed in Rome by members of the families Barberini, Borghese, Chigi, Ludovisi, and Pamphili, who housed their treasures in new imposing Baroque palaces and villas. And in the following century the papal collections were greatly enlarged. During the pontificate of Clement XII (1730–1740) the Vatican acquired the collection assembled by Cardinal Alessandro Albani (1692–1779), some 400 pieces of sculpture, which were housed in the Palazzo Nuovo on the Capitol, inaugurated in 1734 as the Museo Capitolino. Other ancient sculptures were acquired from the Villa Mattei on the Caelian and through excavations in Rome and its immediate neighbourhood, in Hadrian's villa and the so-called Villa of M. Brutus at Tivoli, and also at Palestrina, Civitavecchia, Otricoli and many other places within the Papal State. During the pontificates of Clement XIV (1769–1774) and Pius VI (1775–1799), the problem of housing these sculptures was solved by incorporating the Vatican Belvedere into a new magnificent museum complex, named after the two popes, the Museo Pio-Clementino.

Another important museum was created by Cardinal Alessandro Albani, who after the sale of his first collection soon assembled a new and larger one, for which he built the stately Villa Albani outside the Porta Salaria. For the design of this villa, and the arrangement of the antiques, the Cardinal relied on advice given by Winckelmann, whose epoch-making studies of ancient art were largely based on this collection.

But the eighteenth century also saw whole antique collections being removed from Rome, while others were sold piecemeal to different collectors. In 1728, before the first Albani collection was sold to the Vatican, 32 pieces of it were acquired by the German Elector Friedrich August I of Saxony, who also bought the collection assembled by Prince Agostino Chigi, about 160 pieces, which greatly enriched the modest antique gallery at Dresden. The vast Farnese collection of gems and marbles, having been inherited by Charles of Bourbon, son of Elisabetta Farnese and king of Naples since 1734, was transferred to the new museum erected on the height of Capodimonte and later to the sixteenth-century palace which still houses the magnificent collections of the Museo Archeologico Nazionale di Napoli.

Great numbers of ancient sculptures were also acquired by foreign high-ranking visitors to Rome in the eighteenth century. One of them was King Gustaf III of Sweden (p. 59); but of much greater consequence were the visits of the many English noblemen who completed their education by making the Grand Tour to Italy and, once at home again, adorned their country houses with ancient marbles which they had bought in Rome, from owners of antiques in need of money and with the help of local advisers and middlemen, such as the antiquary Francesco de' Ficoroni, the sculptor and restorer Bartolomeo Cavaceppi, and the English agents Matthew Brettingham, Thomas Jenkins, and Gavin Hamilton. Remaining monuments of this educational tourism are the stately neoclassical sculpture galleries of Holkman Hall, Castle Howard, Newby Hall, Brocklesby Park, and many other English country houses.

In the eighteenth century some diplomats and other distinguished foreigners also used their position and rank for antique hunting through excavations undertaken on their own. Gavin Hamilton excavated in Hadrian's villa at Tivoli, at Ostia, Lanuvio, Palestrina, and in other places in Latium. In the years 1787–1796 the Spanish Cardinal Antonio Despuig y Dameto carried out a series of excavations on the site of the Nemus Aricinum, the sanctuary of Diana on the shore of the Lake of Nemi, discovering, among many other things, the marble relief representing a scene of homicide which is now in the Ny Carlsberg Glyptotek in Copenhagen (p. 80).

The epoch-making excavations started during the reign of Charles of Bourbon, King of Sicily and Naples, on the sites of the Campanian cities buried through the eruption of Vesuvius in 79 A.D., at Resina/Herculaneum in 1738, at Civita/Pompeii in 1748, and at Gragnano/Stabiae in 1749, were also begun and long continued to be made with the sole purpose of finding sculptures, paintings, mosaics and other valuable things, which were summarily registered, gathered and jealously guarded in the royal palace at Portici, and disposed of according to royal whim. Lady Mary W. Montagu, who visited Naples about 1740, narrates in her *Letters from France and Italy* that she tried in vain to be admitted to see the antiquities recently discovered at Herculaneum, and that a beautiful bronze statue of a Vestal from the buried city was melted down to provide metal for medaillons commemorating the christening of a royal baby.

Having become a status symbol for rulers to adorn their castles and palaces with costly works of art, it was soon considered quite normal to also acquire such treasures from conquered states and cities, as booty of war, just as the much-admired ancient Romans had done.

A remarkable instance of art treasures gained in this manner was the enormous quantity of paintings, sculptures and other precious things taken by Swedish troops in Prague, in 1648, mostly from the collections of Emperor Rudolph II. These spoils, housed in the old castle of Stockholm, contained few ancient sculptures; but the young Queen Christina, erudite daughter of Gustavus II Adolphus, already in 1644 and again in 1649 sent one of her courtiers to Italy, Greece, and other Mediterranean countries, with instructions to acquire antiquities, and later on she had several loads of ancient sculptures sent to Stockholm from Nuremberg, Augsburg, The Hague, and Amsterdam.

When Queen Christina abdicated and left Sweden, in 1654, she had sent most of her collections ahead of her to Italy but left the ancient sculptures behind, convinced as she probably was that she would be able to procure other and more valuable antiques in Rome. In the Palazzo Riario, where she lived from 1663 until her death in 1689, she thus complemented the collections brought from Sweden with ancient marbles, coins, gems, and cameos, purchased or presented to her, or even discovered in excavations undertaken on her behalf in Rome, with the sanction of Pope Clement IX.

The Roman collections of Queen Christina were inherited by her friend and advisor Cardinal Decio Azzolino and after him by his nephew Marquis Pompeo Azzolino, who sold the books and manuscripts to the

Vatican and the art collections to Prince Livio Odescalchi. These were housed in the Palazzo Odescalchi, in Piazza Santi Apostoli, until they were dispersed in the eighteenth century. The paintings were acquired by Philippe, Duke of Orléans, the ancient marbles by Philip V of Spain for the palace of San Ildefonso, from where they were transferred in 1830 to the Prado museum in Madrid. The coins and cameos were sold to the Vatican in 1794 and three years later ceded to France. They are now in the Bibliothèque Nationale in Paris, except for the famous Gonzaga cameo with the portraits of Ptolemaeus Philadelphus and Arsinoë, which is now one of the most valuable exhibits of the Hermitage in Leningrad, having been presented by Empress Joséphine to Czar Alexander I of Russia.

The ancient sculptures which Queen Christina had left behind in Stockholm, many of them not even unpacked, were mostly destroyed by the fire which in 1697 laid the old castle in ruin. Saved were only a few marble heads kept in the royal library and two marble statues, representing Hercules and a youthful Caracalla, which had been set up on the western façade of the royal palace of Drottningholm some years before the fire.

Like a victorious Roman imperator, Napoleon Bonaparte also wished to glorify his military achievements by taking famous works of art as booty. A result of his campaigns in Italy was that he ordered a multitude of paintings and ancient sculptures to be carried away from Italian cities to Paris. Among the hundreds of antiques thus taken were the bronze horses of San Marco, the Laokoon and the Apollo Belvedere of the Vatican, the Venus, the Spinario and the Dying Gaul of the Capitoline collections, and all the best sculptures of the Villa Albani. These masterpieces were conveyed to the Musée du Louvre, renamed Musée Napoléon, displayed on wagons drawn by camels and teams of horses, in a triumphal procession which is reproduced in contemporary engravings and on a big vase of Sèvres porcelain. After the fall of Napoleon, however, as a result of negotiations successfully conducted by the sculptor Antonio Canova, the stolen antiques were restored to Italy, except those of the Villa Albani, which Cardinal Giuseppe Albani, then owner of the villa, preferred to sell in Paris, rather than pay for their return transport. Some forty pieces of these marbles were acquired by Ludwig, Crown Prince of Bavaria, for his Glyptothek in Munich.

The violent accumulation and no less violent destruction of the finest art treasures of the Greeks, first in Rome and later in Constantinople, are mainly to blame for the fact that our knowledge of the figurative art created by Greek artists must remain defective, being based on scanty literary and epigraphical information, on rare originals and numberless copies of sculptural works, presenting us with endless problems, and on such imitations of Greek pictorial manners and themes as can be traced in

Etruscan, Lucanian and Apulian tomb paintings, in mosaics and wall paintings chiefly from Herculaneum, Pompeii, Stabiae and Rome, and in figured scenes painted on clay vases.

The many catastrophies that befell Rome are also the cause of deplorable lacunae in our knowledge of Etruscan art and art in early Rome. This is particularly true of the huge triple-cella temple of Jupiter, Juno, and Minerva, built on the Capitoline hill in the age of the Tarquins and destroyed by fire in 83 B.C., together with the colossal terracotta statue of the god, modelled by Vulca of Veii, the only Etruscan artist known by name (Pliny, N.H. XXXV, 157). It is also true of the temple of Ceres, dedicated in 493 B.C. and burnt down in 31 B.C., together with its painted terracotta decoration, executed by two Greek artists, Damphilos and Gorgasos (Pliny, N.H. XXXV, 154). Much to deplore is also the loss of the many bronze statues that were taken from Etruscan cities (p. 6) or made in Rome by unknown artists to commemorate remarkable men and women of the past. Pliny gives much information (N.H. XXXIV, 20–31) on the statues of the Kings of Rome, of Attus Navius, the famous augur in the reign of Tarquinius Priscus, of Horatius Cocles, who single-handed held the Sublician bridge against the soldiers of Porsenna, King of Clusium, of the Vestal Taracia Gaia or Fufetia, of M. Furius Camillus, Gaius Maenius and other heroes of Rome's early wars; but there are no copies to visualize the appearance of these works.

A peculiarity of most present-day collections of Greek and Roman sculpture is that they contain a restricted number of Greek originals in marble, a much greater number of Roman copies, reliefs and portraits in marble, and, at most, one or two large-size figures or portrait heads of bronze.

This state of things is of course due to factors of production and destruction. Greece and the islands of the Aegean were rich in marble, which was largely used for production of votive statues, sepulchral reliefs and architectural decoration, the remains of which are now scattered in different European and American museums. Italy had no marble of importance until, toward the end of the Republic, the many sculptors at work in Rome and other cities were supplied with the milk-white and fine-grained marble quarried in the Apuan Alps at Luna (now Carrara). This marble was nearer at hand, easier to work, and less expensive than the precious coarse-grained marble imported from Paros and other islands of the Aegean, and much cheaper of course than any kind of bronze. In consequence, the production of copies, portraits, reliefs etc. carved in Luna marble was such that, in spite of all medieval lime-making, great quantities of sculptures of this kind have been discovered, especially in Rome and its neighbouring cities, and in Hadrian's enormous villa at Tivoli, which the philhellenic emperor made into a veritable museum of famous Greek statues copied in marble.

· Statuary works of bronze, as shown by literary sources (p. 15), were more liable to be totally destroyed by fire and metal-hunting barbarians than sculptures in marble, which were useless to migrant plunderers and of secondary importance for lime-making, in comparison with the great quantities of revetments and column-drums of marble that were used for this purpose. This obviously accounts for the fact that large-size bronzes are rare or lacking in most antique collections of to-day.

The preponderance of marbles over bronzes is apt to deceive many museum visitors into believing that Greek and Roman sculptors mostly, or exclusively, worked in marble. The fact, however, that ancient authors record a great number of famous bronze statues, and, particularly, that Pliny presents much more information on plastic works and workers in bronze than on those in marble, clearly shows that a majority of Greek masters preferred working in Corinthian, Delian, Aeginetan or other varieties of bronze.

There is, moreover, material evidence of an extensive production of bronze statuary, copies as well as originals, owing to Vesuvius' violent eruption in 79 A.D., through which the cities of Herculaneum and Pompeii were withdrawn from human activities for nearly seventeen centuries. Herculaneum was buried deep in enormous avalanches of hot volcanic matter, which in the course of time solidified into hard tufa, preserving, together with many objects of marble and wood, a considerable number of statues and busts in bronze. Pompeii, which was mainly covered with strata of pumic stone and ash falling from the sky, has yielded a lesser number of such bronzes, owing to the fact that surviving citizens were able to retrieve many precious things from the loose ashes. Together, however, the two buried cities have enriched the Museo Archeologico of Naples with an abundance of ancient large-size bronzes that no other museum can emulate. Of particular interest, besides some bronze statues of members of the Imperial family and prominent citizens of Herculaneum, are the works of plastic art which were brought to light in 1750–1765 from a suburban villa west of the city, the owner of which had a library of papyrus scrolls and adorned his house with some ninety statues, busts and herms, conspicuous among which are a number of fine bronze copies of Greek statues and portraits of famous Greeks. Important among the bronzes found in Pompeii are an Apollo Citharoedus and an Ephebus, copied from Greek fifth-century originals, and degraded to serve as lamp-stands by owners less cultivated than the master of the Villa of the Papyri.

From the art historian's point of view there is something of malicious fate in the fact that the treasured copies and originals of two minor towns have been preserved in great numbers through a catastrophe caused by the forces of nature, while thousands of masterpieces of art made for famous cities and sanctuaries have been irretrievably lost through man's destructive greed. It is only through lucky accidents, again, that a restricted number of very fine bronzes by unknown masters have come down to us, recovered by chance from where they lay well hidden under earth and rubble, or submerged in mud and wreckage on the bottom of the sea.

An early recovery of this kind was that of the Chatsworth Head, a masterpiece of early classical Greek art in bronze which, as demonstrated by Einar Gjerstad, belonged to a life-size bronze statue of Apollo found in 1836 in a river bed near Tamassus in Cyprus by some peasants who, from fear of the Turkish authorities, smashed the body and limbs and sold the fragments piecemeal. Remnants left over from more extensive acts of devastation are the head of an early classical statue of a youth found on the Acropolis of Athens in 1866, the head of a late archaic statue of Zeus discovered at Olympia in 1877, and the head of a fourth-century statue of a boxer found in the same sanctuary in 1880. A surprising discovery was made in Rome in 1884, when excavations in an underground chamber of an ancient building near the Palazzo Colonna brought to light two well-preserved bronze statues: the imposing Hellenistic Ruler and the blow-marked seated Boxer, whose left boxing-glove was once thought to bear the signature of Apollonios, son of Nestor, and master of the Belvedere Torso, until the epigraphist Margherita Guarducci proved the 'signature' to be casual scratches. In 1896 the Charioteer was discovered at Delphi, revealing for the first time since antiquity the full fascination of a Greek masterpiece in bronze of the first half of the fifth century B.C. Another surprising discovery of Greek bronzes was made in 1959, when workmen digging in a street in Piraeus brought to light an archaic statue of Apollo, over life-size, together with a late classical statue of Athena, a late classical statue of Artemis, and early Hellenistic statue of the same goddess, and the reproduction of a tragic actor's mask.

Some very fine bronze statues, most of them Greek originals, have been recovered by chance at different points of the Mediterranean, where ships probably destined for Rome or Constantinople had the bad luck to be wrecked, and their loads of bronzes the good luck to be saved from destruction. Particularly important are the archaic Poseidon from Livadhostro Bay, found in 1897; the late classical statue of a young man (Perseus?, Paris?, Ball Player?) and the head of a statue of a philosopher found off Anticythera in the early 1900's; the Eros Enagonios found together with other bronzes off Mahdia in Tunisia in 1908; the late classical Ephebus recovered from the Bay of Marathon in 1925; the imposing early classical statue of Zeus hurling a thunderbolt and the Hellenistic statue of a boy jockey (with fragments of his horse), which were raised from the deep off Cape Artemision in 1926–1928; the statue of a late fourth century Athlete (the Getty Victor), found in the Adriatic off Numana in 1963; the head of a fifth-century statue of a philosopher, found in the Strait of Messina off Porticello in 1969; and the two impressive Warriors of mid-fifth century date, which were discovered off Riace in Calabria in 1972.

Exceptionally, a few ancient bronze statues have survived unburied through many centuries of destruction, spared by the metal-hunters for quite special reasons. The enigmatic Etruscan She-Wolf, having perhaps passed some length of time in the *favisae* of the Capitoline hill (p. 8), reappears in the Middle Ages, according to chronicles of the tenth century, *in iudiciali loco ad Lateranis,* where she probably stood for a long time past, since the place was designated *ad Lupam, quae mater vocabatur Romanorum.* Though having at that time no figures of suckling twins under her teats, she was regarded as an image of the foster-mother of the Founders of Rome and a symbol of Roman justice, and as such was set up on a tower at the Lateran, to keep watch over the place of executions. She remained in this lofty position until she was removed to the Capitol in 1471 (p. 22), and there eventually supplied with her two chubby Renaissance infants.

Another famous bronze that survived unburied is the equestrian statue of Marcus Aurelius, which stood at the Lateran throughout the Middle Ages, owing its preservation to the common belief that the man on horseback represented Constantine the Great, protector of the Christians. The statue was moved to the Capitol in 1538 and placed in the Piazza designed by Michelangelo.

The four bronze horses of San Marco in Venice have also survived unburied and were probably saved from the general destruction of the bronzes of Constantinople in 1204 (p. 19) only because they did not represent heathen gods or heroes, but the noble animals on whose back warriors and rulers have always loved to show off their bravery.

Some years ago, however, the four horses as well as Marcus Aurelius and his horse had to be removed for repair of damage caused by air pollution, the scourge of our time, which threatens to destroy insidiously all things of beauty that have escaped violent destruction in the past.

Plunder for Cultural Benefit

The many fine specimens of ancient sculpture which were discovered in Latium and Tuscany, and copiously collected especially in Rome and Florence, exercised a profound influence on admiring sculptors and painters of the 14th–17th centuries, and thus became a mighty factor in what was considered in Italy as a *rinascimento,* a rebirth of classical art and letters. In the eighteenth century, owing to increased commercial and military enterprises in the Eastern Mediterranean, and particularly, to the sensational discovery of the Campanian cities buried under the ashes of Vesuvius in 79 A.D., the interest of educated people, not only in Italy, but also in England, France, Bavaria and other German states, turned towards Southern Italy, Sicily, Greece, and the Levant, regions where impressive ruins of Greek temples were the chief attraction.

Winckelmann extolled the art of the Greeks in his epoch-making *Geschichte der Kunst des Alterthums,* published in 1764. Goethe extended his Italian journey to Lucania and Sicily, to see the Greek temples at Paestum, Agrigentum, and Segesta. Giambattista Piranesi engraved on some of his largest plates the massive columns and architraves of the so-called Temple of Neptune at Paestum. The monuments of Athens and other Greek sites were measured, drawn, and engraved by artists and architects engaged by the Society of Dilettanti in London, founded in 1732, which published the results of their activity in a long series of volumes, beginning with J. Stuart's and N. Revett's illustration of *The Antiquities of Athens,* I–IV, 1762–1816. And in Italy the French Abbé J.C. de Saint-Non sent out a staff of travelling artists to draw the sites and monuments of Magna Graecia and Sicily, publishing their work in his *Voyage pittoresque ou Description des Royaumes de Naples et de Sicile,* 1781–1786.

The neoclassic enthusiasm burning in prominent persons of different nationalities also inspired them with the idea that it would be a good thing to improve the taste and artistic ability of their fellow-countrymen by acquainting them with the sublime art of the Greeks not only by means of engravings, casts, and antiques acquired in Italy, but also by bringing before their eyes the best specimens of marble sculpture and other antiquities that could be obtained, in one manner or another, from Greece.

These enthusiasts were of course not the first, since the days of plundering Roman and Byzantine generals and rulers, to covet and carry away precious works of art from Greece and the Levant. The Venetians had done so after the capture of Constantinople in 1204 (p. 19); and owing to their commercial and political interests in the East, and their conflicts with the Turks, they had further opportunities of acquiring such treasures. Thus, in 1687, Venetian troops captured the Acropolis of Athens, having reduced the Parthenon to a ruin through a cannon-shot which detonated the gunpowder kept in the temple; whereupon the victorious general, Francesco Morosini, decided to take home as a trophy a group of marble figures from its western pediment, with the result that the ropes used to lower the heavy statues broke and the whole group was left on the rock as a heap of fragments. Morosini had better luck with a colossal marble lion taken from Piraeus, which was placed before the entrance to the arsenal of Venice and much later revealed as a monument of particular interest, because of two runic inscriptions made on it by Nordic mercenaries in the service of the Byzantine emperor, in memory of their having suppressed a revolt in Athens, in 1040.

The real hunt for antiquities in Greece, however, started only in the last two decades of the eighteenth century, soon taking the character of a competition between prominent and enthusiastic Englishmen, Frenchmen, and Germans, assisted by agents and collaborators of different professions and nationalities. It is a story of rivalry and intrigue among the hunters, of pressure and bribery exerted upon Turkish authorities, who were always willing to take good sums of money for allowing infidels to carry away old rubbish left behind by heathens.

Edward A. Dodwell, a travelling Englishman, thus brought together a fine collection of marble sculptures, bronzes, vases and other antiquities, excavated at Athens, Eleusis, Corinth, Mycenae and other Greek sites; after his death, this collection was acquired by Ludwig, Crown Prince of Bavaria, whose agents were eagerly watching all sales of newly discovered antiques. L-F-S. Fauvel, a French painter living in Athens, was also a shrewd collector and helped the Comte de Choiseul-Gouffier, French ambassador to the Sublime Porte, to assemble a rich collection of antiques, including a slab of the frieze and two metopes which had fallen down from the Parthenon; the slab and one of the metopes are now in the Musée du Louvre, the second metope in the British Museum.

More successful than Choiseul-Gouffier was, however, his British colleague, Lord Elgin, appointed ambassador to the Porte in 1798. Favoured by British victories over Napoleon's forces in Egypt, and bribing generously, he succeeded in getting a *firman* (or decree) from the Porte, permitting him in very ambiguous phrasing to excavate on the Acropolis, to copy in drawing and plaster the 'pictures' remaining there, and also to take away some pieces of stone with inscriptions and figures. Armed with this *firman,* Lord Elgin's assistants, the Reverend Philip Hunt and the Italian painter Giovanni Battista Lusieri, began in 1801 the notorious plunder of the Acropolis, discovering some metopes and parts of the frieze fallen from the Parthenon, excavating some mutilated statues tumbled down from its western pediment by the explosion of 1687, depriving the temple of the greater part of the metopes, frieze slabs, and pedimental figures still remaining in place, and removing four frieze slabs of the temple of Athena Nike from where they were built into the fortifications of the citadel. Later, Lusieri also removed one of the Caryatids of the Erechtheum, ordering a brick pillar to be built as a substitute.

The despatch of the mass of heavy marbles thus assembled, and of other antiquities collected by Lord Elgin, was a very difficult task which mainly fell to the lot of the faithful Lusieri, since his employer, while homeward bound, was taken prisoner of war in France. Fauvel was continually plotting to seize the many cases in which the marbles awaited transport, but at long last the major part of them could be loaded on different ships which by divergent routes, to evade French intervention, brought them safely to England; one vessel, however, was wrecked at the island of Cerigo, but its load of cases was rescued from the sea and eventually picked up by a warship sent by Lord Nelson. Only ten years later could the rest of the cases be shipped over to England, and only in 1816, after long and heated discussions, were the 'Elgin Marbles' acquired for the Nation and placed in the British Museum. The sum paid for them was vastly inferior to that which Elgin had expended from his own purse to secure these invaluable art treasures for his country and his compatriots.

Ten years after Lord Elgin's plunder of the Acropolis, some other enthusiasts, acting much in his manner and spirit, set out to see what could be done with the remains of two other Greek temples. Charles Robert Cockerell, a young student of architecture, and the German baron C. Haller von Hallerstein, together with another Englishman and another German, in 1811 crossed from Piraeus to Aegina in order to study the temple then known as that of Jupiter Panhellenius, much later identified as one dedicated to a local goddess named Aphaea. The party made drawings of its columns and entablature, and digging around its stylobate discovered the major part of the marble statues which once adorned its pediments. Cockerell bought the marbles cheaply from the locals, conveyed them at night to Athens, and soon after sent them to the island of Zante, where they were to be sold at a public auction. Somewhat later, however, a British warship took them for greater safety to Malta, and a representative of the British Museum was sent to the island, authorized to acquire them at any cost – not knowing that the auction was held as arranged at Zante, where the marbles were knocked down to the Bavarian Crown Prince Ludwig, for his Glyptothek in Munich.

In 1812, Cockerell and the other participants in the expedition to Aegina, now accompanied by the Dane P.O. Brøndsted, the German G. Gropius, and the Estonian Baron O.M. von Stackelberg, went down to the remote temple of Apollo at Bassae near Phigaleia in Arcadia, where they excavated the fallen slabs of a fine and well-preserved marble frieze, representing battles of Greeks and Amazons, of Lapiths and Centaurs. In spite of continuous trouble with the Pasha of Morea, with rebellious porters and menacing Turkish troops, during three months of digging and a long and difficult transport of the marbles to the coast, the excavators succeeded in bringing the frieze to Zante, where it was acquired for the British Museum.

During the years of the Napoleonic wars, and of the more or less warlike enterprises intended to secure for a certain country whole sets of architectural sculpture, there were also many amateurs who assembled smaller collections of antiques, buying from treasure-hunters or excavating themselves at different places in Greece and the Levant. In the course of time, their collections were partly dispersed or lost, partly bought by or presented to the British Museum, where some of the items thus acquired are still designated with the names of their former owners. This is the case, for instance, with a marble Apollo from Anaphe and a marble copy of the figured shield of Pheidias' Athena Parthenos, both obtained from the collection of Lord Strangford, British ambassador to the Sublime Porte in 1820–1824.

In those years of plunder the Musée du Louvre, compared with the British Museum and the Munich Glyptothek, only got a small share of spoils, except for the temporary sojourn of the art treasures taken by Napoleon in Italy. Choiseul-Gouffier's aim to forestall Lord Elgin in taking down the sculptures of the Parthenon failed, as did Fauvel's plan to seize them when packed for despatch to England; and when, in 1803, a French frigate picked up Choiseul-Gouffier's own collection, including a metope from the Parthenon, she was captured by one of Nelson's warships, and the collection was sent to London.

Some years later, however, French enterprises had better luck. In 1820, a French warship, after some skirmish, succeeded in taking on board from the island of Melos a marble statue of Aphrodite recently found there by a peasant. It arrived safely in Paris and has ever since been regarded as one of the jewels of the Louvre, the famous Vénus de Milo. Another enrichment of the antique collection of the Louvre was the result of excavations undertaken in 1829 at Olympia by a French expedition to the Peloponnesus, the members of which discovered parts of the metopes of the temple of Zeus, with reliefs representing the exploits of Hercules.

After the War of Independence successfully fought by the Greeks against the Turks, English hunters of antiquities turned their gaze to ancient Asia Minor, where ruined buildings and corruptible officials of the Sublime Porte promised abundant harvests of Greek sculpture. Charles Fellows, a rich amateur archaeologist, travelling in Lycia in the

1840's, enriched the British Museum with the statues and figured friezes taken from two sepulchral buildings known as the Harpy Tomb and the Nereid Monument at Xanthus. Stratford Canning, British ambassador in Constantinople, was permitted in 1846 to remove from the walls of an old fortress twelve relief slabs of marble, which belonged to the Mausoleum erected at Halicarnassus for king Mausolus of Caria and his consort Artemisia about the middle of the fourth century B.C. It is described by Pliny (N.H. XXXVI, 30–31) as one of the seven wonders of the world, decorated by four famous sculptors, Bryaxis, Leochares, Skopas, and Timotheos. Ten years after Canning's achievement, the archaeologist Charles T. Newton, then British consul in Rhodes, was able to excavate the foundations of the Mausoleum, the major part of the colossal statues of Mausolus and Artemisia, and four relief slabs, representing, like those removed from the fortress walls, Greeks and Amazons in combat. After this, the British Museum housed the lion's share of the sculptured marble decoration of some of the most famous buildings of the Greek world: the temple of Athena Parthenos at Athens, that of Apollo at Bassae, and the Mausoleum at Halicarnassus.

Henceforth, the Ottoman Empire remained open to the activities of foreign amateur and professional archaeologists who, backed by powerful States, were permitted to excavate cities and cemeteries of the past and remove the discovered objects to the museums of their own countries. The excavations undertaken by Charles T. Newton at Cnidos, Miletus, and Ephesus in the 1850's–1860's, by Heinrich Schliemann at Troy in the 1870's, and by Alexander Conze and other German archaeologists at Pergamum, Magnesia ad Maeandrum, Priene, and Miletus, from 1878 onwards, meant the beginning of a new era of archaeological research, the attainment of a wealth of new knowledge, and the enrichment of the British Museum and the Berlin museums with magnificent works of Greek art, such as the beautiful marble statue known as Demeter of Cnidos in the former museum and the stupendous marble frieze of gods fighting giants from the Pergamene altar of Zeus, which was reconstructed in the Pergamon Museum in Berlin.

In those years of epoch-making arhaeological progress, Cyprus saw the activities of an antiquity hunter of the old school, Luigi Palma di Cesnola. He was an Italian immigrant to the USA, who in reward for his services in the American Civil War was appointed United States consul to the island. In this capacity he was able to unearth, in the years 1865–1876, with or without Turkish permission, no less than 35,575 Cypriot antiquities of gold, bronze, stone, and terracotta, which he succeeded in shipping off just before the Turks forbade export. His collection was purchased by the newly founded Metropolitan Museum of Art in New York, in competition with the Louvre and the Hermitage of St. Petersburg, and the treasure hunter himself was appointed Director of the new museum.

In the West, on the other hand, Greece after the War of Independence, Italy after its Resurgence as a Nation, and many other countries proud of their past, sooner or later began instituting laws intended to protect sites and monuments of artistic or archaeological importance, regulate excavations, and control sale and export of antiquities and art objects. This, however, was a slow and complicated process, and high-ranking foreigners were often permitted to excavate and export antiquities. Thus, in 1885–1889, the British Ambassador Sir John Savile Lumley and a Signor L. Boccanera, digging on the site of Diana's sanctuary at the Lake of Nemi, unearthed many clay antefixes and thousands of ex-votos of bronze and terracotta, which are now partly in the Museum and Art Gallery of Nottingham, partly in the Museum of Fine Art in Boston.

Nowadays, however, Italy, Greece, Turkey, and other countries rich in remains of a Greek and Roman past, permit foreign cultural institutions and archaeological expeditions to undertake excavations within their boundaries and publish the results of the undertaking, all at the excavators' own expense; but all objects found must remain in the country from whose earth or water they have been brought to light. Exceptions to this rule are rare; one instance was the agreement allowing considerable quantities of vases, terracotta figures, stone sculptures etc., excavated by the Swedish Cyprus Expedition, to be made over to the Museum of Mediterranean and Near Eastern Antiquities in Stockholm.

In our days, moreover, the practice of taking great quantities of precious works of art from vanquished enemies or unreliable allies is no longer considered glorious. After the Vienna Congress in 1814, France had to restore the art treasures taken from Italy by the fallen Emperor. The Russians restored the ancient sculptures which Soviet troops had carried away from Berlin during the last days of the Second World War. In Italy, Signor Rodolfo Siviero, head of the Commission for the Recovery of Works of Art, had great success in the difficult task of tracking down and bringing back numerous works that had been illegally sold or carried away by force to Germany during the years of the Rome-Berlin Axis.

The removal of ancient sculptures and other antiquities from Italy, Greece, and the Levant, carried out by powerful and cunning foreigners in the eighteenth and nineteenth centuries, has resulted in a lasting resentment among culturally or nationalistically motivated citizens of the plundered countries. This is especially manifest in the case of the Elgin Marbles.

Ever since the establishment of Greece as an independent State, Greek governments have repeatedly demanded the restitution of these sculptures, taken from the Acropolis of Athens through arbitrary and unwarranted use of a permit obtained from bribed Turkish authorities. Hitherto, the demands have been constantly refused by the British government; in 1965, for example, with the comment by the prime minister Mr. Harold Wilson that "there is no automatic principle which we should follow that there should be a redeployment of works of art in accordance with their origin". In spite of this, a new demand was made some years ago by the film star Melina Mercouri, in her capacity of Minister of Education, but she was no more successful than her male predecessors.

There are, in fact, many aspects of this long-discussed question. Certainly, Lord Elgin's looting of the Acropolis shocked many of his contemporaries. Lord Byron attacked him vehemently in a poem entitled *The Curse of Minerva,* and in *Childe Harold's Pilgrimage* he wrote of "the modern Pict's ignoble boast, to rive what Goth and Turk and Time hath spared". And when, in 1816, the acquisition of the Marbles for the Nation was debated in Parliament, there was even an M.P. who proposed that they should only be held in trust till they were claimed by the country from which they had been improperly taken. The proposal was not taken seriously.

Lord Elgin, as well as Choiseul-Gouffier, Cockerell, Fellows, and many other contemporary and later amateurs and students of Classical Art, undeniably committed serious plunders facilitated by bribery and deception. But in judging their actions, we ought to consider for what reason and under what conditions they were done, and also what good has come out of them.

Lord Elgin and his confrères and rivals in the game of acquiring antiques were certainly animated by an ardent desire to benefit the cultural development of their countries by their actions, and they accomplished these actions risking health and life in an environment where bribery and deceit were necessary to attain their object, and where they were often dismayed by the sight of how the Turks neglected and destroyed venerable monuments of a glorious past. In fact, Lord Elgin and the other plunderers are worthy of praise for having saved for posterity invaluable art treasures which most probably would have been deplorably reduced or totally destroyed, had they remained any longer in their original surroundings.

For the Turks of the Ottoman Empire regarded the old buildings of the heathens with indifferent disdain and, far from sparing them, they steadily furthered their decay and ruin, using them for different functions, incorporating them into fortifications, or demolishing them to obtain building materials. Engraved drawings by the Jesuit Babin in the 1670's, by Stuart, Dodwell and other travelling artists and explorers, give us invaluable information of the appearance of Athens during the last centuries of the Turkish domination, showing that the Parthenon before the explosion of 1687 was La grande mosquée, with enclosing walls between the columns and a minaret close by; that a smaller mosque stood inside the ruin after 1687; and that the Propylaea and the temple of Athena Nike were incorporated into the mighty fortification walls of the citadel. The fallen marble columns of the gigantic temple of Zeus, the Olympieum, were converted into stone and lime for Turkish buildings, and so were the blocks and column drums of the small Ionic temple at the river Ilissus, which was demolished in 1778. Great damage was also done to the Erechtheum during the War of Independence, when the Turks fired on and recaptured the Acropolis in 1827.

Comparison made several years ago between early casts of the Parthenon frieze and the frieze slabs remaining on the temple has shown, moreover, that the latter have suffered badly from weathering since the time when the casts were taken. And today, air pollution in Athens has reached such degrees that the ancient marble buildings of the city are in danger of being destroyed by corrosion. The remaining Caryatids of the Erechtheum, therefore, have been removed to the Acropolis Museum and substituted with copies. The marbles carried away by Lord Elgin would no doubt have been deplorably disfigured, had they been left until our day in their original positions. And if they one day returned to Athens, it would be unthinkable to replace them on to the Parthenon.

A serious thing to be considered, finally, is the possibility, or probability, that if the Elgin Marbles were restored to Athens, this would give rise to innumerable further appeals, asking for the return of the sculptures from Bassae, Halicarnassus, Xanthus, Cnidos, and Ephesus, of the Aegina pediments, of the Venus de Milo, and of many hundreds of other works of ancient art that were carried into safety by questionable means in the past. Demands that would result in countless speeches in parliaments, pronouncements of governments, diplomatic notes, discussions in mass media and – it is to be hoped – nothing more. For a return to their countries of origin of numberless works of ancient art now widely scattered might prove as fatal as the gathering of art treasures in ancient Rome and Constantinople.

Stealing from Dead and Living

Throughout the ages, while the high and mighty openly carried off rich harvests of precious works of art, humbler people everywhere were secretly searching the earth for buried treasures. Such treasures were mostly to be found in graves, owing to the primaeval and widely spread practice, rooted in religion, of burying with the dead various objects that were thought to be dear and useful to them in the hereafter.

Everywhere in Mediterranean countries, burial places were regarded with awe and veneration, and rituals were performed at the tombs by surviving relatives. But awe and veneration ceased in front of tombs of foreign and long-forgotten dead, especially if the size and outward form of the sepulchres raised greedy hopes of finding rich grave-gifts in them.

An early instance of ancient tombs having been violated in a singularly brutal manner is offered by the Etruscan city of Populonia. This city was built, as accurately stated by Strabo (V, 223), "upon a high promontory that descends sharply into the sea and forms a peninsula". The wealth of the city derived from its iron works. Among the cities of Etruria recorded by Livy (XXVIII, 45) as having contributed to the equipment of Scipio's fleet in 205 B.C., Populonia figures as deliverer of iron; and Strabo, visiting the place in the days of Augustus, still saw people working the iron that was brought over from Elba.

The most lasting product of this iron industry was formerly seen below the promontory, where some twenty-five acres were covered by enormous heaps of black iron slag that had been tipped out from the furnaces in the course of centuries, reaching a height of about twenty-three feet. During World War I, however, the Italians discovered that this slag still contained much badly needed iron, and so began carrying it away to modern iron factories. This work went on for about four decades and yielded not only great quantities of new iron, but also resulted in the recovery of the archaic necropolis of Populonia, which had been plundered by the foundry workers and hidden under gathering masses of slag. The architecture of the tombs, which are built of stone in the form of either circular tumuli or square houses, and the precious grave-gifts which in some tombs had escaped the robbers, show that the necropolis belonged to a rich Etruscan aristocracy of the seventh, the sixth, and the early fifth century B.C.

By desecrating the ancient necropolis of Populonia, the iron workers unintentionally furthered our knowledge of Etruscan art and funerary architecture in the archaic period. A different and more destructive kind of grave-robbing was pursued by the Roman veterans at Capua and Corinth (p. 9), who brought about the disappearance both of the graves and, indirectly, of the grave-gifts, by way of the antique market in Rome. And even more damage has been done by the countless unknown grave-robbers, pagans, christians, and muslims, who everywhere, and for centuries, have done their job so effectively that finding an ancient tomb absolutely intact is a rare archaeological event.

Grave-robbers of all times and countries have usually done their pilfering with no regard as to the remains of the interred bodies, nor to any grave-gifts other than those made of metal that could be converted into money; and the buyers of their goods acquired them for long mostly for their metal value.

There are, however, a few quite early instances of graves and grave-gifts having been looked upon with an interest surpassing that of common greed.

Theodoric the Goth, according to Cassiodorus (*Variae*, IV, 34), permitted objects of metal to be taken from ancient graves, provided that the remains of the dead were left intact, for in his opinion it wasn't cupidity appropriating things that no owner could complain of having lost; or in Cassiodorus' Latin: *non est enim cupiditas eripere quae nullus se dominus gemiscat amisisse.*

Two reports of early discoveries of ancient grave-gifts in Orvieto are especially worth quoting. When digging for the construction of the famous well known as the Pozzo di San Patrizio, situated above the eastern precipice of the isolated tufa plateau on which the city is built, workmen found some objects which attracted the curiosity of a municipal clerk, who described the discovery in the records of 1532, still preserved in the city archives. There were found, *inferius a tufo per maximum spacium*, a number of clay pots, whole and broken, two surgical instruments of iron, and *quaedam navicula parva raminis;* and in a cavity two hundred feet down, there was a clay vase containing many human bones. The objects evidently belonged to graves which, considering the great depth at which the discovery was made, may be supposed to have been tunnelled into the rock from its steep outside; and if the object described as "a little boat of bronze" was a fibula of the type called *a navicella*, 'boat-fibula', or possibly a boat-shaped votive lamp (?) like those found in prehistoric sites of Sardinia, and also at Vetulonia, Populonia, and Graviscae, these Orvietan burials may be ascribed to a remote period of Etruscan civilisation.

Later in the sixteenth century, a learned Orvietan priest named Monaldo Monaldeschi, describing what he pretended to be the history of his native city, in a work entitled *Commentarii Historici della Città d'Orvieto*,

Venetia 1584, attests that "many tombs of the Pagans and the Greeks have been found both within and outside the city, with vases of black clay, formed in various ways, and different figures and other beautiful things, many of which are in the city archives and in the study of Signor Monaldo Monaldeschi della Cervara". The grave-gifts described by the author as originating from "the Pagans and the Greeks" (i.e. from the Romans and the Byzantines) seem to have been mainly composed of the black and multiform Etruscan pottery called bucchero, and were probably mostly found in the Etruscan cemeteries which surrounded the city plateau, with chamber tombs built of stone blocks and aligned along regular sepulchral streets, like row houses of the dead. The information on graves and grave-gifts given by the observant clerk and the learned priest is note-worthy as showing how some enlightened persons already in the sixteenth century took an exceptional interest even in antiquities less remarkable than statues in bronze and marble.

Noteworthy for a similar interest is also a passage in the fifth volume of Père Labat's *Voyages d'Espagne et d'Italie,* printed in 1731, describing how the construction of the aqueduct passing through the Etruscan necro-polis of Tarquinii had brought about the disclosure of many painted tombs, containing human bones of unusual size, corroded iron weapons, and great quantities of clay vases, mostly black-varnished with red orna-ments. Father Labat picked up many such vases for himself and friends but was surprised in finding that the tombs did not contain any objects of gold and silver: "perhaps because the country was short of these metals, or because such precious things were not buried with the dead, or if they were, may have been stolen by the builders of the aqueduct". The first and the second of his guesses are of course wrong, the third may be right; but probably most tombs of this vast necropolis, once studded with tumuli which gave rise to its name of Monterozzi, had been robbed of their metal treasures long before the eighteenth century.

In the course of that century, however, grave-robbers were greatly stimu-lated by learning that such painted clay vases as were formerly left behind in the tombs now were becoming things of value, thanks to the fact that distinguished collectors began turning their eyes towards this kind of antiquities. One of these collectors was the German painter Anton Raphael Mengs who, visiting Naples in 1759–60, acquired about 300 painted vases found in the region of Nola, all of which were sold before his death in 1779 and are now in the Vatican, the Louvre, and other museums. Another prominent collector was Sir William Hamilton, Brit-ish envoy to the King of The Two Sicilies in Naples from 1764 to 1800. He is chiefly remembered as the lovely Lady Emma's tolerant husband, whose only passion was collecting antiquities. He assembled two successive collections, containing marbles, partly originating from Norbert Hadrawa's destructive excavations on the island of Capri (p. 21), thousands of ancient coins, and many hundreds of painted vases, classified as 'Nolan' (Attic red-figure), 'Sicilian' (Attic black-figure), and 'Primitive' (chiefly Corinthian). Owing to financial difficulties, he had to sell his first collection to the British Museum, in 1772; and when for the same reason, twenty years later, his second collection was sent to England to be sold, a third of it was lost at sea, and the rest was bought by the collector Thomas Hope.

In 1828, on the site of the Etruscan city of Vulci, the ground suddenly gave way beneath a ploughing team of oxen and disclosed a grave with two broken clay vases. Prompted by this happening, Lucien Bonaparte, Prince of Canino, and soon other landowners in the district, began digging for buried treasures that could be collected for pleasure, or sold for profit. Every year between harvest and sowing, for many decades running, the Etruscan cemeteries of Vulci were thus robbed of their grave-gifts by ignorant and unskilled labourers in the employ of the landowners. George Dennis, who visited Vulci in the 1840's, saw how the excavations were done and described it in his classic work, *The Cities and Cemeteries of Etruria* (1848; 3rd ed. 1883). The labourers, watched by an overseer with a gun, to keep them from stealing, gathered, by order, all objects of metal and all painted ceramics found in a grave, but left behind unpainted vases, or crushed them under their feet, whereupon the grave was re-filled with earth, so that no surface should be lost for sowing. In 1856, says Dennis, more than 15,000 tombs at Vulci had been opened and rifled in this manner.

In much the same manner, or only a little more carefully, landowners and collectors plundered the cemeteries of Caere and other Etruscan cities of precious grave-gifts, consisting of gold fibulae and other pieces of jewellery, silver vessels, bronze implements, and great quantities of painted clay vases, black-figured and red-figured, which were commonly called Etruscan, although their Greek origin had been established already in 1806 by Luigi Lanzi. Most of these treasures passed into the hands of Lucien Bonaparte and his widow, the brothers Campanari, the Marchese Campana, and many other collectors, and from them, sooner or later, into the Vatican, the Louvre, the British Museum, and other public collections.

Other grave treasures passed into a darkness almost as perpetual as that of the tomb from which they were taken. When, in 1857, the Florentine archaeologist Alessandro François had discovered one of the most important tombs ever found at Vulci, the owner of the ground upon which the discovery was made, the Prince Alessandro Torlonia, had the paintings of the central tomb chamber detached from the walls and removed to his museum in Rome, which was, and long remained, inaccessible, except by special permit, rarely granted. These higly interesting paintings, representing scenes derived from Greek and Etruscan tradition, were thus hidden away for nearly ninety years, until in 1946 they were transferred to the Villa Albani, acquired by Alessandro Torlonia in 1866.

The greatest Roman collector of the nineteenth century, however, was the Marchese already mentioned, Gian Pietro Campana. In addition to a magnificent picture gallery, he owned an enormous collection of antiquities, brought together by digging treasure hunters at work on the sites of Caere, Veii, and Falerii, in the 1830's–1850's. At last he went bankrupt, and his collections were dispersed, the major part of his antiquities being acquired by the Musée du Louvre, in 1861. Some of the monuments he discovered, however, and the antiquities he collected, are still named after him: the early painted tomb at Veii known as the Tomba Campana, the tumulus called the Grotta Campana at Cerveteri, a series of painted terracotta slabs with figure scenes in archaic style, which were disinterred at Cerveteri before 1853, and the numerous Roman terracotta plaques known as Campana reliefs.

A well-known and highly respected figure among Roman antiquaries in the latter half of the nineteenth century was the goldsmith, collector and antique dealer Augusto Castellani. He specialized in making perfect imitations of ancient jewellery – 526 of his pieces are safely kept, fortunately, in the Museo di Villa Giulia. But he was also an assiduous buyer of various antiquities discovered by tomb-robbers in different parts of Italy: select specimens of Greek, Etruscan and Roman jewellery, bronze implements, terracotta figurines, gems, coins, and, principally, painted Greek vases, Corinthian, Attic, and South Italian. He used to select the best vases for his own collection, sell the next best to foreign museums, and keep a lot of mingled sherds in a basket, to be distributed as extras to good customers. A considerable part of his vases and bronzes belong, since 1866, to the collections of the Palazzo dei Conservatori. He died in 1914, leaving a very great and diversified collection, which was acquired by the Italian state for the Museo di Villa Giulia.

Vast treasures of ancient art and craft, Greek, Etruscan, and Roman, have thus been scattered all over the world, passing through the hands of eighteenth and nineteenth century grave-robbers and collectors into various museums of Europe and America, as *disiecta membra,* acquired without any information of either the appearance of the tombs in which the items were discovered or the objects found together with them. What this trafficking has deprived us of, in the matter of archaeological facts, may be vaguely realized when considering the fabulous treasures of wrought gold, silver, bronze, and ivory, which, exceptionally, have been secured in their entirety, together with some knowledge of the arrangement of the burials, from three unrifled tombs: the Tomba Regolini-Galassi at Cerveteri, excavated in 1836, the Tomba Barberini at Palestrina, discovered in 1855, and the Tomba Bernardini, brought to light at Palestrina in 1876. As complete sets of precious grave-gifts, these treasures of the seventh century B.C. are rivalled only by the magnificent ornaments and vessels of fourth-century and Hellenistic date that have been found in Thracian and Scythian cemeteries and in tombs discovered in Thessaly and Macedonia; among the latter are the painted royal (?) chamber tombs excavated by Manolis Andronikos at Vergina.

During the latter half of the nineteenth century the study of ancient artefacts was slowly developing from being an aesthetic hobby of rich collectors, mainly supplied by grave-robbers, into an important branch of the humanities, with methods of research which have been continually refined in the course of the present century. At the same time, most countries have instituted more or less rigorous laws for the protection of their cultural heritage, and officers charged with the maintenance of the laws have shown greater zeal in looking out for illicit excavators and in confiscating what they have found. The archaeologists, for their part, have learnt the importance of registering all particulars of an excavation, of gathering and describing all objects found, and of grouping them separately, according to where they have been discovered. And in the course of time, many technical devices have been employed for facilitating archaeological field work.

Aerial photography has long been used for revealing changes in the growth and colour of vegetation that indicate the existence of subterranean graves, walls, roads, and canals, and also for registering subaqueous remains of ancient harbours, provided that the waters are not too much polluted. By this device we have obtained, for instance, exact and detailed aerial views of Veii, Caere, Tarquinii, Vulci, and many other Etruscan sites, and also of the ancient canal-ways of the city of Spina, west of Comacchio.

Highly effective were the technical devices applied to archaeology in the 1950's–1960's by the Italian engineer and industrialist Carlo Maurilio Lerici. He invented a method of field prospecting with electric resistance measurements registering subsurface objects and formations; and by sinking a periscope with flash-lamp through a hole drilled into a chamber tomb thus located, he was able to obtain photographs of its unopened interior, showing if it was painted or undecorated, untouched or rifled, and if excavation would be remunerative or not. By means of these devices many important archaeological discoveries have been made, such as the location of the ruins of the wealthy Greek colony of Sybaris, covered by immense alluvial deposits, the mapping of about 1000 graves at Cerveteri and some 6000 at Tarquinia, and the discovery at the latter site of many previously unknown painted chamber tombs, such as the Tomba della Nave and the Tomba delle Olimpiadi. Similar and even more ingenious technical devices, such as a so-called subsurface interface radar, have also been very useful in the excavations of a prehistoric settlement conducted by Professor Paul Åström at Hala Sultan Tekke in Cyprus.

Modern technology has also enabled archaeologists to explore the bottom of the sea, by using the equipment of scuba and skin divers. Throughout the ages, the Mediterranean has seen a busy naval traffic, and its bottom must be strewn with remains of wrecked merchant vessels and their cargoes, and of sunken warships and their arms. The exploration of this vast source of material, however, is still at its beginning, and what has hitherto been found and examined are mostly wooden hulls, important for the study of ancient ship-building, and cargoes of plain clay amphorae for liquids, clay lamps, and other ordinary utensils, which are of but little value intrinsically, but important by their shapes and stamps of origin, offering clues as to centres of production and trade routes. Of particular interest are the remains of a Greek ship wrecked off Kyrenia in Cyprus, of a Punic vessel sunk off Marsala, and of Roman ships found off Terrasini, west of Palermo, and in the harbour of Claudius at Ostia. Another interesting discovery recently made is that of a ship wrecked in the fifth century B.C. off the small island of Giglio, at the Tuscan coast, with a cargo containing painted Corinthian and Etruscan vases, a well-preserved Corinthian helmet, and a variety of other objects.

Here may also be mentioned a Roman boat found during excavations initiated in 1982 at the beachfront of Herculaneum, where Italian and American archaeologists have also discovered the skeleton of a horse and, hitherto, about 150 human skeletons, with pieces of jewellery and lots of coins issued in the reign of Nero, all embedded in the hard tufa resulting from the avalanches of hot volcanic ash which engulfed the city in 79 A.D. The victims had taken refuge in a row of chambers along the beach, probably expecting to save themselves by putting out to sea, when they were overwhelmed by what is described by Pliny the Younger (*Epist.* VI, 16) as a landslide which descended from Vesuvius, making the shores inaccessible and forcing his uncle, the Elder Pliny, to steer for Stabiae, where he succumbed to asphyxiation.

Considering the fact that many ancient works of great artistic value have been retrieved by chance from Mediterranean waters – works such as the fine bronze statues already mentioned (p. 30), the marble panels from the harbour of Piraeus, with reliefs of battling Greeks and Amazons copied from the shield of Pheidias' Athena Parthenos, and the Roman marble statues found in the Blue Grotto of Capri and in a submerged Imperial villa at Baiae – it seems reasonable to believe that methodical underwater research in the future, perhaps with techniques yet to be invented, will result in fabulous catches of sunken art treasures. Perhaps one would even be able some day to recover the wrecked cargo of bronze statues carried away from Rome by Gaeseric the Vandal in 455 A.D. (p. 16).

In spite of stricter laws, intensified supervision, and adequate punishment of contravention, the traditional search for buried ancient treasures has been carried on everywhere, mostly by locals who have learnt to read the signs of the terrain, and to keep their occupation as secret as possible. The clandestine excavators, moreover, are stimulated by the development of a thriving international antique market, which supplies a growing number of museums and private collections with a wealth of antiquities, and pays its suppliers much more than the state, even for plain things that were left behind in the graves or thrown away in former days.

The mapping of vast Etruscan cemeteries by scientists equipped with ingenious instruments, and the study of ancient wrecks by other scientists with diving equipment, have also given enterprising grave-robbers and wreck-plunderers valuable hints of where to search, and of what implements to use for searching. A popular and wide-spread sport is the scanning of fields with metal detectors in order to find ancient coins and other loose objects of bronze or silver, which are gathered for pleasure or sold to antique dealers. Another sport, especially popular along the French and Italian Riviera, is diving for wrecked cargoes of oil and wine amphorae and other ceramics, which are sold to rich residents wishing to adorn their villas with something out of the ordinary.

The clandestine antiquity hunters, the suppliers of their equipment, and the dealers who buy what is found, do not understand, or mind, that archaeology suffers great damage by this traffic, in so far as antiquities found together are often dispersed, mingled with others of different origin, and brought on the market without any reliable information about the place where they were discovered, nor of the objects found together with them. This is a great disadvantage when it comes to the question of establishing date and origin of such antiquities. But too many museum officials and private collectors in transalpine and transatlantic countries have shown much the same attitude of mind as their travelling compatriots of old towards the peoples whose ancient art they admire, by trying to get hold of fine specimens of this art by fair means or foul, and caring very little about how and where and in what archaeological context they have been brought to light. These buyers, consequently, are ultimately to blame for encouraging the illegal traffic of treasure hunters, receivers, and smugglers.

Archaeologists and authorities are fighting a loosing battle against this traffic. Now and then they are able to confiscate in time some antiquities illicitly obtained, but far too often the treasure hunters and their confederates have succeeded in smuggling out of the country even large and magnificent works of art, leaving the authorities with small chances, if any, of tracking down and convicting the culprits, or of obtaining any information from the foreign museum implicated in the transaction.

This was the case, for instance, when the Berlin museum, in 1915, acquired the late-archaic statue of a seated goddess from Tarentum and, in 1924, the early-archaic standing goddess said to have been found at Keratea in Attica, and also when the Metropolitan Museum of Art in New York, in 1932, bought its famous Kouros, an early-archaic marble statue of a standing nude youth, which in all probability also came from Attica. In Greece, many lovers of the ancient art of their country perhaps felt a malicious pleasure at hearing that eminent experts on Greek sculpture found the standing goddess in Berlin and the kouros in New York so ugly, and so different from all other archaic sculpture known to them, that they declared both of them to be forgeries. Their verdict was very wrong!

On two occasions, however, Italian authorities reacted strongly upon information received that precious antiquities, in all probability, had been illicitly unearthed in Italy, fraudulently exported, and slyly purchased by foreign museums.

In 1924, the Ny Carlsberg Glyptotek in Copenhagen acquired a large collection of Greek vases and Etruscan antiquities, including architectural terracottas and a number of fine bronze implements. A description of the collection was published in 1927 by the director of the museum, Dr. Frederik Poulsen, under the cautious title *Aus einer alten Etruskerstadt*. Fascist Italy promptly demanded to be told how and from which ancient Etruscan city these antiquities had come into the possession of the Danish museum, but Dr. Poulsen refused to reveal any particulars of the transaction. He was penalized some time later, when he took the train to Rome and was stopped at the Brenner border, as *persona non grata* in Italy. He didn't set foot on Italian soil until after the end of the Second World War.

As a matter of fact, however, he had disclosed the origin of the antiquities already in 1925, publishing a catalogue in Danish of the Etruscan department of the museum, in which the items of the newly acquired collection were said to come from Orvieto. This was of course based on what had been alleged by the sellers; but one of these, later on, asserted that the collection came from Vulci. The sellers were the brothers Riccardi of Orvieto, known in Italy as clandestine dealers in antiquities excavated by themselves or others, with or without permit. In the course of time, they were also revealed as very clever and productive forgers of Etruscan large-size terracotta statues (pp. 69 ff.). Their assertions about the antiquities bought by Dr. Poulsen seem to be partly true, partly false, in so far as the bronzes were probably made in Vulci, the terracottas no doubt in the Etruscan city which preceded Orvieto on its high tufa pedestal. The story may serve as a reminder that the one-word indication of origin often given in museum catalogues for antiquities ultimately obtained from anonymous excavators ought to be taken *cum grano salis*.

Another dubious transaction between sly antique hunters and unscrupulous museum officials was revealed in 1972, with far-reaching consequences. In that year, the Metropolitan Museum of Art in New York acquired a large red-figure calyx krater, signed by two great Athenian ceramists, the potter Euxitheos and the vase painter Euphronios, active in the last decades of the sixth century B.C. The exhibition of the krater was a sensation coupled with suspicion, particularly because two differing stories were told to explain away the fact that this magnificent vase, before its appearance in the American museum, had been unknown even to experts on Greek vase painting. The director of the museum, M. Hoving, declared that the vase had been in a private European collection since about the time of the First World War. The curator of the department of Greek and Roman art, Dr. Dietrich von Bothmer, said that it had been purchased through an American living in Rome, who acted as an intermediary for its owner, an Armenian coin dealer in Beirut, whose father had bought it in London in 1920. For reasons of his own, however, the Armenian had deposited the vase in Zurich, and from there it had been flown over to New York, without any difficulty, since Switzerland has no law prohibiting re-export of imported antiquities.

Italian archaeologists, however, sceptical of the tale of an owner having hidden away the vase for half a century, and knowing that the American living in Rome was a certain Robert E. Hecht, with a record of receiving looted antiquities for sale, were convinced that the krater had been discovered by clandestine excavators at Cerveteri, as late as 1971. Four men, known to be *tombaroli* often at work in Caeretan cemeteries, were brought in by the police, and one of them admitted that the photographs of the Euphronios krater shown to them represented a vase which they had found, broken into several pieces, in a tomb discovered in a terrain called Greppe di Sant' Angelo, to the east of Cerveteri.

Excavations instituted by the Italian authorities in this place brought to sight, in 1974, a rock-face provided with two sculptured false doors, between which an open entrance led into a large chamber tomb. In front of this was an enclosed area, in which were found some figures carved in grey tufa, and placed there to keep watch over the tomb: a winged sphinx, two lions, and a life-size statue representing one of the hook-nosed underworld daemons known both from late Etruscan tomb paintings and two terracotta masks in Orvieto. But the guardians had not been able to deter looters, nor the false doors to deceive them. The tomb had been emptied, probably long ago; and if the excavators had hoped to find in this, or in the smaller tombs discovered on either side, some sherd of the Euphronios krater overlooked by the robbers, they must have been sorely disappointed. The information given by the *tombarolo,* that the vase had been found in the scrubby terrain of the Greppe di Sant' Angelo, was perhaps a lie intended to mislead the police and delay the research of the archaeologists. Anyhow, there seems to be no possibility as yet to prove where and when the vase was brought to light, and to reclaim it from the American museum.

The treasures of ancient art and craft assembled in European and American museums and private collections have of course also whetted the desire of people anxious to get hold of such valuables, but without the toil of grave-robbery and wreck-plunder, and with the possibility of choosing in advance what objects to steal. Many antiquities are thus in risk of being stolen twice, first from owners long since dead, and later on from their present-day possessors. In fact, the museums never subjected to theft are becoming very rare nowadays.

The thieves are often experts who know what to take and how to outwit monitoring televison cameras, electronic alarm-bells, and complicated locking devices. They are generally collaborating with receivers but not seldom also working for wealthy and unscrupulous gentlemen coveting exquisite pieces for their collections, well guarded from the eyes of experts.

Most frequently stolen are, of course, small objects of great artistic and commercial value, such as ancient jewellery, gold and silver coins, bronze statuettes, and painted pottery. Bronze and marble statues are not easily stolen from ordinary museums; but in 1962 the mayor's office in Castelvetrano, Sicily, was visited by a gang of thieves who carried away an archaic bronze statue of a youth, known as the Ephebus of Selinunte, where it was discovered in 1886. The thieves could not find a buyer, until eventually they contacted a respectable Florentine dealer, who promised to send a nephew of his to inspect the statue in Agrigento. The 'nephew', however, was no other than Rodolfo Siviero, head of Italy's Commission for the Recovery of Works of Art (p. 37), who arrested the six robbers and recovered the statue, which is now in the museum of Castelvetrano.

Imitation and Deception

When the supply of an article cannot keep pace with the demand for it, the item will become expensive and imitated, for honest or deceptive purposes. This is particularly true of fine works of ancient art and craft, the supply of which ultimately depends on chance. The rarity of such works, and the high prices paid for those available, account for the production of copies and forgeries.

It is not always possible to state precisely whether a certain work ought to be defined as a copy or a forgery. An exact copy may be offered for sale as an original, through ignorance or by fraud; but it becomes a forgery if it is treated so as to look more or less timeworn.

Most forgeries, however, have been made by free imitation of the style of a certain artist, or of a certain period, and their chances of deceiving depend on the makers' feeling for style and their experience in modelling, painting, carving, and metallurgy. In consequence, forgeries of all kinds have been and are being made, ranging from monstrosities acquired only by ignorant and unsuspicious buyers to sophisticated and sometimes beautiful creations, calculated to deceive even eminent art experts.

The activities of skilled forgers in art are more dangerous and damaging than stealing from museums and plundering graves, ruins, and wrecks. The museum or private collection visited by thieves suffers the loss of valuable art objects, but these are seldom damaged and may even be recovered, sooner or later, thanks to their having been described and reproduced in books and periodicals or advertised as missing in widely circulated museum publications. The museums and collectors that buy in the open antique market usually receive dispersed and unpedigreed antiquities brought to light by anonymous finders, but if the sellers are reputable firms of dealers, no antiquities are offered for sale before having been examined and declared genuine by experts.

If, on the other hand, a museum or a private collector is tempted to buy what seems to be a remarkable piece of ancient art secretely offered for sale in the store-room of some obscure antique dealer, there is great risk of acquiring a forgery, and of paying a large sum of money for a piece worth nothing. And, what is worse, if the article acquired is made by a skilled forger, it has great chances of being accepted as genuine by leading art experts, exhibited as a fine specimen of ancient art, and illustrated as such in journals and manuals of art and archaeology, giving students all over the world a false conception of a certain artist or a certain school.

The worst thing that can happen is, however, when a professional or amateur archaeologist yields to the temptation of gaining money, fame, and promotion, or of fooling colleagues, by devoting himself to forgery or other fraudolent activities. The consequences will be detrimental, not only to the reputation of the culprit, but above all to the progress of historical and archaeological studies and research. Scholars and scientists, always depending on results presented by colleagues, have to presuppose that their confrères are scrupulously honest and reliable; but if one of them deviates from honesty, presenting forgeries, wittingly, as genuine antiquities, or manipulating ancient artefacts in order to make them more important, or giving false information about the origin and context of his exhibits, many wrong theories and conclusions may be made on the basis of evidence thus fabricated.

The history of deception in classical art and antiquities offers many examples of how clever professional forgers and unscrupulous scholars have duped a majority of experts, and how their frauds have been definitely exposed only after years or decades of scholarly polemics, difficult investigations, and various laboratory tests, not always of undisputed reliability.

The history begins in ancient Rome, where a growing collection mania, a flourishing antique market, and an enormous production of so-called Roman copies, to be used for the decoration of both public and private buildings, constituted a hot bed for all kinds of deception.

The term 'Roman copies' is generally used to designate statuary executed in imitation of Greek models during the centuries of Roman domination, either as intentionally exact reproductions of Greek originals, or as intentional adaptions, variations, and eclectic contaminations of Greek themes and styles, all mostly made by Greek artists, who had no conception of what we call plagiarism and often signed their works with their own name. The production of Roman copies presents us with many difficult problems of how far lost prototypes can be recognized and reconstructed with the help of such copies as happen to have survived, of what methods were employed for reproduction, and of what criteria were mostly used by the Romans for choosing works to be taken and copied: material value, artist's fame, or subject suited for temples, thermae, palaestrae, libraries, etc. These and related problems have been dealt with by eminent archaeologists specialized in Greek and Roman art, from Adolf Furtwängler to Brunilde Sismondo Ridgway, who has lately advanced many fresh and controversial ideas and interpretations, which cannot be discussed here. Complete and definite solutions are of course unattainable, because of the inadequacy of sources and material.

A circumstance of fundamental importance is the fact that the copyists of sculpture could hardly travel about with their manifold equipment of tools and other requisites in order to make replicas by direct transference of form from originals placed in different buildings of different and widely distant cities. The copyists obviously had to make the replicas in their workshops, and generally with the help of casts of the originals which were used as models.

The practice of making casts by means of moulds taken off originals modelled by hand was in use from early archaic times onwards, especially for the production of antefixes, acroteria, relief friezes and other architectural decoration in terracotta. According to a tradition retold by Pliny (N.H. XXXV, 151–152) the art of modelling life-size figures in clay was invented by a Sicyonian potter named Butades who, working in Corinth (probably in the 7th/6th century B.C.), first adorned the tile-fronts along the eaves of buildings with heads (*antefixa*), which he first made as *prostypa* modelled by hand, later as *ectypa* cast from moulds.

In the course of time, casts were also made of statues and even of living models, which, according to Pliny (N.H. XXXV, 153), was invented by Lysistratos of Sicyon, a brother of Lysippos. Anyhow, this method had great success. Lucian, writing in the second century A.D., in his dialogue *Zeus Tragodos* (33) speaks of a bronze statue of Hermes in the Agora of Athens which was "covered with pitch because of the moulds that were being taken from it every day". Material evidence of the practice is given, moreover, by the discovery in a thermal complex at Baiae of about 290 fragments of plaster moulds and casts, once used for reproduction of a great number of famous statues, among which have been recognized the Aristogeiton of Antenor's group, the Doryphoros, the Athena of Velletri, and the three Amazons at Ephesus attributed to Polykleitos, Pheidias, and Kresilas (of the four recorded by Pliny, N.H. XXXIV, 53).

From such casts, distributed to workshops in Rome and other cities, unlimited numbers of reproductions could be made: fairly exact marble copies, such as the well-known ones of the Diskobolos, the Doryphoros, the Diadoumenos, made with the aid of the so-called pointing system, the use of which is traceable in ancient sculptures left unfinished; exact bronze copies, probably made with new moulds taken from the casts and used to form the wax in the bronze casting process called *à cire perdue* (p. 82); and free-hand adaptions and variants, such as, for instance, the many varied marble statues of the 'Crouching Aphrodite', the prototype of which was thought to have been a statue described by Pliny (N.H. XXXVI, 35) as "a Venus washing herself" and ascribed to one Doidalsas of Bithynia, whose name was restored from the corrupt text.

Adaptations of a special kind were certain eclectic works which were in vogue in the last century B.C. and a speciality, it seems, of the praised Pasiteles, modeller, sculptor, and chaser. A typical work of his school is the Ephebus of the Villa Albani in Rome, a mannered marble youth signed by Stephanus, pupil of Pasiteles, and much admired by neoclassic critics.

The colossal chryselephantine statues were hardly available for mechanical copying, since taking of moulds from them could not be done without scaffolding and risk of damage to the gold and ivory laminae. Our knowledge of Pheidias' Zeus in Olympia and his Athena Parthenos in Athens is therefore primarily based on Pausanias' detailed descriptions (V, 11, I and I, 24, 5, supplemented by Pliny and other authors), which have permitted us to recognize a number of reproductions, more or less reduced in size and simplified in detail, and probably executed on the basis of sketches in clay and drawing. The Killing of the Niobids represented on the armrests of Zeus' throne are thus reproduced in Neo-Attic relief panels; the Athena is rendered in a number of statuettes; and the figures of the Amazonomachy represented on her shield are reproduced on the Strangford Shield in the British Museum and the relief panels found in the harbour of Piraeus (pp. 46).

How a rich and cultivated man could adorn his house with bronze and marble copies of Greek busts and statues is illustrated by the discovery of the Villa dei Papiri at Herculaneum, referred to above (p. 29). Proud possessors of such copies were probably often showing off their treasures in the manner described in Lucian's dialogue *Philopseudes* (18), which takes place in a private house where Myron's Diskobolos, Polykleitos' Diadoumenos, Kritios' and Nesiotes' Tyrannicides and some other famous works are described as if they were the originals. Well-informed contemporaries of Lucian probably knew that the original Tyrannicides stood in the Agora of Athens, perhaps also where the other originals mentioned in the dialogue were to be seen.

The enormous quantities of exact copies, adaptions, variations, and eclectic contaminations, emanating from hundreds of sculptors' workshops in Rome and other cities of the Roman Empire, constituted a market where buyers were often deceived, and the scattered remains of this production present today abundant possibilities of dubiety and misinterpretation. Two remarkable examples may be adduced.

In the early 1830's a well preserved bronze statue was raised from the bottom of the sea off Populonia by some fishermen from Piombino, on the Tuscan coast. It was acquired in 1834 by the Musée du Louvre and has since then been known by the improper name of 'Apollo of Piombino'. It represents a nude youth standing in a frontal pose, and an inscription on its left foot, which reads ATHANAIA DEKATAN, denotes that it was made from a tenth part of war booty and dedicated to the goddess Athena. The Doric spelling of the inscription and the modelling of the statue, showing a curious medley of late archaic and more developed forms, led to the assumption that it was executed in the first half of the fifth century B.C. in one of the Doric colonies of Sicily or Magna Graecia. In 1967, however, the archaeologist Brunilde Sismondo Ridgway and the epigraphist L.H. Jeffery were able to demonstrate that it was made in the last century B.C. by two Greek artists, who had written their names on a lead tablet hidden in the interior of the figure; one of them was a certain Menodotos of Tyre, the other a certain . . . phon of Rhodes. They must have been very proud of their work, superstitiously anxious to make it preserve their names, and confident that its true character would be difficult to reveal – and they proved to be right! The statue may have passed today as an eclectic work, were it not for the false dedicatory inscription, which definitely brands it as a forgery.

In 1877 German archaeologists excavating the remains of the temple of Hera at Olympia discovered the marble statue of Hermes with the infant Dionysus, which was immediately recognized as the one described by Pausanias (V, 17, 3), who saw it in this very temple, stating that its *techne,* its execution, was that of Praxiteles. Because of this evidence the statue was commonly accepted as an original revealing the great fourth-century sculptor's supreme skill in making hard marble look like soft living flesh. In the course of time, however, this interpretation has been called in question. Pausanias' phrase, and the work itself, admit of doubt of whether we are dealing with an original of the great Praxiteles or with an original made by a second-century sculptor of the same name, or rather with a fine replacement copy of a looted work, as suggested by the fact that the god's back is partly left unfinished and the drapery hanging down from the infant's legs is supported by a tree-trunk united to the god's left hip, in a manner typical of Roman copies. Or is the Hermes an eclectic work perhaps created by a younger descendant of the famous master, as advocated by Brunilde S. Ridgway?

Greek decorative metalware, particularly vases of gold, silver, and bronze, embossed, chased, and often ornamented with figurative appliqués, were in great demand and sold at high prices in the Roman antique market, especially since the days of King Attalus' bequest (p. 9) and the inflow of Corinthian bronze vessels (p. 9). Pliny informs us of many famous Greek silver chasers and the prices paid for their works, annotating, for example (N.H. XXXIII, 147 and 156), that the orator Lucius Crassus had a pair of chased silver goblets made by Mentor, which he had bought for 100,000 sesterces and never had the heart to use; that two goblets by Zopyros, with scenes representing the Areopagus and the Trial of Orestes, were valued at 12,000 sesterces; and that an embossed silver bowl by Pytheas, showing Odysseus and Diomedes in the act of stealing the Palladium, was sold at the price of 10,000 denarii.

Such precious metal vessels were frequently copied, by menas of moulds of clay or plaster made over the originals. Reproductions thus made could be confusingly like the originals, as is shown by extant replicas and Pliny's statement (N.H. XXXIV, 47) that Zenodoros, who made the colossal bronze statue of Nero (p. 15), also copied two cups by Kalamis so skilfully that there was scarcely any difference between the imitations and the originals. Such copies were of course often sold as originals. The above-mentioned Pytheas, however, made certain small drinking cups which, says Pliny (N.H. XXXIII, 157), were so thin and liable to damage that no casts could be taken of them.

In the antique market of ancient Rome there were of course many smart dealers who understood how to fleece snobbish collectors, by making them believe that a vessel offered for sale, genuine or not, was made by a renowned Greek silversmith or had belonged to a famous ruler in the distant past.

Horace, in his *Satire* I, 3, 90 f., speaks of the happy owner of "a dish worn by the hands of Evander" (meaning the Arcadian Evander, said to have been the first settler on the Palatine, not the sculptor Avianius Evander, as Porphyrio explains). And in the *Satire* II, 3, 16 ff., the poet portrays the bankrupt speculator and art collector Damasippus, who before the crash took pleasure in hunting for "the bronze basin in which the cunning Sisyphus washed his feet" and in pointing out careless carving and coarse casting, while cleverly investing a hundred-thousand in a statue.

The growing demand for very old silverware is sarcastically described by Pliny, saying (N.H. XXXIII, 157) that in his time value was attached only to specimens so much worn by use that the decoration was no longer discernible. Martial, too, gives some interesting glimpses of contemporary art collectors, presenting (VIII, 6) an owner of two goblets, each decorated with "a dove worn by the thumb of Nestor" (and thus both pretended to be the famous goblet of King Nestor of Pylos, described in the *Iliad,* XI, 632 ff.); saying of a certain Paulus (XII, 69) that his friends are as genuine as his pictures and cups; asking (VIII, 34) if a vase attributed to the famous silversmith Mys is more authentic because the owner wasn't present at its making; and portraying (IX, 59) a purchaser who used to sniff up the smell of the bronzes to ascertain if they were real Corinthian.

Pliny speaks (N.H. XXXIV, 6) of the many collectors who pretended to be connoisseurs of Corinthian bronzes without having any insight in the matter; but the olfactory test of authenticity described by Martial was probably no sham. The bronze vases gathered from the ancient graves of Corinth and specified by the name of *necrocorinthia*, 'Corinthian death-vessels' (p. 9), presumably retained a smell of death and decay, to judge from a passage in Petronius' *Satyricon* (50), where the rich upstart Trimalchio, having displayed his silly humor and solid ignorance speaking of Corinthian bronzes, concludes by saying that he, personally, prefers glassware, which at least doesn't smell: *ego malo mihi vitrea, certe non olunt.*

During the Middle Ages there was a large market for faked and ficticious relics of Saints but none for forgeries in art, since no one collected things of beauty: ancient marbles and bronzes were destroyed, medieval carvings and paintings belonged to the churches.

The Renaissance brought a revaluation: works of medieval figurative art were now looked upon as clumsy and defective products of a dark intermediate period and were largely superseded by creations of the new era, inspired by, and made to compete with, the marvelous works of Antiquity which had survived destruction and now began to be collected both by leaders of the Church and by secular rulers and noblemen.

This collecting activity continued well into the nineteenth century, motivated by a lasting admiration for all things Greek and Roman, and pursued according to the concepts of the august collectors, who, as a rule, were chiefly interested in adorning their parks and palaces with statues and busts representing such characters of Greek and Roman myth and history as were familiar to them through classical authors and contemporary poetry, plays and operas. They were less concerned with the artistic qualitites of their antiques and, of course, had no possibility of judging the style and date of the works, or whether they were originals or ancient copies. But they had a firm opinion concerning mutilated sculptures, finding it quite unthinkable to adorn their aristocratic homes with portrait busts lacking nose and ears, or with statues deprived of their head or other parts of the body. Many of them, therefore, seem to have been no less eager to acquire contemporary copies or casts of the Laokoon and other very famous works than to buy ancient marbles, always more or less damaged.

Thanks to the taste of the collectors, Italian sculptors were secured full employment for five hundred years, copying ancient sculptures and restoring them to what had been, or was thought to have been, their original appearance.

The complicated Laokoon group, discovered in 1506, was very soon used for testing the talent and ability of sculptors. Vasari narrates that Bramante arranged a competition between some artists in making wax copies of the Laokoon, and that Raphael declared young Jacopo Sansovino to have made the best model, which was also cast in bronze. In the 1520's Baccio Bandinelli made a marble copy of the group, in the size of the original, and representing its three figures as they were then restored, each of them raising their right arm in the air (p. 65). Bandinelli proudly and honestly put his signature to the copy; other sculptors of the sixteenth and seventeenth centuries produced anonymously a great number of free, reduced and more or less debased copies of the group, which were spread all over Europe and sometimes believed to be antique. One of them was acquired for Queen Christina of Sweden, according to a list of purchases made at Augsburg in 1650, which records "den Laucont sampt 2 Kindern von Schlangen gebissen, von Stein".

A purchase of antiques characteristic of the time was the one made in Rome for Francis I of France (p. 24), which consisted of 125 pieces of ancient marbles and moulds of the most famous statues of the Roman collections. The King, says Vasari, was thus able to adorn the garden of the Fontainebleau château with bronze copies of these celebrated works, "making the place look like a new Rome". For similar purpose Louis XIV of France purchased from Italy many hundreds of statues, busts and decorative vases of marble, both ancient and less ancient, which were used for the embellishment of the park of Versailles. The collection assembled by Queen Christina in Stockholm was also a mixture of ancient and less ancient antiques, to judge from the twelve marble heads saved from the fire of 1697, five of which are ancient, while the other seven are antiques probably dating from the seventeenth century.

The sculptors engaged in the repair of ancient marbles performed their work with drastic thoroughness. Grey, mottled and corroded surfaces were polished till the marble was white and smooth. Breaks were planed off to obtain even surfaces for attaching new parts of the body in place of lost ones. A missing head was replaced by another one, ancient or made *ad hoc,* with no attention paid to whether the combination was stylistically admissible or not. And a badly mutilated statue could be 'restored' to any imaginable shape except the original one.

Innumerable ancient marbles have been treated in the manner described, but some of the cases are more significant, and curious, than others.

In his famous autobiography Benvenuto Cellini narrates (II, ch. 10) how he had placed his great skill at the disposal of Cosimo de' Medici, by restoring an ancient marble torso of a boy, providing it with a new head, new arms and legs, and an eagle at its side, "so that we could name him Ganymede".

The marble copies of the Tyrannicides in Naples had a curious appearance in former times, since the statue of Aristogeiton had been provided with a curly head of fourth-century type, strongly contrasting with the hair and features of Harmodios, modelled in the style of the 470's B.C. It was only after the discovery that a bearded marble head in the store-rooms of the Vatican museums belonged to another marble copy of Aristogeiton, found in 1938 during the excavations at the church of Sant' Omobono in

Rome, that the statue in Naples was correctly restored, by means of a cast of the Vatican head.

Three ancient marble copies of Myron's Discobolus, all lacking legs, arms and head, were 'restored' in three different ways in the eighteenth century. One of these torsos, formerly in the possession of Giulio Romano, was acquired by the French sculptor Pierre Étienne Monnot (1657–1733), who converted it into the body of a falling warrior, now in the Capitoline Museum. Another torso was 'restored' as Endymion regarding Selene, now in the Uffizi Gallery in Florence. The third torso was used to make a Diomedes carrying off the Palladium, formerly in the Lansdowne collection (now dispersed). This last-mentioned 'restoration' was the work of Monnot's pupil, the sculptor Bartolomeo Cavaceppi (1716–1798), who collected and restored countless quantities of ancient marbles, sold them to prominent collectors in different countries, and reproduced the best of his works in his *Raccolta d'antiche statue,* etc., Vols. I–III, Roma 1768–1772.

The three torsos were restored according to the erudite fancy of the sculptors, who had no idea of what sort of figure they belonged to. This became evident only after the discovery on the Esquiline, in 1781, of the well-preserved marble statue of a discus-thrower, which was identified two years later by the Italian archaeologist Carlo Fea as a copy of Myron's famous bronze Discobolus, described in Lucian's *Philopseudes* (p. 54). After this discovery, correct restorations could be made of two other marble copies of the Discobolus, found in Hadrian's villa at Tivoli in 1791, one of which is now in the Vatican, the other in the British Museum.

The precious copy from the Esquiline, however, was long withdrawn from all further examination, being hidden away in the Palazzo Massimi-Lancelotti until, in 1938, it was illegally sold to the Glyptothek in Munich, whence it was recovered in 1948; it is now exhibited in the Museo delle Terme in Rome, together with another very fine marble copy of the Discobolus, found at Castelporziano.

Another typical example of how ancient marble fragments could be used to form what an erudite eighteenth century artist thought to be a beautiful composition is the so-called Piranesi pastiche in the Villa Albani in Rome. It is a relief panel composed by the great engraver, combining a Greek fragment of the fifth century B.C. representing a seated woman and a thymiaterion, a Roman fragment with an archaistic Athena, and a 'restored' architectural background.

A typical eighteenth-century collection of antiques is the one assembled by Gustaf III of Sweden, a monarch with a passion for literature, theatre, and classical art. During his tour in Italy in 1783–1784, the King, guided and advised by the eminent Swedish sculptor Johan Tobias Sergel, acquired from Cavaceppi and the engraver G. Volpato a set of marble

Muses, a Minerva, and a Diana, all restored and partly composed of disparate bodies and heads. Sergel also exerted himself, but in vain, to acquire for the King the above-mentioned excellent marble copy of Myron's Discobolus, recently discovered on the Esquiline. After his return from Italy, the King made two more acquisitions in Rome. One of them, strongly applauded by Sergel, was a marble statue of the sleeping Endymion, said to have been found in Hadrian's villa at Tivoli; later on, however, Sergel came to the conclusion that it was "restored and not antique", and he was probably right. The other acquisition, made in spite of Sergel's dissuasion, was that of Gian Battista Piranesi's collection of antiques, offered for sale by the engraver's son, Francesco; and this time Sergel was manifestly right, for the collection consists mainly of decorative marbles, extensively restored, reworked, and often made up of different fragments, like the Piranesi pastiche just described. The collection assembled by Gustaf III, now back in its original place and order in the Royal Palace of Stockholm, is of no great artistic value, but interesting by showing us an eighteenth-century museum of antiques, typifying the august collector's taste and cultural ambition.

The traditional treatment of mutilated ancient marbles was practised long after the turn of the eighteenth century. When the pedimental sculptures of the temple of Aphaea in Aegina had been acquired for the Glyptothek in Munich, they were sent to Rome to be restored by the famous Danish sculptor Bertel Thorvaldsen who, after two years' work on them, is said to have declared that he had carried out the task so well that he could not distinguish between the original parts of the figures and his own additions. At the same time, however, some voices were raised against this practice; and when the question was discussed of whether the Elgin Marbles should be restored, "to increase their value", as somebody said, the sculptor Antonio Canova, fortunately, was successful in his opposition to restoration.

Most collectors, however, maintained the time-honoured opinion that ancient marbles ought to be completed, preferably so that restored parts differed as little as possible from the rest of a figure, to attain which, drastic means were sometimes used. The Norwegian archaeologist Ingvald Undset, father of the great authoress, relates in a book of memories entitled *Fra Akershus til Akropolis* (1892) that the rich banker Alessandro Torlonia, busily increasing the large collection of ancient sculpture housed in the family palace at the Lungara in Rome, used to bury the marbles in a big dunghill, to give the original and the restored parts an all over blond tonality.

Considering the fact that restoration of mutilated ancient sculptures was required for at least four centuries, it seems a miracle that the famous Torso of the Vatican Belvedere has been spared from being supplied with a new head, new arms, new shanks and feet, and some conjectured additional attribute. The miracle is probably due to the fact that no one has been able to settle the question of how the huge marble figure was posed and whom it represented (Hercules?, Marsyas?, Philoctetes?), as is shown by the many reconstructions in clay, plaster and drawing that have been made of it, from the Renaissance down to the present time.

The sculptors of the Renaissance, Baroque, Rococo, and Neo-Classical periods, owing much of their formal training to the study, copying and restoring of ancient sculptures, not infrequently also used their skill in making statues and reliefs of gods and heroes, and portraits of prominent Greeks and Romans, basing their work on ancient models, or on their own fantasy. Such 'antiques' were easily sold to distinguished collectors who wished to have a Venus, a Minerva, a Caesar, a Caracalla, and so on.

Vasari narrates that Michelangelo as a young man made a Sleeping Cupid in marble and was persuaded by Pierfrancesco de' Medici to treat the figure so as to give it the appearance of being antique, whereupon another person brought it to Rome, buried it in a garden, and in due time sold it to a Cardinal. His Eminence, however, found out that he had been cheated, returned the figure, and compelled the seller to pay back the sum he had received for it; which Vasari criticizes, with the significant argument that "a modern work may be just as perfect as an ancient one, provided that it is made with excellent skill".

Michelangelo nevermore lent himself to such activities; but many minor artists, Tullio Lombardo, Simone Bianco, Gian Cristoforo Romano, Giovan Battista della Porta and other Renaissance sculptors, the brilliant seventeenth-century portrait sculptor Alessandro Algardi, and the prolific eighteenth-century sculptor and restorer Bartolomeo Cavaceppi (p. 59), dedicated themselves to an abundant production of 'antiques' made in their own workshops.

Works of this kind found their way into private and public antique collections in many countries. Some of them show clear signs of having been treated intentionally to defraud, by such means as artificial corrosion and tinting, restoration of damage made on purpose, or tooled lines imitating joints of non-existent restorations. Others may arouse suspicion by being unusually well preserved, or by exhibiting very few, small, and judiciously placed restorations. But there is no reason to assume that all such 'antiques' were intended to deceive. Many were made to order, as for instance the eighteenth-century portrait busts of Suetonius' twelve Caesars in the Galleria degli Imperatori of the Casino Borghese in Rome. Anyhow, it is generally not very difficult to pick out such 'antiques' on the basis of stylistic criteria, for the executing sculptors seldom contrived to liberate themselves completely from the artistic mode of their time.

This is well illustrated by two marble busts, the so-called Clythia in the

British Museum and the portrait of the young Octavian in the Vatican.

The first-mentioned bust came to the British Museum in the collection of Charles Townley, who had bought it in Naples in 1772. It represents a lovely young lady with bare shoulders and scarcely covered bosom, above a corolla of large petals. It has been thought to be a contemporary portrait of Antonia, consort of the elder Drusus; but the sentimental and sensual sweetness of the girl, and the idea of letting her emerge from a flower, definitely speak in favour of the supposition that we are dealing with an eighteenth-century work, perhaps by the sculptor Antonio Corradini.

The Vatican bust, alleged to have been found at Ostia in the early nineteenth century, has been admired as an idealized portrait of the future Emperor Augustus in his teens, made in his later years or in the age of Hadrian. In 1949, however, Paolino Mingazzini argued for its having been made by Canova, especially on account of its resemblance to the sculptor's portrait of Napoleon. This is a convincing theory; and the discovery in Mainz in 1961 of a marble head which was claimed to be a Roman copy of the Vatican bust is no proof of the antiquity of the latter, since the head turned out to be one of the many modern copies made of it. Canova probably carved the imaginary portrait of a teen-age Octavian, basing it on the well-known features of Augustus, restored some damages judiciously made on purpose (tip of nose, edges of ears, breast and front of neck), and put the bust on the market as a precious antique, perhaps just to satisfy himself as being the equal of the famous sculptors of old.

The excavations begun at Herculaneum in 1738 and at Pompeii in 1748 brought to light wall paintings and mosaics which aroused amazement and admiration among the very few who were admitted to see them (p. 26). Some privileged painters, however, soon began making imitations, although with little success, owing to the complicated technique of the ancient paintings, which were often erroneously described as 'frescoes'. In his *Sendschreiben über die Herculanischen Entdeckungen* Winckelmann condemns the poor 'Herculanean' paintings made by Giuseppe Guerra, a pupil of the renowned Neapolitan painter Francesco Solimena. But at the same time, in letters and in his *Geschichte der Kunst des Alterthums,* he glorifies what he believed to be an ancient Herculanean painting, representing Jupiter and Ganymede, a luscious composition which the painter Raphael Mengs, when dying, confessed to have made.

In later times, probably because of the difficulties involved in executing the imitations, there has been no great production of 'Herculanean' and 'Pompeian' paintings. The mosaic pavements, on the other hand, which were continually discovered in the buried Campanian cities and in Hadrian's villa at Tivoli, often tempted restorers of such tesselated floors to make various 'antique' compositions in this special medium, which has a long tradition in Mediterranean countries.

Clever forgers, however, found it much more profitable and interesting to display their skill in counterfeiting ancient small-sized objects, especially engraved gems and fine coins, which were eagerly collected, both for their costly material and for their artistic quality.

Engraved gems, made of semiprecious stones, chalcedony, carnelian, jasper, lapis lazuli, etc., and generally used for signet rings by Greeks, Etruscans, and Romans, were imitated with great skill by Italian gem cutters, especially in the eighteenth century. Toward the end of the following century, however, the brilliant German archaeologist Adolf Furtwängler was able to single out the imitations from the ancient gems, which he presented in his fundamental work entitled *Die antiken Gemmen*, I–III, published in 1900.

Coins have been forged in two different ways, and for two different reasons. They have been made of adulterated metal for circulation at normal value, or of alloys and with designs simulating those of ancient coins, to be sold as genuine pieces to collectors.

Counterfeiting of the former kind has often been resorted to, for reasons of State, by rulers who ran no risk of being punished for it, unlike ordinary people caught doing such things. A certain maestro Adamo was burnt at the stake for this crime in 1280, and Dante placed him among other forgers tormented by eternal thirst in Hell. Benvenuto Cellini tells with relish (I, ch. 11) of a die engraver who was hanged for having forged the coins he, Benvenuto, had made for Pope Clement VII.

Far lesser risk was run by those who furnished collectors with ancient coins of their own making. Clever men of the Renaissance, considering the art of the ancients as the standard for imitation, were also tempted to produce ancient coins. The architect Pirro Ligorio (1510–1583), who made drawings of the ruins of Rome and sketches for the restoration of the ancient marbles collected by Cardinal Ippolito d' Este, also produced spurious Latin inscriptions and counterfeit Roman coins. His contemporary Giovanni dal Cavino (1500–1570), working with a team of collaborators in Padua, produced the so-called Paduans, counterfeit Imperial sesterces, skilfully imitating genuine coins and filling gaps in the series with pieces designed by himself. Cavino's coins are recognizable by containing more zinc than authentic sesterces, and by the fact that his dies and punches are preserved in the Bibliothèque Nationale in Paris.

The most remarkable coin forger of all times was Carl Wilhelm Becker (1772–1830). While still in his early youth he took a vivid interest in numismatics, and after his career in a line of ordinary business had come to an abrupt end in 1803, he pursued whole-heartedly his numismatical studies and established himself in Munich as a dealer in ancient coins. He had a keen eye for quality and supplied the most fastidious collectors of Europe with Greek and Roman gold coins of great beauty and in excellent state of preservation. He is described as a brilliant and charming man who received a noble title from a German prince and welcomed Goethe and other distinguished friends in his home. In the course of time, however, he began satisfying the demands of his clients by using his skill and knowledge to counterfeit ancient coins. He made his own dies and punches with which he struck coins in all metals, confusingly similar to the genuine pieces copied, even displaying, like some of these, the double contours of the design resulting from the flan having been slightly moved before a second blow on the punch. He also gave his coins the appearance of having been in circulation some time, by putting them in a box filled with iron filings and fixed to the axle of his carriage. But his profitable business and life of elegance came to a calamitous end in 1819, after he had tried to sell some of his products to the eminent numismatic expert and collector C.H. Haeberlin. His forgeries are well known, through imprints in lead from his stamps, and by being illustrated and described by another eminent numismatist, Sir George F. Hill, in a work entitled *Becker the Counterfeiter,* I–II, 1924–1925.

In the course of the nineteenth century, archaeologists and art historians learnt, gradually, to pursue their activities with stricter criticism and method, to regard products of ancient art and craft as material of historical importance not to be tampered with, and to base the arrangement of museum collections not on aesthetic criteria alone, but on historical and educational considerations as well.

In consequence, the traditional practice of restoring, disputed already in the early decades of the century (p. 60), went slowly out of use, and scholars and cultivated museum visitors became accustomed to seeing mutilated antiques, and even to discovering the artistic qualities of fragmentary works.

As a result of all this, ancient marble sculptures discovered today are exhibited in much the same condition as when they came to light, retaining breaks, corrosions, stains, and marks of plant roots, all attesting to their age and authenticity. Ancient statues and reliefs of terracotta, mostly discovered as scattered fragments, are usually completed only so far as is necessary to keep the preserved pieces together; and when terracotta reliefs made with a mould are completed with the aid of the best preserved specimens of the series, the plaster used in the restoration is generally of a different colour to that of the terracotta.

Unlike the marbles, ancient bronzes were seldom exposed to hard cleaning after the discovery, and their patina, smooth or rough, dark or bright, was generally regarded as an aesthetic quality added by nature, especially if it had the character of an enamel-like *aerugo nobilis,* shining in various shades of blue, green or reddish-brown.

To remove the patina from ancient bronzes in order to recover the original golden lustre of the alloy, as has been done in some cases by modern archaeologists, is comparable to the hard polishing of ancient marbles, abandoned long ago. It cannot be justified by referring to the fact that the Greeks appreciated the untarnished colour of the bronze, as is shown by papyri and inscriptions telling us of bronze statues being cleaned of rust and polished with olive oil, as well as by Pliny's comments on different kinds and colours of Corinthian bronze (p. 9). But the same author's information (N.H. XXXIV, 8) about a certain liver-coloured bronze used for images and statues, and a passage in one of Dio Chryso-stomus' orations (*Or.* 28, 289 M), in which a young athlete is said to resemble well-modelled statues and the colour of his skin to be like "blended copper", suggest that Greek bronze statues of nude males usually had a colour of sunburn, similar to the reddish-brown given to the nude parts of male figures in terracotta.

In the course of time, the opinion that mutilated ancient sculptures ought not to be restored gave rise to the idea that all parts added to such sculptures by restorers should be removed. This is of course justified when an incongruous addition can be exchanged for an appropriate one, as was done in the case of the statue of Aristogeiton in Naples (p. 58).

A similar case is that of the Laokoon group which, when discovered in 1506, was incomplete in so far as the right arm of the father, the fingers of the right hand of the elder son, and the right arm of his younger brother were missing. Michelangelo made what was probably a trial piece for a restoration of the father, carving too large an arm, fully bent and gripping a coil of the attacking serpent. This work was left unfinished, and the restoration of the group was carried out by Baccio Bandinelli and G. Montorsoli, who had the father lift a coil of the serpent high above his head, gave the elder son a new hand, and let the younger one raise his right arm in the air. Michelangelo's conception of the father's posture was confirmed, however, when the German archaeologist Ludwig Pollak, in 1905, found a fully bent marble arm with traces of a serpent and rightly recognized the piece as the missing arm of Laokoon. But Pollak, and others, considered the arm to be a fragment of an ancient copy of the group; and it was only in the 1950's that it was identified as part of the original and put back in place, after the removal of the restored extremities of the three figures. In this way Laokoon himself has resumed the attitude decided on by the three Rhodian sculptors who made the group (p. 13), which implies that the right arm of the younger son must have been bent towards his head, as shown by an integrated cast of the group.

Less justified was the treatment of another famous statue of the Vatican, the Apollo Belvedere, restored by Montorsoli, who completed the god's extended left arm with a hand holding a bow and added to his lowered right upper arm a forearm and a hand opened in an elegant gesture. After the removal of these additions in 1924, unnumbered crowds of museum visitors gazed at the mutilated god without any idea of what he was doing, until in 1979 it was decided to give him back his left hand with the bow and let him hold an arrow in his right.

After the Second World War visitors to the Glyptothek in Munich were taken by surprise to find Thorvaldsen's restorations audaciously removed from the pedimental sculptures of the Aeginetan temple of Aphaea, which now appeared as two groups of warriors supported by metal props and badly marred by planed-down breaks with dowel holes where restored parts of their bodies had been attached. Many art-lovers protested vehemently against what they called destruction of aesthetic values but could not prevent the similar treatment of another famous statue of the Glyptothek, the Sleeping Satyr, generally known as the Barberini Faun, restored by the great Gian Lorenzo Bernini; this sculpture, however, has regained a new right leg, in plaster.

There can be no general rule for or against the removal of restored parts from ancient sculptures. It is advisable, however, to abstain from substituting tolerably matching restorations with metal props and wires, and to only remove such additions as are strikingly incongruous, disfiguring, and misleading; and even in cases of this kind, deliberation is commendable. If, for instance, some eminent stickler for archaeological purism were able to have the head, arms and legs removed from the 'restored' Falling Warrior of the Capitoline Museum (p. 59), the remaining tooled torso of one more copy of Myron's Discobolus would be small gain compared to the loss of an interesting example of how a skilled eighteenth-century sculptor solved the problem of converting a fragment of a then unidentified antique statue into a significant whole.

Instead of trying to undo what has been done by restorers in thousands of cases, keepers of collections containing restored ancient sculptures will do enough by indicating in catalogues and guide books what parts of such works are restored, whether the restorations are acceptable or not, and also, whether a certain sculpture is really antique, or perchance, an 'antique' made by a clever sculptor during the periods of classical imitation.

The intensified excavating activity during the nineteenth century, bringing to light increasing quantities of ancient works of art and craft, also accounts for the appearance of professional forgers, generally involved in a prospering clandestine antique market, and specialized in imitating such antiquities as were well paid for by a growing number of museums and private collections.

For many reasons, forgers frequently tried their skill in imitating Etruscan plastic works in painted terracotta and Greek figurines in the same material. They found an abundance of models thanks to excavations carried out in different parts of Etruria, from the 1820's onwards. In Orvieto, diggings at a place called Il Belvedere, near the Pozzo di San Patrizio (p. 41), in 1828 and again in 1879, brought to light some remarkable terracotta figures which, through methodical excavations in the 1920's, were shown to have decorated the pediments of a triple-cella temple richly adorned with antefixes and friezes in terracotta. Great quantities of Etruscan terracottas of different kinds were also unearthed at Cerveteri by diggers employed by the Marchese Campana in the 1830's–1850's (p. 44) and later by regular excavations in Veii and many other Etruscan sites. Other excavations, legal and illegal, were undertaken in the cemeteries of Tanagra and Myrina in the 1870's and 1880's, unearthing great numbers of the graceful Hellenistic terracotta figurines which were named after the two cities and soon became the rage of museums and private collectors, and a favourite theme for forgers.

The abundant production of forgeries in terracotta is obviously also accounted for by the fact that clay is a common, cheap and tractable material, the preparing and baking of which can be learnt in any pottery at hand; and furthermore, by the fact that ancient terracottas are generally discovered as fragments and have to be reconstructed by restorers who were often tempted to make money by modelling figures similar to those they had pieced together and completed.

Young men of that profession found plenty of work thanks to the excavations undertaken by the Marchese Campana, especially at Cerveteri, where his diggers and tomb-pilferers discovered, in addition to the archaic painted terracotta slabs mentioned above (p. 44), a large archaic terracotta sarcophagus, modelled in the shape of a couch, with a lid in the form of a mattress on which are two reclining life-size figures, representing the married couple for whom the sarcophagus was made. This sarcophagus, together with the major part of the Campana collection of antiques, was acquired in 1861 by the Musée du Louvre, where it is still an exhibit worth seeing, especially after the removal, some years ago, of the clumsy repairs and retouches to the painted decoration made by the restorers employed by the Marchese.

This sarcophagus was unique until the British Museum in 1873 acquired a collection assembled by the Roman antique dealer Alessandro Castellani, a brother of the well-known goldsmith and collector Augusto Castellani (p. 44). The purchase included the fragments of a large terracotta sarcophagus which, pieced together in the museum, appeared as even more remarkable than the Campana specimen, having figured relief panels all round the coffin, corner pedestals each masked by the bust of a Siren or Harpy, a naked male and a dressed female figure above, and an

Etruscan inscription painted along and below the front edge of the lid.

The sarcophagus thus restored was described in C.T. Newton's publication of the Castellani collection, printed in 1874, where the author states that "the style of these figures is archaic, the treatment throughout very naturalistic, in which a curious striving after truth in anatomical details gives animation to the group, in spite of extreme ungainliness of form, and ungraceful composition"; adding that "the inscription is very similar to that on a gold fibula found at Chiusi, but its interpretation is not yet determined".

This was a kind of similarity that inevitably aroused suspicion. The Italian epigraphist Ariodante Fabretti pronounced the inscription to be a forgery; but this did not preclude the possibility that the sarcophagus itself could be genuine, and provided with a modern inscription to increase its market value. According to Alessandro Castellani, the sarcophagus, broken in pieces, had been sold to him by a certain Pietro Pennelli, who said he had discovered it at Cerveteri in 1856. But the year after its publication in 1874, Newton visiting Paris learnt that Pennelli's brother Enrico, who had restored antiquities for the Marchese Campana with Pietro, and entered into the Musée du Louvre as restorer together with the Campana collection, openly boasted of having made the sarcophagus of the British Museum and duped the antiquaries by breaking it and burying the pieces in the earth for some time. Newton instituted inquiries that resulted in a heated quarrel between the two brothers regarding which of them was telling lies, until Enrico, threatened with legal action by Pietro, acknowledged himself, in writing, to be the liar.

In spite of all this, and although true examples of archaic Etruscan style were represented by the Campana sarcophagus and, since 1898, by the similar and only moderately restored Caeretan sarcophagus of the Museo di Villa Giulia in Rome, scholarly opinions differed in regard to the authenticity of the Castellani sarcophagus, which, therefore, continued to be exhibited in the British Museum right up to 1935, when it was removed to the store-rooms in the basement. By that time, all critics of ancient art had at last become aware of the fact that the sarcophagus was an ugly forgery, and that "the extreme ungainliness of form and ungraceful composition" of the two grotesque figures on its lid were not due to the shortcoming of a primitive Etruscan artist, as many scholars thought, but to Enrico Pennelli's and his brother's inadequate capacity of imitating archaic Etruscan style. The sarcophagus, however, was permitted to return to daylight for a limited time in 1961, when it occupied a prominent place in an exhibition of various kinds of forgeries acquired by the museum in the course of two centuries.

Besides the two Pennellis, Rome in the latter half of the nineteenth century had many other craftsmen who used their skill in restoring and fabricating antiquities. One of them was a goldsmith named Pio Riccardi, who worked for two widely known antique dealers, Francesco Martinetti in Rome, and Domenico Fuschini in Orvieto. A late work of Pio's was a 'repaired' bronze chariot which was sold to the British Museum by Fuschini, as having been found in 1908 at Prodo, between Orvieto and Todi; it was exhibited for a much shorter time than the Castellani sarcophagus, before being likewise removed to the basement as a pastiche. After the construction of the chariot, Pio Riccardi and his family moved to Orvieto, where his sons and two nephews devoted themselves to various secret activities, which were disclosed only after the lapse of many decades.

From the 1890's onwards, the English archaeologist John Marshall, who lived in Rome from 1906 until his death in 1928, was engaged in buying antiquities, for the Museum of Fine Arts in Boston in collaboration with the American collector Edward P. Warren (p. 76 f.), and later as purchasing agent for the Metropolitan Museum of Art in New York. In this latter capacity, he acquired in 1915 the fragments of a terracotta statue well over life-size representing a lean old warrior with a white beard, in 1916 the fragments of a colossal helmeted head of the same material, and in 1921 the fragments of a huge terracotta warrior in the attitude of fighting.

It appears from Marshall's correspondence and diaries, and from sellers' receipts, that the old warrior and the colossal head were acquired through the antique dealer Pietro Stettiner in Rome, from whom Marshall also bought a series of seven terracotta slabs "from Cerveteri", decorated with sea monsters and dolphins in relief, and the upper part of a life-size terracotta statue of a woman wearing Etruscan necklaces. The statue and the slabs were exhibited in the Metropolitan Museum and included in the *Handbook of the Classical Collection* published in 1917 by Gisela M.A. Richter, then Assistant Curator of Classical Art. The statue is carefully modelled in a classicistic manner and displays so many stylistic inconsistencies that it was withdrawn sometime before 1927 as a forgery. The slabs were exhibited as genuine until, in 1960/61, they too were revealed as forgeries, through cleaning and technical examination.

While Marshall was negotiating the purchase and export of these objects, Italian archaeologists excavating in Veii discovered the foundation walls of an Etruscan temple and three fragmentary archaic terracotta statues, representing Hercules carrying away the sacred hind of Apollo, the god striding out to recover the animal, and Hermes wearing his winged hat. These statues, which were later found to have been placed along the roof ridge of the temple, were generally hailed as a marvellous confirmation of Varro's statement, quoted by Pliny (N.H. XXXV, 157–158), that the art of modelling statues of clay was brought to perfection especially in Etruria; that Tarquinius Priscus summoned Vulca from Veii to receive the contract for the clay statue of Jupiter to be consecrated in the Capitoline temple; and that the same artist made a Hercules which was still known in Rome as the Clay Hercules. Many scholars regarded the Veientine statues as works by Vulca himself; anyhow, they must come from the workshop of a great Etruscan modeller active in Veii about 500 B.C.

Marshall, for his part, tried to settle the provenance of the old warrior and the colossal head bought in 1915–1916, and of the big fighting warrior purchased five years later, by friendly contact with the persons who were said to have discovered the statues. These claimed to have unearthed the fragments during clandestine excavations of a temple at Boccaporco, between Orvieto and Bolsena; but they pointed out that the excavated place had been covered up and sown over, and when he asked them to show him the spot, they were unable to do so on the plea of sickness. At last, resenting their having sold behind his back a large collection of ancient vases, bronzes and terracottas to the Ny Carlsberg Glyptotek (p. 48), Marshall cut all relations with "my Orvietans". The identity of these Orvietans was revealed after his death in 1928, in a letter written by his secretary: they were the Riccardi brothers, who at that time, however, being suspect of illicit excavations, had left Orvieto for Florence and Siena.

There were thus reasons enough for the experts of the Metropolitan Museum to look at the terracotta fragments "from Boccaporco" with suspicion; but after a technical examination the warriors were pieced together and exhibited in 1933. Four years later they were published in a richly illustrated monograph by Gisela Richter, by then Curator of the Classical Department of the museum.

Many reviewers congratulated the author and the museum on the acquisition of these magnificent specimens of Etruscan plastic art: two warriors of terracotta, bigger than life-size, each wearing cuirass, greaves, and a crested helmet, all ornamented in painting or relief; and in addition, a colossal warrior's head of the same material, and with a similar helmet.

In Italy, however, where archaeologists were closely acquainted both with Etrusco-Italic terracottas and the shrewdness of forgers and clandestine excavators, the warriors were mostly regarded with smiling scepticism. The etruscologist Massimo Pallottino promptly condemned them as forgeries and even pointed out the prototypes used by the forgers: a well-known bronze statuette from Dodona, which Gisela Richter had adduced as an example of the type of fighting warrior reproduced by the imaginary Etruscan modeller; certain Eastern Greek aryballoi (round clay flasks for perfume) in the shape of helmeted heads; and a well-known type of Etrusco-Italic bronze statuette, representing a very lank warrior with a helmet crest of abnormal size.

In spite of this, opinions continued to be divided about the huge warriors. Some scholars argued that they were forged, others were convinced of their authenticity and tried to explain away their anomalies. As late as in 1955, Gisela Richter described them, in a book entitled *Ancient Italy,* as artistic as well as technical masterpieces of Etruscan art.

Only after a long and complicated investigation of the history of the purchase, a new technical examination of how the statues had been made and painted, and the disclosure of all this, verbally and in writing, by a certain Alfredo Adolfo Fioravanti of Rome, could definitive proof of the unauthenticity of the warriors be obtained and the particulars of a sensational fraud be told, in a report issued in 1961 by the archaeologist Dietrich von Bothmer, Curator of Greek and Roman Art, and the technician Joseph V. Noble, Operating Administrator of the Metropolitan Museum of Art.

Fioravanti described how he had begun in the early 1910's as an apprentice in Orvieto at the workshop of Riccardo, the eldest son of Pio Riccardi; how he had made and helped to make a great number of Etruscan relief slabs of terracotta; and how he had made the Etruscan warriors in collaboration with Riccardo and his two cousins.

Four series of relief slabs were produced, one with sea monsters, two others with palmetto and lotus flower designs, and still another with two daemon's heads, male and female. The slabs were made with the help of moulds obtained from originals in the Museo Civico and the Museo Faina in Orvieto. Most of the forged slabs, alleged to have been found at Bolsena, were sold to the antique dealers Elio and Ugo Jandolo in Rome, from whom many of them were acquired by different museums, including the Museo Gregoriano Etrusco of the Vatican, the Museo di Villa Giulia and the Palazzo dei Conservatori in Rome, and the National Museum in Copenhagen. The slabs bought by Marshall for the Metropolitan Museum of New York evidently came from the same Orvietan workshop. A slab with the daemon's heads was still offered for sale in the 1930's.

Fioravanti also recounted in detail how the warriors were made. The forgers built up the hollow clay statues from the floor of their workshop, supporting them with wooden scaffolding, and modelling them after photographic reproductions and originals of the statuettes and vases which were later correctly identified by Pallottino. When making the big fighting warrior, however, they had to shrink the body from the waist up, finding that the ceiling of their workroom was too low for a statue of the intended proportions. For the glaze and painted decoration they used manganese dioxide; and when the glaze had developed a net of cracks in drying, they pushed the statues to the floor so that they broke into many pieces, which were then fired batch-wise in an ordinary kiln for ceramics.

Fioravanti's account tallies with the evidence of the technical examination and explains certain anomalies of the warriors. The spectographic analysis established that the black glaze of the statues contained manganese dioxide, which was used as colouring agent by forgers of Orvietan maiolica, but not for ancient painted vases and terracottas. The difficulty in building the huge fighting warrior accounts for the stocky proportions of the figure, which had not been adequately explained before. The statement that the statues were broken before firing, and the pieces fired in several batches, explains why the forgers made the telling mistake of not providing the figures with ventholes, as was regularly done in hollow ancient clay statues and statuettes meant to be baked in one piece, to allow access of the hot air to their interior and prevent cracking during the firing. But the forgers spared themselves the trouble and risk of building a kiln big enough to take the statues whole, as some scholars thought the Etruscan master modeller had done.

Signor Fioravanti, being informed of the technical evidence of the unauthenticity of the warriors, apparently decided to make a clean breast of his collaboration with the Riccardi family some fifty years before. But he said nothing about his doings after Riccardo Riccardi's sudden death in the winter 1918/19 and the completion of the fighting warrior. This was revealed, however, shortly after the disclosure of the forgery of the warriors.

In 1930 the Ny Carlsberg Glyptotek in Copenhagen acquired a small mutilated terracotta statue representing a young girl in the attitude and dress of the archaic Greek korai. The statue was described by the director of the museum, Dr. Frederik Poulsen, as an Etruscan masterpiece probably from the same workshop as the archaic terracotta statues found at Veii in 1916. In the wake of the inquiries into the forgery of the warriors in New York, however, the authenticity of the Copenhagen kore was also called in question, and she was classed as a forgery in consequence of comparative spectographic analyses made by J.V. Noble. Her origin was demonstrated by the American archaeologist Harold W. Parsons who, in an article entitled *The Art of Fake Etruscan Art,* published in 1962, reproduced three photographs taken in Fioravanti's workshop in Rome and showing the kore in three stages of production: before firing, after firing and mutilation, and pieced together and restored. Some years ago she was submitted to a thermoluminescence test (p. 95) which gave her an age of 48 years.

After the death of his master in the art of faking Etruscan art, Fioravanti had carried on the trade on his own, evidently, as shown by his kore, making great progress in the matter of style by studying the Veientine statues in the Museo di Villa Giulia. The kore seems to be intended to represent a votary statue from the temple which carried these on its roof ridge. The imitation was so successful that it deceived many eminent experts in Etruscan art for some thirty years.

Fioravanti, however, had a formidable rival, endowed with a marvellous versatility and a remarkable capacity for deceiving distinguished archaeologists and art historians.

In 1952 the City Art Museum of St. Louis acquired at a very high price a small polychromed terracotta statue of Diana the Huntress, representing the goddess striding out in a long garb, with a fawn at her side. The statue was bought in the Roman antique market as an archaic Etruscan masterpiece. Italian archaeologists, however, contested its authenticity, and the art export office of Bologna let it depart from Italy as a forgery. Such being the case, the direction of the American museum applied to a non-Italian authority for expertise, in the hope of seeing the dear Diana cleared of suspicion.

Hence it came about that Professor Reinhard Herbig, then Director of the German Archaeological Institute in Rome, presented the result of his examination of the statue and inquiry as to its origin in a lengthy article, published in 1956. In this article Professor Herbig emphasized that the statue, according to "sworn statements of honest persons of Italian birth, whose love of truth cannot reasonably be questioned", had been discovered in 1872 near Civita Castellana and since then had been preserved in a secluded private collection, until some sixty years later it was offered for sale in Rome.

This was obviously a tale fabricated for trusting presumptive buyers; and it was incompatible with the fact that among the photographs of forgeries collected in the photo archive of the German Archaeological Institute there was one taken in 1936/37, showing the Diana mutilated and roped round for coherence. In spite of this, and although he observed that the statue was restored and repainted, and that its garments presented anomalies, Herbig declared himself to be convinced of its authenticity and tried to explain away its irregularities by pointing out that it did not come from Etruria, but from Civita Castellana, the site of ancient Falerii, capital of the Faliscans. Concluding, he expressed his firm belief that the St. Louis Diana was going to take her place in the history of ancient art as well as the imposing Etruscan warriors in New York.

Six years later, however, the Diana took her place in the history of forgery as well as the warriors. In his paper cited above, H.W. Parsons reproduced two photographs taken in the 1930's in the studio of Alceo Dossena in the Via del Vantaggio in Rome, showing the Diana smashed and roped up and accompanied, in one of them, by a gorgon antefix of terracotta, which is now exhibited as an unmistakable forgery in the study series of the Nelson Art Gallery in Kansas City. A thermoluminescence test of the Diana made some years ago gave her an age of 40 years.

Alceo Dossena (1878–1937) was a sculptor who won fame and notoriety in the 1920's – 30's through his great productivity, manual skill, and uncanny capacity for imitation. He used to emphasize that his works were never copies but original creations of his own in the styles of different periods, and that unscrupulous dealers mutilated them and put them on the market as ancient sculptures. This, however, cannot be the whole truth, to judge from the case of the Diana. Anyhow, he certainly knew that smart vendors sold his works ostensibly as Renaissance sculptures, Greek votive and pedimental statues, Etruscan terracottas etc., and for sums far greater than the payments he received for them. He also made a portrait bust of Mussolini and was honoured after his death by a retrospective exhibition and a book on his life and work, published in 1955 by his son Walter Lusetti. His talent is shown at its best in some of his 'Renaissance' and 'Greek' sculptures in marble; his 'Etruscan' Diana looks like a caricature of the Veientine Apollo.

In the wake of the successful sales of the forgeries made by the Riccardis, Fioravanti, and Dossena, some clever forgers eventually started producing imitations of the archaic painted terracotta slabs found by the Marchese Campana in the Banditaccia necropolis of Cerveteri and transferred to the Louvre in 1861 (p. 44). According to Dennis, suspicion was thrown upon these slabs by the appearance in Rome, a few years after their discovery, of another series of painted terracotta slabs said to have been found at Cerveteri but evidently forged. The authenticity of the Campana slabs, however, is corroborated by the fact that no slabs of this type are known to have been found earlier, and also by the discovery in the same Caeretan necropolis in 1874 of a series of similar slabs, the so-called Boccanera plaques in the British Museum. Most of the Campana slabs, however, have been repaired, redrawn and repainted by the Marchese's restorers to such an extent that their figured scenes only retain a narrative value. The later forgers of this type of Etruscan terracotta decoration generally betray a keener eye for style, and many of their products could only be unmasked by means of thermoluminescence tests performed in 1972.

The traditional fabrication of antiques in marble was kept alive in nineteenth-century Italy, especially in Rome, where numerous *scalpellini,* stone carvers, found work and tempting examples for imitation in the many museums and good chances of procuring ancient blocks of Greek or Luna marble at reasonable prices.

The producers of forged marbles preferably worked in what was called "classical" or "Praxitelean" style, but late archaic Greek sculpture had also caught their interest in the years when Thorvaldsen was restoring the Aeginetan pediments in Rome. Many such forgeries were exposed by Adolf Furtwängler's keen eye: a colossal female head in Berlin and a helmeted head of Athena, both made in imitation of Aeginetan sculptures; a head known as "Hera of Girgenti", acquired by the British Museum from Alessando Castellani (p. 67), and a "Praxitelean" head in the same antique dealer's collection; and also a statue alleged to be an ancient copy of Polykleitos' famous Diadoumenos, bought by the rich Danish brewery owner Carl Jacobsen for the Glyptotek he was creating in Copenhagen.

This statue was acquired through the German archaeologist Wolfgang Helbig, who acted as Jacobsen's purchasing agent in Rome and said he had found it in the store shed of the antique dealer Francesco Martinetti after his death in 1895, immediately recognizing it as an excellent Roman copy of Polykleitos' bronze statue of an athlete in the act of binding a fillet round his head. From Martinetti's store shed came also another marble athlete which Helbig sold to Jacobsen in 1893 as a precious sculpture found at Formia; it consisted of an ancient torso completed with a head, a right arm with a palm twig, part of a left arm, and the lower parts of the legs, all made *ad hoc* in the time-honoured manner of Roman restorers. The forged Diadoumenos and the 'restored' athlete were probably made by a Roman *scalpellino* named Pacifico Piroli, after ideas and designs originating from Helbig and Martinetti.

The illustrious Helbig and the shady Martinetti were the most successful of the foreign archaeologists and native antique dealers who operated together in Rome during the latter half of the nineteenth century, unscrupulously and for mutual profit, in order to provide transalpine and transatlantic museums with antiquities from Italy, genuine or forged, and exported by fair means or foul. Both of them took part in the underhand designs made for the acquisition of two remarkable three-sided marble reliefs which in the course of time were to be the objects of much discussion.

In 1887, during the parcelling out of the ground of the Villa Ludovisi on the Monte Pincio in Rome, once the site of the beautiful Horti Sallustiani, some workmen unearthed a strange piece of sculptured marble which was thought to have been part of a throne for a big statue of a god or goddess. It was cut out of one square-hewn block of Greek marble and decorated with reliefs on the outer surfaces of two sloping side panels and a gable-shaped back, the top of which was unfortunately destroyed by the pick-axes at the moment of discovery. The piece was added to the antique collection of the Ludovisi family and is customarily referred to as the Ludovisi Throne, although the first guess as to its use is evidently wrong and a more plausible conjecture is that it served as a parapet at one end of a long rectangular altar.

Seven years later two Roman antique dealers, Antonio and Alessandro Jandolo, were found to be in possession of another triple marble relief, which was said to have been unearthed in the same area as the Ludovisi

Throne and seemed to be its companion-piece. This marble was acquired in 1896 for the Museum of Fine Arts in Boston and is since then generally referred to as the Boston Throne.

The Ludovisi Throne is universally regarded as the most charming example of Greek relief sculpture that has come down to us from the time about 470–460 B.C. The meaning of its reliefs, on the other hand, has been the object of different interpretations, not to be related here. A most plausible theory is that the scene on its long side represents Aphrodite being born from the sea and received on a pebbly shore by two Horae, as described in the sixth Homeric hymn, and that the figures on the two shorter sides represent worshippers of the goddess, a nude hetaera playing the flute and a draped bride offering incense.

The Boston Throne presents even more difficult problems. Many distinguished experts in ancient art have hailed it as a Greek masterpiece dating from the same time as the Ludovisi Throne, with reliefs corresponding to the Birth of Aphrodite. The scene on the long side is thus usually interpreted as a representation of Eros in the shape of a nude winged boy weighing two male figures carved on the weights, in the presence of two women, seated and draped, one of which is raising her hand in a gesture of pleasure at the turn of the scales, while the other bows her head in grief. On the short sides a nude boy playing a lyre corresponds to the flute-playing hetaera, and a crouching old woman to the incense-offering bride of the Ludovisi Throne.

Other eminent experts have disputed the authenticity of the Boston Throne, basing their arguments on observations of its style and execution, and consideration of its mysterious appearance in the antique market. This, in fact, and the secret activities of those interested in its sale, offer so many discrepancies that, in spite of Ernest Nash's thorough investigation, it is hard to believe even those assertions that the investigator regarded as reliable.

The sale of the two 'thrones' is an interesting chapter in the long history of antique hunting in Italy. The two purchasing agents of the Boston Museum, E.P. Warren and J. Marshall (pp. 69 f.), had great chances of making two important acquisitions, first when Don Rudolfo Boncompagni-Ludovisi in 1892 had to look for buyers of the family collection of ancient sculpture, including the Ludovisi Throne, and two years later when the other 'throne' was secretly offered for sale. At that time it had passed from the Jandolo brothers into the possession of Francesco Martinetti and the German archaeologist Paul Hartwig, who were now negotiating for its sale either to the Museum of Fine Arts in Boston or to the Staatliche Museen in Berlin, while Martinetti's other German friend, Wolfgang Helbig, was acting in the background to facilitate export. In 1896 the sellers accepted the higher bid of the American museum, thereby bringing down upon themselves the wrath of German archaeologists; the sum paid was divided between Hartwig, a brother of Martinetti (the dealer himself having died in 1895), and "a person unknown", whose share was handed over to Helbig; and the 'throne' was sent to Warren's residence in England, from where, some years later, it was forwarded to Boston. Helbig and Warren also tried to purchase the Ludovisi collection for division between the Boston Museum and Carl Jacobsen's Glyptotek in Copenhagen, but this plan was frustrated in 1901, when the Italian State acquired the whole collection for the Museo Nazionale delle Terme in Rome.

What first aroused suspicion regarding the authenticity of the Boston Throne was of course its timely appearance in the antique market as an almost undamaged counterpart to the so far unparalleled Ludovisi Throne and the discrepant statements about when and where exactly it was discovered. But these circumstances prove nothing as to the question of its being genuine or a forgery. The Ludovisi Throne, too, except for certain excisions made in antiquity, would have been almost undamaged if the top of its long side had not been inadvertently smashed at the moment of discovery; and those who had an economic interest in the Boston Throne quite naturally gave vague and varied answers to questions about its provenance, being probably well aware of the fact that the owner of the Villa Ludovisi could make a legal claim for antiquities found even in areas parcelled out of the estate.

Among the arguments advanced to establish the unauthenticity of the Boston Throne the most serious are those based on observations of its style and execution. But these arguments, and some others, are nullified as the result of a thorough technical and stylistic examination carried out in 1966 by the physicist William J. Young and the archaeologist Bernard Ashmole, the latter having acquired special experience of forgeries in marble by his scrutiny of the once famous portrait head of Julius Caesar in the British Museum, some relief fragments with heads copied from the Parthenon frieze, and some 'archaic' statues made by Alceo Dossena.

The scientific examination of the Boston Throne and a fragment of the Ludovisi Throne, as well as samples of marble from Paros, Naxos, Siphnos, Thasos and Pentelikon, by means of microscope, ultraviolet rays, and spectographic analysis, enabled Mr. Young to state that the Boston Throne is made of the same sort of marble, probably Thasian, and presents similar corrosion by earth and ground water as the Ludovisi Throne; that its surface in many areas has marks of roots whose stains penetrate into the marble and fossiliferous incrustations with frail remains of snails; and that the marble under ultraviolet light fluoresced amber and light purple, indicating that it was hewn and carved a very long time ago.

Mr. Ashmole, for his part, was able to disprove Fiorenza Baroni's claims of finding errors in the execution of the lyre played by the boy on the right-hand wing of the Boston Throne, especially by pointing out a thin raised line running along the horns of the sculptured lyre, a detail paralleled in Greek vase paintings and a wooden Greek lyre in the British Museum. It is not very likely that a forger would have known of this tiny detail or troubled himself to reproduce it, had he even been informed of its existence by some learned antiquarian.

Mr. Ashmole also demonstrated that the two 'thrones', shown by corrosion, root-marks and incrustations to have been long buried probably near one another in Rome, were evidently used together in Roman times, when the rectangular side panels on both of them, for unknown but similar reasons, were cut down slopewise, regard taken to the figures; and further, that the 'thrones' were most probably together in Greek times also, since it is "in the highest degree unlikely that a Roman collector could have procured two similar Greek pieces of almost identical but otherwise unparalleled character, of closely similar marble and of almost the same size, from different places".

Some Italian scholars, however, ignoring or ignorant of these results, persisted and still persist in regarding the Boston Throne as a forgery, sometimes even described as *falsissimo*. The archaeologists Giovanni Becatti and Licia Vlad Borelli, while not doubting the validity of the scientific examinations, tried to uphold this opinion by assuming that a forger could have carved the Boston Throne on the end of an ancient marble sarcophagus or from an ancient block of marble, which would explain its being marked by plant roots and fossiliferous incrustations. This theory, however, is refuted by the fact that the root-marks and incrustations are also to be found on the reliefs, supposed to have been carved by a forger in the 1890's. And it is hard to believe that this forger could have had such remarkable luck in finding not only an ancient sarcophagus or block of just the same sort of marble as the one used for the Ludovisi Throne, but also just the size needed to make another 'throne' of about the same dimensions, and just in time to have this new 'throne' ready when the sale of the Ludovisi collection was of current interest.

And, what's more, it seems quite unbelievable that any forger active in the 1890's would have been able to make an imitation of such amazing quality as the Boston Throne, not even with the help of ideas and sketches supplied by some friendly archaeologist. This will be evident by comparing its reliefs with the many forged 'Greek' marble sculptures that were made during the late nineteenth and the first four decades of the twentieth century, sculptures such as the 'archaic' heads and the Diadoumenos condemned by Furtwängler, the 'restored' head of the 'Athlete' sold to Carl Jacobsen, the relief fragments 'from the Parthenon' unmasked by

Ashmole, the 'archaic' sculptures made by Alceo Dossena, and the 'antiques' collected by the Russian baron Wladimir de Grueneisen.

The sculptures of the Grueneisen collection, published in 1925 by the owner as *Art Classique,* with a eulogizing preface by the renowned French archaeologist Salomon Reinach, were promptly condemned as forgeries by German and Italian art experts, which gave rise to much scholarly altercation. An important contribution to the discussion was made by Franz Studniczka, who in a lengthy article, published in 1928, surveyed a number of forged marble sculptures, including a loathsome 'archaic' Athena in the Grueneisen collection, a miserable kore made by a restorer in Rome and purchased by "a Nordic museum" (viz. the National Museum in Stockholm), and two 'pedimental statues' by Dossena, one representing Athena striding out in battle, the other a Goddess fighting a Giant, of whom only a leg was extant.

These and other 'archaic' marbles by Dossena appeared in the Roman antique market about 1926. One of them, a small kore of excessive slenderness, said to come from Etruria, was bought that year by John Marshall for the Metropolitan Museum of New York but was soon withdrawn from exhibition on the advice of the buyer himself. In 1927 the Athena just mentioned, together with a fragmentary group consisting of the upper part of a woman and the head and shoulders of a man, were offered to the same museum by dealers who alleged that these marbles had been found at Velia, south of Paestum. The Metropolitan Museum refused them and the Cleveland Museum bought the Athena but was eventually glad to see her taken back by the vendor, after representations by Marshall, whereupon the batch was sent back to Europe.

The extraordinary thing in this tangle of fraud was that Studniczka, while condemning Dossena's Athena and his Goddess battling a Giant, tried to rehabilitate the fragmentary group "from Velia" which, together with the Athena, had been refused by the New York museum and was suspected to be a forgery by most other archaeologists. In spite of this, Studniczka was convinced of its genuineness, had a plaster reconstruction made of it in Munich, adding a third figure, and tried to prove that this "Entführungsgruppe" was a "durchaus stilreine, frischfröhlich kühne Schöpfung der Zeit um 500 vor Christus", and that his sceptical colleagues were thrown into a fever of panic and suspicion because of the current traffic in forgeries. The group, however, as pointed out by Bernard Ashmole, betrays itself as a forgery by its sham archaic style typical of Dossena's works, its artificial breaks and weathering, and its groves made by means of a running drill, a technique not used in the archaic age.

Ashmole was also able to demonstrate that Dossena possessed a couple of fascicles of F. Winter's *Kunstgeschichte in Bildern* and used its small photographic reproductions of archaic Greek sculptures as models for his works. Dossena's insistence on being a creative artist, whose works were mutilated, artificially weathered and sold as antiques by unscrupulous dealers, was all evidently part of his deceptive activities.

The successful productivity of Pio Riccardi and his sons and nephews, of Fioravanti, Dossena, and many other forgers, whose works were accepted and defended as genuine by distinguished art experts and exhibited in renowned museums, ought to be a useful lesson about the necessity of scrutinizing with eyes sharpened by suspicion all unpedigreed works sold or offered for sale as antiques. Suspicion, however, ought to be counterbalanced by an awareness of the fact that our knowledge of Greek art and its offshoots in different countries of the Mediterranean world is and always will be fragmentary. Otherwise, important ancient works of art run the risk of being condemned as spurious by experts who find them too divergent from what happens to be known today of comparable works of ancient art. This was the case, for instance, with the early archaic standing goddess in Berlin and the early archaic kouros in New York (p. 48), which are now considered as excellent examples of how Athenian sculptors represented the draped female and the nude male figure about 600 B.C.

This was also the case with the well-known marble relief in the Ny Carlsberg Glyptotek, representing a peculiar scene of homicide so difficult to interpret, date and classify that, perhaps as a way out, the possibility of its being a forgery has been considered. It belonged formerly to the collection of the Cardinal Antonio Despuig, having been discovered during his excavations 1787–1796 on the site of the *Nemus Aricinum,* Diana's grove and sanctuary at Lake Nemi (p. 26). It was reproduced in 1791 by the engraver Pietro Fontana, with the legend *Rex Nemorensis.* The relief was thus regarded at that time as an illustration of how, according to a custom of remote antiquity, an escaped slave attained the office of priest to Diana, with the title King of the Grove, by killing his predecessor. More probable interpretations have been suggested in later times; usually, the scene is thought to represent Orestes (assumed to have been the founder of the sanctuary) in the act of murdering Aegisthus in the presence of Clytemnestra, Electra, and two maid-servants.

The relief was formerly regarded as an archaic Greek or archaistic Roman work, until Furtwängler rightly pointed out, in *Die antiken Gemmen,* published in 1900, that its style is neither pure archaic Greek nor archaistic Roman, but similar to that of Etruscoid gems of the third and second centuries B.C.; and considering also that it is made of Italian marble, he classified it as an indigenous archaized work of the said period. Other scholars, however, falling back upon the common belief that marble was not used in Italy until the first century B.C., tried to show that the relief was a much later Roman copy of an earlier work, archaic Cypriot according to Maurizio Borda, late archaic Greek in the opinion of Gisela Richter.

The material of the relief, however, provides no valid argument against its assignment to an earlier period, since at least some ten sculptures of Greek or indigenous marble have been discovered in Etruria, ranging in date from the late archaic to the late Hellenistic age. All except three of them are evidently made by Etruscan sculptors who, with modest results, ventured to work in this hard material, the measure-bound carving of which seems to have been against the grain of Etruscan artists, who preferred freely modelling in clay and wax, for statues and reliefs in bronze and terracotta.

F. Altheim's theory that the relief could have been made about 500 B.C. by a Greek sculptor working in Italy, and using the marble of the country, is thus acceptable as far as the material is concerned, and also in view of the fact that the presence of Greek artists in Etruria and Rome was a prerequisite, born out by literary tradition and archaeological evidence, for the development of the Hellenized Etruscan art; one of these artists probably made the small archaic marble statue of a female nude, found in the sanctuary of the Cannicella necropolis at Orvieto and identified as a cult image of the Etruscan goddess Vei. But Altheim's attempt to explain the somewhat ambiguous archaism of the relief as due to a supposed retooling soon after its discovery is far from convincing; and its authenticity is corroborated by strongly adhering rootmarks, and also by the unlikeliness of an eighteenth-century forger being interested in producing, and able to execute, a composite scene in archaic style such as the Despuig relief.

The most plausible judgement has been pronounced by German Hafner who, on the basis of comparison between the relief and early Etrusco-Latial sculptures, inferred that the former was made in the fifth century B.C., probably in Rome. The sculptor may have been an Etruscan working in the style and manner he had learnt in the workshop of an immigrant Greek master.

Ancient bronze figurines, Greek, Etruscan, and Roman, have frequently been used as models by forgers working in the same metal. The reasons are obvious. The original bronzes, produced to serve as votive offerings or decorative details of mirrors, candelabra, kottaboi, incense-stands, and vessels of various kinds, are small, solid, and widely differing in style and quality, which permits forgers of moderate resources to fabricate great numbers of imitations, saleable, if not otherwise, in junk markets, together with second-rate antiquities from illicit excavations.

Forged bronzes of larger dimensions, on the other hand, seem to have become less common in later times. This may be due, in some degree, to the costliness of the metal, but the main reason is no doubt the fact that ancient bronzes of some size were made hollow by casting *à cire perdue* (lost-wax), which implies that an imitation of such a bronze, to have a chance of deceiving present-day experts, must be made by the same process.

This process was a succession of delicate procedures. The first thing to do was to make a core of coarse clay roughly in the shape of the prospective bronze figure. When the core was dry and hard it was covered with a layer of beeswax as thick as the figure's bronze shell was to be. The wax layer was given the definite form intended for the bronze, either while it was still soft, by free-hand modelling or with moulds made from an exact model, or else, when the wax had hardened, by carving as in wood or stone. The wax layer was then covered with successive coats of diluted clay forming a mantle which, to prevent displacement, was fixed to the core with bronze nails. The whole, having been provided with vents and pouring channels, was fired till the wax melted and drained off, whereupon molten bronze was poured in to take its place between the core and mantle. When the metal had cooled, the mantle was broken away, the core removed as far as possible, and the bronze was given an elaborate finish. Protruding parts of the nails and the metal solidified in the vents and pouring channels were cut away; flaws due to gas bubbles were excised and repaired with thin pieces of bronze; the hair and other details were perfected by chasing; the nipples, lips and eyebrows were often indicated by inlays of copper. In fine Greek bronze statues the eye-sockets were empty to receive eyeballs of white and coloured materials and eyelashes of copper. Sometimes, bronze statues were made in parts cast separately in diversified lost-wax processes, as demonstrated through F. Roncalli's thorough examination of the so-called Mars of Todi in the Museo Gregoriano Etrusco of the Vatican.

A forger, consequently, must have great antiquarian knowledge and remarkable skill in modelling and metallurgy to be able to make a large-size bronze figure in the manner described, in a style convincingly Greek, Etruscan, or Roman, and in addition, with an artificial patina that seems to be produced by millennial oxidation. Lacking this skill, and casting with the help of moulds, a technique unknown in Europe until the fourteenth century, he will produce bronzes with mould-marks proving them to be forgeries.

Adolf Furtwängler, more than eighty years ago, pointed out some badly cast bronze forgeries, including a statuette known as the Apollo Stroganoff, modelled on the Apollo Belvedere, and a number of female heads reproducing the Greek type of head traditionally known as 'Sappho'.

At the same time Furtwängler vindicated the authenticity (questioned by some French scholars) of a large bronze head of a female wearing a city-wall crown, found in Paris in 1675 and preserved in the Bibliothèque Nationale, declaring it to be a representation of Lutetia Parisiorum made in the age of Augustus, probably after a statue by the fifth-century sculptor Alkamenes.

Another bronze work erroneously thought to be a modern forgery is the famous statuette of a horse in the Metropolitan Museum of New York. Acquired in 1923 from a Paris art dealer, it was admired and much reproduced as a Greek masterpiece of about 470 B.C., vying with or even surpassing the bronze statuette of a horse found fifteen years later in Olympia. But in 1956 the technician J.V. Noble noticed a fine line running down the horse's spine and along its belly, and interpreting this mark as an indication that the statuette had been cast between two moulds, he concluded that it must be a modern forgery. This seemed to be confirmed by other observations. A small hole in the horse's mane, considered to have held a separately made head-stall, was placed too low for this purpose, as shown by the modelled head-stall of the Olympia horse. Another hole on top of the horse's head, thought to have held a *meniskos,* a spike like those placed on the heads of Greek outdoor statues to discourage bird droppings, was found to have no *raison d'être* in a statuette. In 1967 the horse was submitted to examination with a magnet and gamma-rays, which revealed that the sandy core remaining in its interior contained pieces of iron wire, the protruding ends of which had been cut off and concealed with bronze tacks, formerly thought to be repairs of flaws proving the genuineness of the figure. All this was now looked upon as an illustration of how even a master forger was liable to make tale-telling mistakes.

The German archaeologist Carl Blümel, however, who was also a practising sculptor, upheld the authenticity of the statuette, pointing out that several Greek bronzes were supplied with interior iron stays. On closer inspection, moreover, the presumed mould-marks seen on the horse turned out to be thin wax ridges resulting from the many reproduction casts made of it for the museum's souvenir shop. Finally in 1971 some grains of quarts and zircon taken from the core of the horse were submitted to a thermoluminescence test which, allowing for the radiation produced when taking the gamma-ray shadowgraph, demonstrated that the horse was between 2,000 and 4,000 years old.

This, however, does not imply that it must be a Greek original of the fifth century B.C. Its sleek over-elegant form, the hole in its mane and the other on top of its head, both difficult to explain, perhaps also the absence of a modelled head-stall, suggest that it might be a late Hellenistic work based on Greek models of the early fifth century, just as the 'Apollo of Piombino' already described (pp. 54 f.).

Gold is costlier than any other material traditionally used for ornaments and fine utensils of different kinds. But the high prices paid for ancient gold jewellery have made it profitable for skilled forgers to work even in this precious metal, which also has the advantage of being very ductile and unaffected by oxidation. The forger in gold, consequently, unlike his colleagues working in bronze, is spared the trouble of bringing about some sort of artificial patina, but may content himself with giving his products a thin coating of dirt or an imitation of the reddish film often seen on gold objects taken from ancient graves.

The marvellous gold treasures discovered ever since the early nineteenth century in ancient tombs of Etruria, Latium and Magna Graecia, of Rhodes, Thessaly, Macedonia, and southern Russia, soon tempted clever goldsmiths to test their skill by making imitations of these beautiful things, for profit but not always for fraud. The imitators, however, were faced with immense difficulties because of the advanced techniques used by their ancient colleagues, in decorating jewellery and gold vessels with figures and ornaments executed in repoussé and stamping, as filigree work, and in granulation. This last-mentioned embellishment, consisting of minute balls of gold fixed closely-packed to a gold surface, was used by Greek goldsmiths and perfected in Etruria in the archaic period; the granulation of some pieces of Etruscan jewellery looks like mist formed on a cold metal sheet or glass pane.

In the course of time, however, these difficulties were gradually overcome, especially since the Roman goldsmith Fortunato Castellani in about 1830 succeeded in imitating Etruscan granulation and his son Augusto (pp. 44, 67) improved on the father's invention. In consequence of this and other technical copying methods, great numbers of 'Greek' and 'Etruscan' gold diadems, necklaces, earrings, bracelets, medallions, fibulae, finger-rings etc. have nowadays passed from the workshops of unscrupulous goldsmiths into the show-cases of many museums and, especially, into the hands of rich, unsuspecting and self-assured private collectors. Fortunately, it happens that the forgers in gold also make telling mistakes, formal, stylistic, or technical.

The appearance in the 1880's and 1890's of a great number of magnificent gold objects alleged to come from Scythian graves in southern Russia was highly sensational. They were acquired with enthusiasm by many museums, probably because the museum experts were not sufficiently acquainted with the character of Scythian art, which represents a mixture of Greek, Persian, Central Asiatic and indigenous styles and subjects. Furtwängler effectively warned the Berlin museum against the intended acquisition of a splendid gold crown with a Greek votive inscription stating that it was made by "Kallinikos, son of Euxenor, goldsmith in Olbia". But he got involved in a hot controversy with his French colleagues, the brothers Salomon and Theodore Reinach, by declaring that the Musée du Louvre in purchasing a magnificent gold headgear, beehive-shaped and inscribed with the name of Saitapharnes, had in reality acquired a forgery, revealed as such by sundry anomalies in its encircling zones of embossed figured and ornamental decoration. Furtwängler's conclusion, though, was soon confirmed by a Russian goldsmith, Israel Ruchomovsky of Odessa, who proudly declared that he had made the Tiara of Saitapharnes and many other Graeco-Scythian ornaments at the orders of antique dealers, decorating his masterpieces with the help of illustrations found in various archaeological publications, among others a work entitled *Antiquités de la Russie méridionale,* edited in 1891 by N. Kondakoff, J. Tolstoy, and Salomon Reinach.

Ordinary forgers work for profit and as secretly as possible, and what they may feel of pride in having duped eminent art experts must be enjoyed within a strictly limited circle. When a professional or amateur archaeologist follows the path of deception – which, alas!, has happened more than once – he does it less, or not at all, for the sake of pecuniary gain, but primarily to win himself a name or increase the fame he has already won, and the means used to reach this goal may be of many kinds.

Amateur archaeologists, who often are or have been engaged in occupations in which a certain amount of shrewdness and showing off is required, seem to yield more easily than professionals to the temptation of using fraud for the sake of aggrandizement in the world of learning.

This is well illustrated, to begin with, by the life and epoch-making activities of the most renowned of all amateur archaeologists, the German Heinrich Schliemann, who fulfilled the dream of his early years of poverty and self-instruction by using the fortune he had amassed in trade to excavate the ruins of Troy and the tombs of Mycenae, in order to prove the historicity of the Iliad and make himself an honoured and world-famous man. He achieved all this, as recently revealed, with a resolution that did not shrink from falsifying not only documents regarding his private life, but also the reports of his excavations. His accounts of how he discovered "Priam's Treasure" at the city wall of what he thought had once been Homer's Troy, secretly and in danger removing the precious objects with the help of his loving Greek born wife Sophia (who was demonstrably in Athens at the time of the alleged assistance), contain so many other lies and discrepancies, regarding the find-spot, the date of discovery, and even the shape of the gold vessel said to have been found together with the famous jewellery, that there is strong reason to suspect that Schliemann assembled artefacts from different places to form one large and spectacular treasure, the discovery of which would permanently glorify his name.

A great name in the history of archaeology seemed also to be assured an English lawyer and amateur archaeologist named Charles Dawson. In the early years of the twentieth century he appeared at various learned societies, lecturing on the remarkable discoveries he had made near his home in Sussex, where he had found figurines of cast iron, being the first proof of the early use of this metal in Europe, and also some fragments of roof tiles stamped with Latin inscriptions testifying to Stilicho's victories over the Irish and the Picts in the reign of the Emperor Honorius (395–423).

In 1912, Dawson and the paleontologist A. Smith-Woodward created still greater sensation by exhibiting to the members of the Royal Geological Society in London a prognathous human skull, said to have been found by Dawson in a gravel-pit at Piltdown in Sussex: here at long last was material proof of the existence of "the missing link" in the evolution from ape to man! To make doubly sure, Dawson continued his excavations, finding teeth and bones of extinct animals in the gravel-pit, and discovering in another place not far off other skeletal remains of the Piltdown type of ape-like man, now termed *Eoanthropus Dawsoni*, "Dawson's Man of Dawn".

After long and heated disputes the alleged discoveries of Charles Dawson have been definitely exposed as frauds. A thermoluminescence test of the tiles proved that they were made only a short time before being displayed and discussed at the Society of Antiquaries in London, in 1907. Chemical, microscopic and other examinations of the Piltdown skull revealed that it consisted of the subfossil brain-pan of a fully developed specimen of *Homo sapiens* combined with the lower jaw of an orang-outan, the teeth of which had been filed into appropriate shape.

Dawson was unquestionably guilty of fraud and forgery. But he does not seem to have been alone in this affair of deception. According to a statement tape recorded shortly before his death in 1980, J.A. Douglas, professor of geology at Oxford university, had reasons to suspect that his predecessor, professor W.J. Sollas, had played a trick on his antagonist Smith-Woodward by supplying Dawson with skeletal remains with which he larded the gravel-pit at Piltdown. When the practical joke caused more turmoil than the joker had foreseen, he preferred to keep silent, and professor Douglas to have his suspicion revealed posthumously.

Highly sensational, and giving rise to much lively scholarly and even judicial controversy, were the reports issued in the 1920's of the remarkable discoveries made at Glozel, a hamlet near Vichy in central France, where a young peasant named Émile Fradin and a physician interested in archaeology, Dr. Antoine Morlet of Vichy, had unearthed fragments of glass and glazed bricks, implements of stone and bone, coarse clay vases, stones with incised figures of animals, and clay tablets with incised graphic symbols. Fradin had made the first discoveries in 1921; Dr Morlet, enthusiastic, imaginative, and ambitious, provided him with archaeological literature, incited him to undertake new excavations, summoned journalists to write of the enterprise, and in printed papers described the discovered artefacts as originating from a neolithic civilization which had flourished in the region of Glozel many thousands of years before and had invented the art of glass-making and a writing system of its own.

These conclusions were of course contrary to the accumulated evidence of the spread of culture from the East toward the West but corresponded with Salomon Reinach's ideas about a diffusion of culture in the opposite direction. Reinach's judgement of the style and execution of ancient artefacts was not on a level with his vast learning, and having seen young Fradin excavating at Glozel, he became a firm champion of Dr. Morlet's theories. The archaeologists O.G.S. Crawford and A. Vayson de Pradenne, on the other hand, having made researches of their own on the find-spot, concluded that it had been larded with objects made by Fradin.

The sequel was a long and heated argumentation in favour of or against the asserted neolithic origin of the artefacts unearthed at Glozel. In 1927 an international commission of eminent archaeologists, having examined the excavated objects and made new excavations at the find-spot, formally stated that the alleged neolithic artefacts were forgeries. Whereupon Reinach and two other French scholars who had taken sides with him published a manifesto declaring that in the future these foreign archaeologists would appear just as ridiculous as the inquisitors who condemned Galilei.

In 1928 a new commission headed by Reinach made yet another excavation at Glozel, finding, among other things, a clay tablet on which the Swedish criminal investigator Harry Söderman discovered a fingerprint that did not match any of those taken from Dr Morlet and the members of the Fradin family.

In the same year the family brought an action against the French archaeologist René Dussaud for having accused its members of forgery; and at this juncture a statement by a famous forensic chemist was produced, who had found that certain clay objects excavated at Glozel contained cotton fibres and pieces of grass and moss retaining the chlorophyll, and that the clay dissolved in water within a few hours. At last, the court of appeal at Riom decreed that the objects alleged to be ancient artefacts discovered at Glozel were to be regarded as forgeries, but that no one could be found guilty of the fraud.

In spite of this, Dr Morlet continued deciphering his "neolithic" inscriptions until his death, confident that his ideas would be confirmed in the future; and at the same time and later on other amateur linguists tried to interpret the mysterious script with the help of different languages, Phoenician, Hebrew, Arabic, Basque, etc.

A few years ago, however, some typical clay artefacts from Glozel were submitted to thermoluminescence tests, on the basis of which they were referred to dates between 700 B.C. and 100 A.D.; and at the same time it was observed that the glaze of a clay fragment covered its inscription. The conclusion drawn was that the tested objects could not possibly have been made in the neolithic age, nor only some fifty or sixty years ago; that they could not have been inscribed a long time after they were made; and that they probably dated from the La Tène or the Celtic-Roman period.

These results, though, were soon called in question. Physicists pointed out that the tests were unreliable because no allowance had been made for the possibility that the tested objects could have been exposed to nuclear radiation from uraniferous ground not far from the find-spot. Archaeologists emphasized that the artefacts from Glozel consisted of objects that did not belong together or to any of the periods suggested. An important observation was also made by the linguist T.D. Crawford, who pointed out that as the Glozel inscriptions contain at least 133 different signs, they cannot possibly have been symbols of the sounds of a spoken language.

In 1927 the French historian C. Jullian tried to interpret the curiously mixed artefacts at Glozel as a Celtic magician's professional equipment. But the magician of Glozel was most probably the young peasant, who having found some pieces of old glass and curiously incised clay objects, may have been induced by the doctor's enthusiasm and archaeological pictures to enhance the value of his discovery by larding the find-spot with home-made antiquities, conspicuous among which are the mysterious inscriptions, in which O's, T's, X's and other Latin letters are well mixed with swastikas, sun-wheels, crescents, zigzags and other figures, all written in rows, as by a schoolboy.

The most sensational fraud that ever occurred in the history of classical archaeology was perpetrated in the 1880's and remained unrevealed till long after the death of the culprits. It will be described at some length here, because a renowned professional archaeologist was the protagonist and the *corpus delicti* figured as a document of great historical and philological importance for almost a century, until the deception was definitely unmasked, in 1980.

The *corpus delicti* is the so-called *Fibula Praenestina*. It is a gold fibula of a type dated to the seventh century B.C. and generally called *a drago*, dragon-fibula, because of its serpentine bow. It owes its fame to the fact that its long catch bears an engraved inscription in what seemed to be archaic Latin, running from right to left: MANIOS:MED:FHE: FHAKED:NUMASIOI. This was usually rendered in classical Latin as *Manius me fecit Numerio* and supposed to mean that the fibula told the reader that Manios, a goldsmith in Praeneste, now Palestrina, where the fibula was said to have been found, made it for Numasios, a citizen of Praeneste, whose name was considered to be the archaic equivalent of Numerius, a name known from Cicero's narrative, *De divinatione,* II, 85, of how the oracular *sortes Praenestinae* were found by a certain Numerius Suffustius.

The inscription has been quoted, interpreted, and used as basis for historical and linguistic inferences in countless university lectures, dissertations and textbooks, as the earliest known specimen of written Latin, with archaisms such as the accusative *med* for *me,* the dative termination *-oi,* and the reduplicated perfect *fhefhaked.*

The fibula was presented to the world of learning in 1887 through lectures and printed articles by the well-known German archaeologist Wolfgang Helbig, assisted in part by his compatriot, the epigraphist Ferdinand Dümmler. From the beginning, however, there was something disquieting in Helbig's vague and varied information as to the provenance of the fibula. He stated at first that it had been found at Palestrina in a tomb of the same type as the rich Tomba Bernardini, discovered there in 1876. Later on he said that the fibula belonged to a friend of his, who had bought it in Palestrina in 1871. Soon after it was revealed that this friend was the antique dealer Francesco Martinetti (p. 75), who in 1889 presented the fibula to the Museo di Villa Giulia, and in acknowledgement received the title of *cavaliere.*

In the sequel new disconcerting statements were made. In 1898 the German archaeologist Georg Karo published an article in which he alleged that the inscribed fibula came from no other tomb than the Tomba Bernardini, and in the next year, therefore, Emil Reisch repeated this statement, with some reserve, in the second edition of Helbig's *Führer durch die öffentlichen Sammlungen klassischer Altertümer in Rom.* In 1900 Karo informed the director of the Museo Preistorico in Rom, Luigi Pigorini, in writing, that Helbig had assured him that the fibula had been stolen from the Tomba Bernardini and sold to Martinetti by the foreman superintending the excavation of the tomb, and that Helbig only at this time, after the death of Martinetti and the foreman, thought fit to reveal the truth. In consequence, the fibula was associated with the grave-gifts of the Tomba Bernardini in the Museo Preistorico; and Karo repeated his statement about its provenance in the first part of his study of Etruscan jewellery, entitled *Le oreficerie di Vetulonia.*

Ever since its first mysterious appearance in 1887, the authenticity of the fibula, or at least its inscription, was discussed by eminent archaeologists and philologists, Giovanni Pinza, Charles D. Curtis, David Randall-MacIver, Vittore Pisano, A.E. Gordon, and others; and the fibula was left behind in the Museo Preistorico when the grave-gifts of the Tomba

Bernardini were transferred to the Museo di Villa Giulia in 1960.

In spite of all suspicious circumstances, the authenticity of the fibula and its inscription, as well as its belonging to the Tomba Bernardini, have been upheld by other eminent scholars, most emphatically by Giovanni Colonna, in the periodical *Epigraphia,* 1976 and 1979, and in the catalogue of the exhibition *Civiltà del Lazio primitivo,* organized in Rome in 1976. In the same catalogue, Massimo Pallottino even ventured the conclusion that "the earliest written document in Latin so far known, the fibula of Praeneste, seems to show East Italic linguistic influences that to a certain degree accord with the literary evidence of the Sabines being drawn to and penetrating into the plains of Latium as early as the time of the foundation of Rome".

The suspicions, however, have been definitely confirmed by the eminent epigraphist Margherita Guarducci, who in 1980 published an exhaustive memoir entitled *La cosiddetta Fibula Praenestina,* containing the results of thorough examinations of the fibula and its inscription as well as a diligent inquiry into the activities of certain archaeologists, collectors and antique dealers living in Rome during the latter half of the nineteenth century. This memoir was followed by another in 1984, in which Professor Guarducci presents the results of further research in the matter.

The learned authoress advances many arguments against the authenticity of the inscription, and of these the following are decisive. The inscription, as revealed by magnifying lenses, was engraved by an unskilled and unsteady hand, incising lines of different depth, sometimes tremulous, sometimes doubled, thus producing very irregular letters, strikingly different from the exact lettering of archaic incised inscriptions, such as the owner's name *Fetusia* discovered in 1949 on a silver bowl from the Tomba Bernardini of Praeneste and the *mi mamerces artesi* on a gold fibula from Vulci. An ancient Praenestine goldsmith can hardly be supposed to have scratched his precious work as if it were a simple clay pot.

The words of the inscription are divided from each other by punctuation-marks consisting of two points placed vertically, and the perfect *fhefhaked* has also an inner punctuation, as sometimes seen in early Etruscan inscriptions. But this inner punctuation, which divides the reduplication from the stem, consists of three vertical points; and after these, the writer first engraved the letters FHF, probably intending to write a second FHE, but seeing his mistake, changed them into FHA. The letter F, the Greek digamma, which in archaic Latin denotes the semivocal V (the Fetusia of the silver bowl just mentioned thus stands for Vetusia = Veturia), is marked as aspirated by an added H, a writing common in early Greek inscriptions but unknown, apart from the fibula, in Latin epigraphy.

These observations, together with the fact that the name Numerius, as demonstrated by the linguist W. Belardi, cannot be derived from an archaic Numasios, prove that the inscription of the fibula was composed and executed by a person unpractised in engraving but acquainted with Praenestine tradition and well versed in Latin epigraphy and philology, though not as thoroughly as to be able to avoid telling mistakes.

The observations here summarized all and sundry betoken that the Manios inscription is a forgery. There was always the possibility, however, that the forger could have engraved the inscription on an ancient gold fibula, to raise its value and importance, since fibulae of this type are not rare. But if the fibula could also be shown to be a forgery, it would mean that the inscription must needs be spurious. Professor Guarducci, therefore, had the fibula submitted to technical tests, to be compared with similar tests of gold objects of undoubted antiquity.

The chief results of these tests, executed by means of microscope, X-ray fluorescence, and ultra-violet rays, may be summarized as follows. The Manios fibula is made of an alloy composed of $83,3\pm2$ % gold, $13\pm1,5$ % silver, and $0,7\pm0,2$ % copper, whereas a fibula of the same type from the Tomba Bernardini consists of 92 ± 1 % gold, 8 ± 1 % silver, and $0,3$ % copper. Owing to a different micro-structure, the Manios fibula lacks the stiffness and brittleness shown by gold objects found in archaic graves: its pin can be bent and straightened without snapping. The surface of the fibula has corroded cavities from having been treated with acids, both before the inscription was made, as shown by the fact that some engraved lines traverse corroded spots, and also after the engraving was completed. The fibula has no traces of a calcareous deposit like the one generally formed on long-buried gold objects, but was smeared over with an artificial 'patina' composed of gum-lac, grease, wax and resin; and it also shows some traces of gilding, used to hide faulty casting and soldered joints.

The accumulated evidence, epigraphical, linguistic, and technical, leaves no opening for reasonable contradiction. The Fibula Praenestina and its famous inscription are forgeries. And this leads to the question of why and by whom this painful fraud was perpetrated.

On the basis of oral tradition, newspaper articles, correspondence between Wolfgang Helbig and Carl Jacobsen, and the unpublished memoirs of the German archaeologist Ludwig Pollak, Margherita Guarducci draws a highly interesting and informative picture of the dimmed Roman scene in which the antique dealer Francesco Martinetti (1833–1895) played an important part. He is described as a peculiar type, morbidly greedy and suspicious, wealthy through dubious dealings in genuine and less genuine antiquities, a skilful restorer and gem engraver, assisted by certain goldsmiths and sculptors, and by his friend, adviser and commercial partner, the German archaeologist Wolfgang Helbig.

Wolfgang Helbig (1839–1915) was to all appearances a complex personality, gifted, inventive, ambitious, and unscrupulous. He arrived in Italy in 1862, twenty-three years old, with a doctor's degree from the university of Bonn and a scholarship at the German Archaeological Institute in Rome. Three years later he was appointed to the post of Second Secretary (=Director) of the Institute, and in the following year he married the Russian princess Nadejda Schakowskoy. Through her he made the acquaintance of many rich Italian land-owners, who informed him of archaeological discoveries on their estates. He now also became a friend of some distinguished collectors of art and antiquities, the Count Michel Tyskiewicz, the Baron Giovanni Barracco, the Marchese Chigi Zondadari, and the Count Grégoire Stroganoff, who used to meet every Sunday and discuss their latest acquisitions with each other and Helbig, over a glass of champagne. In 1887 he also came into friendly contact with Carl Jacobsen and procured for his Glyptotek in Copenhagen a great number of large copies in colour of Etruscan tomb paintings at Tarquinia, Chiusi, and Orvieto. In the same year he resigned his post at the German Archaeological Institute and took up residence with his family in the Vil. Lante on the Gianicolo, built and decorated by Giulio Romano.

All this according to Helbig's brief autobiography, written in 1911 for Jacobsen's catalogue of the Etruscan department of his museum, which was largely created with antiquities purchased by Helbig and therefore called the Helbig Museum. In this autobiography, Helbig also dwells upon his scholarly works, of which the aforementioned *Führer* is still very useful, thanks to new, revised and amplified editions, the fourth published in the years 1963–1972, in four volumes. But he says nothing of his activities as a purchasing agent for the Ny Carlsberg Glyptotek and other foreign museums (pp. 75 ff.), nothing of his friend Martinetti, nothing of the famous fibula.

In the autobiography Helbig also states that he resigned his post at the German Archaeological Institute because of disagreement with certain bureaucratic members of the Central Direction in Berlin. But in Lothar Wickert's *Beiträge zur Geschichte des Deutschen Archäologischen Instituts 1870–1920* (1979) it is made clear that Helbig left the institute in anger at not having been promoted to the post of First Secretary, and that the reason of his being passed over was that the Central Direction considered him unfit for this position because of his behaviour and his activities as middleman between Roman antique dealers and foreign collectors.

Some great German scholars, Otto Jahn, Theodor Mommsen, and Ulrich von Wilamowitz-Moellendorff, also pronounced themselves on Helbig's character in terms that explain how he came to be a learned and diligent archaeologist, a capricious bon vivant, and an unscrupulous partner of shady antique dealers. There is some reason to believe that

Helbig soon after his arrival in Rome in 1862 got involved in the activities of such dealers, particularly in the trade with the much admired *cistae Praenestinae*, large toilet boxes of bronze, generally cylindrical, sometimes oval or rectangular, and mostly decorated with engraved figure scenes round the sides and on the lid.

One of these cistae, oval and adorned on the cover with an engraved composition showing Aeneas, Latinus, Turnus, and other figures of the Aeneid, was lectured on the 21st of April 1864 by the learned Heinrich Brunn, Second Secretary of the German Archaeological Institute, who found that this scene illustrating traditions of early Rome seemed "almost made to offer the subject of a lecture on the Birthday of the City". So it was perhaps, but later than Brunn imagined. The cista was sold to the British Museum through the antique dealer Pasinati; and it was only after the lapse of fifty-five years, in 1919, that the figured scene was exposed as a forgery, in Carl Robert's *Archäologische Hermeneutik*. It is engraved by a sure hand on a genuine undecorated cista, to raise its market value; but the design was no doubt composed by a person more intimately acquainted with the Aeneid than the engraver may be reasonably supposed to have been. Margherita Guarducci thinks that this person was no other than Helbig but is unwilling to believe that the forgery was part of a planned intrigue. Anyhow, less than a year after he lectured on the cista Brunn was transferred to a professorship in Munich, and Helbig was appointed his successor in Rome.

The profitable treatment of the Pasinati cista seems to have encouraged Martinetti to have other undecorated Praenestine cistae embellished in the same manner. Two of these cistae were published by Helbig in 1871 and sold by Martinetti, one to the British Museum, the other to the Czartoryski Museum in Cracow.

Helbig took but small risks in helping Martinetti, as he probably did, by composing mythological scenes to be engraved on undecorated cistae from Praeneste. But he took great risks when he sold to Carl Jacobsen the miserably 'restored' marble athlete "from Formia" and the forged Diadoumenos mentioned above (p. 75). The last-mentioned statue was promptly condemned as a forgery by Pollak and Furtwängler; and Helbig, author of the guide to the antique collections of Rome, can hardly have acted in good faith.

In spite of Margherita Guarducci's thorough inquiry, the maker of the fibula remains unknown. He must have been a goldsmith by trade, dabbling in the art of imitating ancient jewellery, without ever reaching the mastery of Augusto Castellani (p. 44), to judge from the technical faults found in the fibula. Castellani, however, on condition that it be kept secret, revealed the name of the maker to the archaeologist Giovanni Pinza and also told him of "a foreign scholar" as the creator of the inscription.

The identification of this foreign scholar is not very difficult. Helbig's specific qualifications, his participation in Martinetti's shady transactions, his conflicting statements as to when and how the fibula was found and came into the hands of the dealer, and his need to win the favour of the members of the Central Direction in Berlin through a remarkable contribution to historical and philological studies, in order to be promoted to the post, vacant in 1887, of First Secretary of the German Archaeological Institute in Rome, are all circumstances that make it more than probable that he decided to convert the plain newly-made fibula into a document of paramount importance, by scratching the fateful dedicatory inscription on to its pin-catch. This circumstantial evidence, moreover, is strengthened by the fact that, according to a renowned expert in graphology, most of the letters of the fibula correspond to those written by Helbig in his copies of ancient inscriptions.

The fraud did not help him to reach the goal he desired; but having left his institute in angry disappointment, he was able to continue his lucrative trade and his fashionable life as a venerated scholar in the Villa Lante, thinking perhaps at times with secret pleasure of how capitally he had deceived those supercilious colleagues of his who had dared to criticize him.

The method of raising the market value of plain antiquities by added decoration was used by nineteenth-century antique dealers and their assistants not only in the case of undecorated bronze cistae but also, and prevalently, in that of worn or unadorned clay vases, which were made saleable by touching up their paintings or embellishing them with freshly painted ornaments and figures.

A typical example of the last-mentioned kind of forgery is the so-called Nephele dish, once owned by the Count Tyskiewicz, from whose collection it passed into the possession of an English private collector. It is decorated with four figures outlined in black on a white ground, with coloured details and a name written by each figure, indicating that the scene represents Ino, Athamas, Phrixus, and Helle; and below the figures is what looks like the vase painter's half-effaced signature.

One of Helbig's colleagues in Rome, the German archaeologist Paul Hartwig, expert in Greek vase painting, had certified the authenticity of the dish; but Furtwängler was able to establish the fact, on basis of a close examination, that the dish itself is certainly genuine, while the white ground, the four figures, their names and the 'signature' show every sign of being a clever forgery. This is also suggested by the fact that one side of the dish has been broken into small pieces, while the central part with the figures is almost intact.

The person who designed and named these figures must have been thoroughly acquainted with Greek mythology and vase painting, the one who executed them had a sure hand guided by a keen eye. There is no proof of who perpetrated this forgery; but the fact that Hartwig had commercial interests in common with Martinetti (p. 76) and, with his special expertness, vouched for the authenticity of the faked dish, suggests that he may have had a hand in this fraud.

It has been aptly said, by Karl E. Meyer, *The Plundered Past* (1973 and 1977), that "the prevalence of fakes is the venereal disorder of the illicit art market – the punishment for excessive desire and bad judgement". During the last fifty years, however, thanks to a number of discoveries and inventions, particularly in chemistry, optics, nuclear physics, and radioactivity, archaeologists and art historians have received valuable help in dating ancient artefacts and weeding out forgeries made in later times.

Radiocarbon dating, based on the measurable disintegration of the radioactive isotope C 14 after the death of an organism, has been in common use some fifty years for determining the age of objects of wood, bone and other organic substances. The method, however, is complicated by variations in the absorption of the atmosphere's carbon dioxide according to where and under what conditions plants and animals have lived; and its use for dating and authentication of art objects is restricted owing to wide plus or minus limits and the fact that the analyses require taking of large samples which are destroyed in the process.

Dendrochronology, or tree-ring dating, based on the variation of ring-width in objects of wood, is also of limited use in classical archaeology, except for the study of wrecked ships.

The thermoluminescence (TL) analysis, on the other hand, has proved very serviceable for accurate dating of art objects and has also the advantage of requiring very small samples. This analysis is based on the fact that the clay fabric of ancient pottery, terracottas, and cores of bronze figures, which has lost its natural radioactivity in the process of kiln firing and subsequently re-accumulated nuclear energy in the earth, when heated to 500°C in a laboratory releases this new energy in the form of light, by which the time elapsed between the first and the second firing is measurable. A black-figured amphora in the Ashmolean Museum in Oxford, dated c. 540 B.C. on stylistic grounds, was thus shown by a TL test to be 2460 years old and genuine; whereas a black-figured column krater in the Metropolitan Museum of Art in New York was shown by a similar test to be only 102 years old and a forgery. Other TL tests executed in the 1970's have confirmed the unauthenticity of a number of terracottas already condemned as forgeries, showing that Dossena's Diana in St. Louis was then 40 years old, that Fioravanti's kore in Copenhagen had an age of 48 years, that his and Riccardo Riccardi's warriors in New York were about

60 years old, and that a number of painted 'Etruscan' terracotta slabs (p. 74) were also of recent manufacture.

In addition to these dating methods, archaeologists have at their disposal a great many laboratory devices for the detection of forgeries of different kinds. Spectographic and X-ray crystallographic analyses are used for determining the composition of the clay fabric and the glaze of vases and terracottas; X-ray fluorescence and atomic absorption spectometry for determining the elements of metal alloys; gamma ray shadowgraphy for examining the interior of bronzes cast hollow (as in the case of the bronze horse in New York, p. 83); scanning with ordinary or electron microscopes and microchemical tests for examining jewellery and simulated patination in bronzes; spectographic analyses and ultraviolet rays for examining sculptures in marble (as in the case of the Boston Throne, p. 77).

In spite of the possibilities now at hand of having forgeries detected through laboratory tests, the expert or amateur of ancient art is often faced with a difficult choice of buying or not buying an unpedigreed work which, if genuine, would be an important addition to his museum or private collection, and if not genuine, would mean a serious loss of money and reputation. The seller, of course, is unwilling to submit his ware to laboratory tests and has other presumptive buyers waiting. And the expert knows that clever forgers, learning from mistakes made by colleagues, and keeping up with the progress of art criticism and science, have found many new ways to deceive him: by studying more carefully the style and execution of ancient works suited for imitation; by learning how to prepare clay and glazes for vases and terracottas intended to be sold as Greek or Etruscan; by procuring alloys properly composed by melting down ancient coins, pieces of jewellery and bronze figures or implements that are unsaleable from wear and damage; by learning which tools to use, and which to avoid using, for making marble sculptures in archaic style; and by exposing forged clay vases and terracottas to nuclear radiation in order to frustrate possible thermoluminescence tests.

In the permanent conflict between zealous museum curators and private collectors, on one hand, and unscrupulous forgers and dealers, on the other hand, the former are thus justified in not trusting blindly in the infallibility of scientific authenticity tests, which, moreover, are too expensive to be used for examining the many thousands of unpedigreed artefacts that have been gathered and are steadily gathering in antique collections all over the world. The primary judgement, anyhow, of whether such an artefact is genuine or not will always depend on the scrutinizing expert's eye and experience in the matter of style and artistic merit (of which scientific tests can of course say nothing), of modelling, carving, painting, and metallurgy, and of the effects of oxidation and corrosion. In a majority of cases, experts in ancient art and craft first observed and pointed out anomalies or anachronisms in a work which was therefore submitted to laboratory tests and definitely revealed to be a forgery. Unfortunately, such revelations too often take place after years and decades of scholarly dispute, while the suspected work is still exhibited and described as a masterpiece of ancient art.

The experts who made the mistake of buying, accepting and defending works that are at long last exposed as forgeries are often criticized by people ignorant of the difficulty of stylistic judgement and wise after the event. This is very unfair. No expert is able to acquire perfect expertise of all kinds of artefacts that were made and all materials and techniques that were used at different times in different parts of the vast Mediterranean world which saw the birth, growth and spread of Greek civilization. Judgement is particularly difficult in the case of works created under Greek influence among Etruscans and Italic tribes, Gauls, Iberians, Thracians, Scythians and other peoples collectively called barbarians by the Greeks. Forgers imitating works of such hybrid art have the advantage that their mistakes and shortcomings may be interpreted as marks attesting the authenticity and alleged origin of the product.

This is probably the reason why eminent experts in Greek art have been repeatedly deceived by forgeries of the said kind, declaring the tiara and other gold ornaments made by Israel Ruchomovsky of Odessa to be masterpieces of Graeco-Scythian art (p. 85), considering the ugly figures of the terracotta sarcophagus made by the Pennelli brothers to be the result of coarse Etruscan modelling (pp. 67 f.), and praising the monstrous dark-hued terracotta warriors from the Riccardi-Fioravanti workshop as artistic and technical masterpieces of Etruscan art (pp. 69 ff.).

When a work of disputed antiquity is finally exposed as a forgery, through inquiries into its origin and scientific tests of its make and material, the policy pursued by annoyed museum directors caring for the reputation of their institution and its staff is to hide away the piece in locked up rooms where other fakes are usually awaiting its arrival. It would be a better policy, however, if all public museums of importance followed the example set by the British Museum in 1961 (p. 68), by exhibiting their forgeries in special rooms open to visitors. By this arrangement old mistakes could be useful lessons, in all senses of the word, for all serious students of classical art and antiquities.

Notes

To avoid a superabundance of bibliography, references are only made, as a rule, to early publications of documentary importance, to relevant works of later date, and to three other works in which the reader will find: ancient authors' statements about Greek art and artists; excellent photographic reproductions of Greek sculptures, with comments and bibliography; and explanatory descriptions, with extensive bibliographies, of numerous works of ancient art, Greek, Etruscan, and Roman, preserved in the museums of Rome. These publications are cited with the names of the authors:

Overbeck = **J. Overbeck,** Die antiken Schriftquellen zur Geschichte der bildenden Künste bei den Griechen, Leipzig 1868. Nachdruck Hildesheim 1959.

Lullies = **R. Lullies,** Griechische Plastik, von den Anfängen bis zum Beginn der römischen Kaiserzeit. Aufnahmen von **Max** und **Albert Hirmer.** Neuausgabe München 1979.

Helbig = **W. Helbig,** Führer durch die öffentlichen Sammlungen klassischer Altertümer in Rom. Vierte, völlig neu bearbeitete Auflage herausgegeben von **Hermine Speier,** I–IV, Tübingen 1963–1972.

Titles of periodicals are cited in full, in the interest of readers not acquainted with usual (more or less cryptic) abbreviations.

P. 5   Croesus' offerings to Delphi: **Herodotus,** I, 50 f., describing the figures and vessels of gold, silver and electrum which were presented to the oracle by the Lydian king and partly saved from the fire which destroyed the original temple of Apollo in 548 B.C.

P. 5   Archaic marbles of the Acropolis: **H. Payne – G. Mackworth-Young,** Archaic Marble Sculpture from the Acropolis, 1936, 2nd ed. 1950; **E. Langlotz – W.H. Schuchhardt,** Archaische Plastik auf der Akropolis, 1938; **H. Schrader** (with **Langlotz** and **Schuchhardt**), Die archaischen Marmorbildwerke der Akropolis, 1939.

P. 5   Apollo Philesios: **Overbeck,** Nos. 403–407.

P. 5   Tyrannicides: **Overbeck,** Nos. 443–447, 457; **G. Becatti,** I Tirannicidi di Antenore, in Archeologia Classica, 9, 1957; **S. Brunnsåker,** The Tyrant-Slayers of Kritios and Nesiotes: A Critical Study of the Sources and the Restorations, Skrifter utgivna av Svenska Institutet i Athen, 4°, XVII, 1955, 2nd ed. 1971. In his list of bronzes made by Praxiteles, **Pliny,** N.H. XXXIV, 69–70, includes "the statues of Harmodios and Aristogeiton, the Slayers of the Tyrant, which were carried off by Xerxes, king of the Persians, and restored to Athens by Alexander the Great after his conquest of Persia". Since Pliny states, N.H. XXXIV, 17, that the Tyrant-Slayers (of Antenor) were set up "in the year in which the kings were expelled from Rome" and dates the *floruit* of Praxiteles, N.H. XXXIV, 50, in the 104th Olympiad (364–361 B.C.), the absurd attribution of the famous group to Praxiteles cannot be ascribed to ignorance but is probably due to a displacement of what belongs to N.H. XXXIV, 72, where the author describes the monument of Leaina, a courtesan who refused to betray Harmodios and Aristogeiton, although tortured to death by the tyrants.

P. 5 Pausanias: **H. Hitzig – H. Blümner,** Des Pausanias Beschreibung von Griechenland, mit kritischem Apparat . . . (und) erklärenden Anmerkungen . . ., Band 1–3, 1896–1910; **J.G. Frazer,** Pausanias' Description of Greece, Text, Translation and Commentary, I–IV, 1898; **W.H.S. Jones,** Pausanias: Description of Greece, 5 Vols. and Companion Vol. arranged by **R.E. Wycherley** (The Loeb Classical Library); **Pausanias,** Guide to Greece, translated with an introduction by **P. Levi,** The Penguin Classics, 1971; **Pausanias,** Beschreibung Griechenlands, übersetzt und herausgegeben von **Ernst Meyer,** 1–2, 1972; **Pausanias,** Graeciae Descriptio, edidit **Maria Helena da Rocha-Pereira,** 1–2, Bibliotheca Teubneriana, 1973, 1977; **Christian Habicht,** Pausanias und seine "Beschreibung Griechenlands", 1985.

P. 6 Evocatio: **Pliny,** N.H. XXVIII, 18, quoting Verrius Flaccus.

P. 6 Volsinii: The location of the Etruscan city of Volsinii, destroyed and depopulated by the Romans in spite of its strong defensive wall, expressively mentioned by Zonaras, has been the matter of much scholarly discussion, with more or less weighty arguments, advanced to prove either that the old city lay on the lofty rock of Orvieto, or at Bolsena, the site of Roman Volsinii on the Lacus Volsiniensis. The discovery of an imposing Etruscan city wall and early tombs at Bolsena, and the absence of a ring-wall on Orvieto's naturally protected site, have been adduced in support of the last-mentioned opinion; see **R. Enking,** s.v. Volsinii, in Pauly-Wissowa, Realencyklopädie der classischen Altertumswissenschaft, 2. Reihe, IX:1, 1961; **R. Bloch,** in Studi Etruschi, 31, 1963, pp. 399 ff. But the abundance and quality of the Etruscan antiquities found in Orvieto, its medieval name *Urbs vetus,* which suggests that we have to do with an abandoned and resettled city, and the discovery within the city of remains and traces of two Etruscan defensive walls, speak strongly in favour of the first-mentioned theory; see **F. Gamurrini,** Volsinii etrusca in Orvieto, in Annali dell'Instituto di Corrispondenza Archeologica, 53, 1881, pp. 42, 55, 58 f.; **M. Bizzarri,** Una importante scoperta per l'antica topografia di Orvieto, in Bollettino dell'Istituto Storico Artistico Orvietano, 19–20, 1963–1964, pp. 118 ff.; **Id.**, Trovato in Orvieto il teichos di Zonara?, in Studi sulla città antica, Bologna 1970, pp. 153 ff.; **J. Heurgon**, in Un trentennio di collaborazione italo-francese nel campo dell'archeologia, Atti dei Convegni Lincei, 54, 1983, pp. 97 ff.; **A. Andrén**, Orvieto, Studies in Mediterranean Archaeology, Pocket-book 27, Göteborg 1984.

P. 7 M. Fulvius Flaccus' votive inscriptions: **M. Torelli,** in Roma Medio Repubblicana, exhibition catalogue, Rome 1973, pp. 103 f., fig. 10.

P. 7 Lupa Capitolina: **L. Goldscheider,** Etruscan Sculpture, 1941, pls. 98–99; **E. Simon,** in **Helbig,** II, No. 1454; **C. Dulière,** Lupa Romana, Recherches d'iconographie et essai d'interprétation, I–II, Études de philologie, d'archéologie et d'histoire anciennes publiées par l'Institut Historique Belge de Rome, 18, 1979.

P. 8 Spoils from Syracuse and Tarentum: **Livy,** XXV, 40, XXVII, 16, 7.

P. 9 Necrocorinthia: For the term, see **H. Payne,** Necrocorinthia, 1931, Appendix III.

P. 9 Verres: The works of art stolen by Verres are catalogued by **H. Habermehl,** Pauly-Wissowa, Realencyklopädie etc., 2. Reihe, VIII, 1958, coll. 1593–1602. On Verres' impudent decoration of the Comitium, Forum Romanum and Vicus Tuscus with stolen statues, see **Robert E.A. Palmer,** C. Verres' Legacy of Charm and Love to the City of Rome: A New Document, in Rendiconti della Pontificia Accademia Romana di Archeologia, 51–52, 1982, pp. 111–136.

P. 10 Apollo Temenites: Accordig to **A. Boëthius,** The Golden House of Nero, 1960, p. 24, note 37, Pliny used the word *Tuscanicus* not to designate the statue as Etruscan, but as a term denoting its archaic style. **G. Becatti,** Opere di arte greca nella Roma di Tiberio, in Archeologia Classica, 25–26, 1973–1974, p. 43, considered the statue to have been a Greek work of the archaic or early classical period. In late Republican and early Imperial times archaic rigidity and schematic anatomy were regarded as typical of Etruscan works of art, to judge from the fact that **Strabo,** XVII, 1, 28, compares Egyptian reliefs with Etruscan sculptures, and **Quintilian,** Inst.Or., XII, 10, 7, characterizes the works of the archaic sculptors Kallon and Hegesias as *duriora et Tuscanicis proxima.* But it is hard to believe that the Apollo Temenites/Tuscanicus would have been admired as a work of great beauty by Cicero, Pliny, and their contemporaries, had it presented the stance and features of an archaic or early classical statue.

P. 10   Dionysius' raid upon Pyrgi: **F. Prayon,** Historische Daten zur Geschichte von Caere und Pyrgi, in Akten des Kolloquiums zum Thema Die Göttin von Pyrgi, Biblioteca di "Studi Etruschi", 12, Firenze 1981, pp. 39 ff. The remarkable results of the excavations at Pyrgi are fully described by G. Colonna and others in Notizie degli Scavi di Antichità, Serie VIII, Vol. XXIV, 1970, II Supplemento (printed in two volumes in 1972).

P. 11   Lucian on chryselephantine statues: Gallus, 24, speaking of "the great colossi that Phidias or Myron or Praxiteles made, each of which outwardly is a beautiful Poseidon or a Zeus, made of ivory and gold, with a thunderbolt or a flash of lightning or a trident in his right hand; but if you stoop down and look inside, you will se bars and props and nails driven clear through, and beams and wedges and pitch and clay and a quantity of such ugly stuff housing within, not to mention numbers of mice and rats that keep their court in them sometimes" (tr. A.M. Harmon, The Loeb Classical Library).

P. 11   Gauls raiding Delphi: Ancient authors have different accounts of the event, some stating that the barbarians sacked the sanctuary, others that they were prevented from plunder by gods and heroes; whereas Calenan relief vases, Etruscan ash-urns, and a terracotta frieze from Civita Alba present a combination of the two versions, showing Gauls being put to flight during the pillage; see **P. Biénkowski,** Die Darstellungen der Gallier in der hellenistischen Kunst, 1908, pp. 93–104, figs. 106–112; **A. Andrén,** Architectural Terracottas from Etrusco-Italic Temples, 1940, pp. 301–308, pl. 101.

P. 11   Jewish temple treasures: **Leon Yarden,** Work in Progress: The Spoils of Jerusalem on the Arch of Titus, A Reinvestigation, in Skrifter utgivna av Svenska Institutet i Rom, 4°, XXXIX, Opuscula Romana, XIV, 1983.

P. 11   Pliny the Elder; C. Plini Secundi Naturalis Historiae Libri XXXVII, recensuit **I. Sillig,** vols. I–VIII, 1851–1858, with a useful index quoting all passages regarding persons, places and subjects mentioned in the work. For Pliny's chapters on metals and minerals and their application in art, see The Elder Pliny's Chapters on the History of Art, translated by **K. Jex-Blake,** with Commentary and Historical Introduction by **E. Sellers,** 1896; **S. Ferri,** Plinio il Vecchio, Storia delle arti antiche, testo, traduzione e note, 1946; Pline l'Ancien, Histoire Naturelle, Livre XXXIV, Livre XXXVI, Texte établi et traduit par **H. Le Bonniec,** commenté par **H. Gallet de Santerre** et **H. le Bonniec,** 1953, 1981. The Elder Pliny's way of living, his eager pursuit of knowledge through assiduous reading, and his death while studying the eruption of Vesuvius in 79 A.D.

are vividly described in three letters by his nephew and adopted son, Pliny the Younger (III, 6; VI, 16 and 20). For the reliability of Pliny's chapters on Greek and Roman sculpture, see **William D.E. Coulson,** in The Classical World, 69, March 1976, pp. 361–372, who tries to correct earlier views of the polyhistor as an indiscriminate excerpter relying very little on personal observation.

P. 12   Polykleitos the Younger: **Overbeck,** Nos. 995, 1004–1005.

P. 12   Alexander and his body-guard: **Overbeck,** Nos. 1485–1489.

P. 12   Vatican copy of Lysippos' Apoxymenos: **W. Fuchs, in Helbig,** I, No. 254; **Lullies,** fig. 232.

P. 13   Apelles' Anadyomene: **Overbeck,** Nos. 1847–1863.

P. 13   Asinius Pollio's gallery: **G. Becatti,** Letture Pliniane: le opere d'arte nei monumenta Asini Pollionis e negli Horti Serviliani, in Studi in onore di Aristide Calderini e Roberto Paribeni, III, 1958; **G. Gualandi, in** Annuario della Scuola Archeologica di Atene, 54, n.s. 38, 1976, pp. 56 ff., discussing the relationship of the Toro Farnese to the marble group described by Pliny.

P. 13   Laokoon: **Overbeck,** Nos. 2031–2037; **W. Fuchs, in Helbig,** I, No. 219; **Lullies,** figs. 302–303.

P. 15   Eros of Thespiae: **Overbeck,** Nos. 1249–1262.

P. 15   Wounded Bitch: **H. von Steuben,** in **Helbig,** II, No. 1913.

P. 11 ff.   Greek art treasures in ancient Rome: **L. Urlichs,** Griechische Statuen im republikanischen Rom, 13. Programm zur Stiftungsfeier des v. Wagnerschen Kunstinstituts, Würzburg 1880; **F. Jacobi,** Grundzüge einer Museographie der Stadt Rom zur Zeit des Augustus, I, 1884; **L. Homo,** Les musées de la Rome impériale, in Gazette des Beaux-Arts, 61, 1919; **W. Wunderer,** Manibiae Alexandrinae, Eine Studie zur Geschichte des römischen Kunstraubes, 1948; **H. Jucker,** Vom Verhältnis der Römer zur bildenden Kunst der Griechen, 1950; **G. Becatti,** Arte e gusto negli scrittori latini, 1951; **R. Lullies – J. Le Brun,** Griechische Bildwerke in Rom, 1955; **D.E. Strong,** Roman Museums, in Archaeological Theory and Practice, Essays presented to W.F. Grimes, 1973; **M. Pape,** Griechische Kunstwerke aus Kriegsbeute und ihre öffentliche Aufstellung in Rom, von der Eroberung von Syrakus bis in Augusteische Zeit, Diss. Hamburg 1975; **G. Waurick,** Kunstraub der Römer: Untersuchungen zu seinen Anfängen anhand der Inschriften, in Jahrbuch des Römisch-Germanischen Zentralmuseums Mainz, 22, 1975.

P. 15 f.   Colossus Neronis: **Overbeck,** 2273–2276; **F. Préchac,** Le colosse de Néron, son attitude et ses vicissitudes, Paris 1920; **Margaret R.**

Scherer, Marvels of Ancient Rome, 1955, pp. 135 f., with notes p. 392. Cf. **Pliny,** N.H. XXXIV, 5, on the contemporary decline of the art of alloying and founding valuable bronze.

P. 17   Bronze Heifer by Myron: **Overbeck,** Nos. 550–591; **H. von Steuben,** in **Helbig,** II, No. 1472.

P. 18   Spelunca/Sperlonga: **Tacitus,** Ann. IV, 59; **Suetonius,** Tib., 39. **B. Conticello – B. Andreae,** Die Skulpturen von Sperlonga, Antike Plastik, Lieferung XIV, 1974; **H. Riemann,** Sperlongaprobleme, in Forschungen und Funde, Festschrift B. Neutsch, Innsbruck 1980.

P. 18 f.   Destruction of Greek statues in Constantinople: **Overbeck,** Nos. 754, 1244, 1467, quoting Kedrenos on Pheidias' Zeus, Praxiteles' Aphrodite, and Lysippos' Kairos, No. 1472, quoting Choniates on Lysippos' Hercules. **Franz Grabler,** Die Kreuzfahrer erobern Konstantinopel, Byzantinische Geschichtschreiber, Band IX, 1958, presents a translation of Choniates' description (pp. 854–868) of the looting of Constantinople and destruction of its statues in 1204. On the colossal bronze Athena destroyed in 1203 (Choniates, pp. 738 f.) and its possible identity with Pheidias' Athena Promachos, see **G. Becatti,** Problemi Fidiaci, 1951, pp. 161 ff.

P. 19   Bronze Horses of San Marco: The removal of the Horses from the church to save them from further damage through air pollution, and the exhibition of one of them in the Metropolitan Museum of Art in New York, offered the possibility of examining them thoroughly, with regard to their origin, style, workmanship and historical importance, all of which is described by the experts involved in a work entitled The Horses of San Marco, Venice, published in 1979, with a wealth of illustrations and bibliographical references.

P. 20   Athens during the Turkish domination: **J. Stuart – N. Revett,** Antiquities of Athens, I–IV, London 1762–1816, 2nd ed. 1825–1830; **Comte de la Borde,** Athènes aux XV:e, XVI:e et XVII:e siècles, Paris 1854; **H. Omont,** Athènes au XVII:e siècle, Paris 1898.

P. 20   Monuments and city-planning of ancient Rome: **F. Castagnoli, C. Cecchelli, G. Giovannoni, M. Zocca,** Topografia e urbanistica di Roma, Istituto di Studi Romani, Storia di Roma, Vol. XXII, 1958; **L. Castagnoli, L. Cozza,** and others, Roma antica e paleocristiana, 1965 (being a collection of articles by various authors published in the Enciclopedia dell'Arte Antica Classica e Orientale, vols. I–VI, with extensive bibliographies and numerous illustrations).

P. 20 f.   Early excavations at Veii: **R. Lanciani,** Pagan and Christian Rome, 1893, pp. 64 ff., quoting Pietro Sante Bartoli's account of the seventeenth-century excavations on the Piazza d'Armi. For the marble portraits from the site of Roman Veii, see **Helga von Heintze,** in **Helbig,** I, Nos. 347–349.

P. 21   Hadrawa's excavations on the island of Capri: Ragguagli di varii scavi, e scoverte di antichità fatte nell'Isola di Capri dal Sig. **Hadrava,** e dal medesimo comunicati per lettere ad un suo amico in Vienna, Napoli 1793; **Norbert Hadrawa's** freundschaftliche Briefe über verschiedene auf der Insel Capri entdeckte und ausgegrabene Alterthümer, aus dem Italiänischen übersetzt, mit Kupfern, Dresden 1794. For a judgement on Hadrawa's activities, see **A. Andrén,** Capri: From the Stone Age to the Tourist Age, Studies in Mediterranean Archaeology, Pocket-books, 13, 1980, pp. 65–67.

P. 21   Forma Urbis: **G. Carettoni, A.M. Colini, L. Cozza, G. Gatti,** La pianta marmorea di Roma Antica, 1960.

P. 21   Early drawings and engravings of ancient monuments in Rome: **A. Bartoli,** Cento vedute di Roma antica, 1911; **H. Egger,** Römische Veduten, I–II, 1911, 1931; **A. Bartoli,** I monumenti antichi di Roma nei disegni degli Uffizi, I–IV, 1914 ff.; **Th. Ashby,** Topographical Study in Rome 1581: A series of views with fragmentary text by Étienne Dupérac, 1916; **C. Hülsen – H. Egger,** Die römischen Skizzenbücher von Marten van Heemskerck, I–II, 1916; **M. Chiarini,** Vedute Romane, Disegni dal XVI al XVIII secolo, 1971.

P. 22 ff.   Antique collections in 14th–18th century Rome: U. **Aldrovandi,** Delle statue antiche che per tutta Roma in diuersi luoghi & case si ueggono, in **Lucio Mauro,** Le antichità della città di Roma, Venetia 1542; **J. Fichard,** Italia, in Frankfurtisches Archiv für ältere deutsche Litteratur und Geschichte, 3, 1815; **E. Müntz,** Le musée du Capitole et les autres collections romaines à la fin du XVe et au commencement du XVIe siècle, in Revue Archéologique, 43, 1882; **A. Michaelis,** Geschichte des Statuenhofes im vatikanischen Belvedere, in Jahrbuch des Deutschen Archäologischen Instituts, 5, 1890; **Id.,** Storia della collezione capitolina di antichità fino alla inaugurazione del museo nel 1734, in Mitteilungen des Deutschen Archäologischen Instituts, Römische Abteilung, 6, 1891; **R. Lanciani,** Storia degli scavi di Roma e notizie intorno le collezioni romane di antichità, I–IV, 1902–1912, reprint 1975; **P.G. Hübner,** Le Statue di Roma, Grundlagen für eine Geschichte der antiken Monumente in der Renaissance, I, Quellen und Sammlungen, Römische Forschungen herausgegeben von der Bibliotheca Hertziana, II, 1912; **Chr. Hülsen,** Römische Antikengärten des XVI. Jahrhunderts, in Abhandlungen der Heidelberger Akademie der Wissenschaften, Philosophisch-historische Klasse, 4, 1917; **L. von Pastor,** Die Stadt Rom zu Ende der Renaissance,

4.–6. Aufl., 1925; **B. Nogara,** Origine e sviluppo dei Musei e Gallerie Pontificie, 1948; **C. Pietrangeli,** Il Museo Clementino Vaticano, in Rendiconti della Pontificia Accademia Romana di Archeologia, 27, 1951–1952; **Id.,** I Musei vaticani al tempo di Pio VI, ibid., 49, 1976–1977; **H. Wrede,** Der Antikengarten der Del Bufalo bei der Fontana Trevi, Trierer Winckelmannsprogramme, Heft 4, 1982.

P. 22   Spinario: **W. Fuchs,** in **Helbig,** II, No. 1448.

P. 23   Influence of famous classical sculptures: **M. Bieber,** Laocoon, The Influence of the Group since its Rediscovery, New York 1942; **A. von Salis,** Antike und Renaissance, Erlenbach-Zürich 1947; **H. Ladendorf,** Antikenstudium und Antikenkopie, Leipzig 1953; **F. Haskell – N. Penny,** Taste and the Antique, Yale University Press, 1981.

P. 23   Hercules Farnese: **C.C. Vermeule,** The Weary Herakles of Lysippos, in American Journal of Archaeology, 79, 1975.

P. 23   Florentine antique collections: **G.A. Mansuelli,** Galleria degli Uffizi, Le sculture, I, 1958. Etruscan bronzes: **L. Goldscheider,** op.cit., pls. 95–97, 120, 122–124; **W. Llewellyn Brown,** The Etruscan Lion, 1960, pp. 155 ff.; **T. Dohrn,** Der Arringatore, Monumenta Artis Romanae, VIII, 1968.

P. 24   Barberini collection: An inventory of the antiquities of the collection, now dispersed, was compiled in 1738 and is printed in the Documenti per servire alla Storia dei Musei d'Italia, vol. IV, 1880, pp. 19–76.

P. 24   Borghese collection: **E.Q. Visconti,** Sculture del Palazzo della Villa Borghese a Porta Pinciana, 1798.

P. 24 f.   Eighteenth-century antique collections in Italy, Germany, and England: Antikensammlungen im 18. Jahrhundert, herausgegeben von **H. Beck, P.C. Bol, W. Printz, H. von Steuben,** Frankfurther Forschungen zur Kunst, Band 9, 1981, containing a great number of articles by different authors, with extensive bibliographies; Eighteenth Century Restorations of Ancient Marble Sculpture from English Private Collections, Exhibition Catalogue, London 1983.

P. 26   Early excavations at Herculaneum: **U. Pannuti,** Il "Giornale degli scavi" di Ercolano, Memorie della Accademia Nazionale dei Lincei, Serie VIII, Vol. XXVI, Fasc. 3, 1983.

P. 26 f.   Queen Christina's collections of antiques: **Chr. Callmer,** Drottning Kristinas samlingar av antik konst, Svenska Humanistiska Förbundets skrifter, 63, 1954; **H.H. Brummer,** Till belysning av drottning Christinas antiksamling i Stockholm, in Konsthistorisk Tidskrift, 32, 1963; **A. Andrén,** Antik skulptur i svenska samlingar (with an English summary and extensive bibliographical references), 1964, pp. 13–21, figs. 1–6.

P. 27   Napoleon's acquisitions of antiques: Les Monuments Antiques du
Musée Napoléon, dessinées et gravées par **Thomas Piroli,** avec une ex-
plication par **J.G. Schweighaeuser,** publiées par **F.** et **P. Piranesi,** frères,
Tomes 1–4, Paris 1804–1806; **F. Boyer,** Les transferts d'antiques d'Italie
en France entre 1796 et 1814, in Comptes Rendus de l'Academie des
Inscriptions et Belles Lettres, Sept. 1914; **Id.,** L'achats des antiques
Borghèse par Napoléon, ibid., 1937, pp. 405 ff.; **L. Berra,** Opere d'arte
asportate dai Francesi da Roma e dallo Stato Pontificio e restituite nel
1815 dopo il Congresso di Vienna, in Rendiconti della Pontificia
Accademia Romana di Archeologia, 27, 1952–1954; **C. Pietrangeli,** Sculture capitoline a Parigi, in Bollettino dei Musei Comunali di Roma, 14,
1967; **A. Busiri Vici,** Un vaso di Sèvres documenta le asportazioni
Napoleoniche dall'Italia, in Antichità Viva, 3, 1971.

P.28   Vulca of Veii: **A. Andrén,** In Quest of Vulca, in Rendiconti della
Pontificia Accademia Romana di Archeologia, 49, 1976–1977.

P. 28   Bronze statues of early Romans: The statue of Attus Navius, said
to have been set up by Tarquinius Priscus in the Comitium on the spot
where the augur wrought the miracle of cutting a whetstone in two with a
razor, is recorded by **Livy,** I, 36, 5, as having disappeared (*fuit*) from its
place on the left of the steps leading up to the Curia. **Pliny,** N.H. XXXIV,
21, also speaks of the statue as no longer to be seen in front of the Curia,
adding that its base was destroyed by fire when the Senate House was
burnt down at the funeral of Publius Clodius (52 B.C.). But **Dionysius,**
III, 71, 5, attests that the statue remained down to his own time, standing
in front of the Senate House near the sacred fig-tree, and representing the
augur as a man under average height, with the mantle drawn up above his
head. The statue was probably removed after the fire in 52 B.C. and
temporarily replaced on a new base. The statue of Horatius Cocles,
according to **Livy,** II, 10, 12, was also erected in the Comitium; it is
described by **Dionysius,** V, 25, 2, as showing the hero fully armed, and
Pliny, N.H. XXXIV, 22, mentions it as still standing in his time. Pliny's
interest in the statues made in or for Rome is confined, upon the whole, to
the reason of why they were erected, and sometimes, to some peculiarity
in a figure's dress. In N.H. XXXIV, 23, he tells us that the statues of
Romulus and Tatius on the Capitol and that of Camillus on the Rostra had
no tunic. And in N.H. XXXIV, 31, he describes the statue of Cornelia,
the mother of the Gracchi and daughter of the elder Africanus, as a seated
figure, remarkable by having shoes without thongs. The inscribed base of
this statue was found in 1878 in the Porticus Octaviae, where it stood in
Pliny's time; see **E. Meinhardt,** in **Helbig,** II, No. 1679.

P. 28   Marble copies from Hadrian's villa at Tivoli: **S. Aurigemma.** Villa
Adriana, 1961, figs. 197–205.

P. 29   Herculaneum and Pompeii: **M. Ruggiero,** Storia degli scavi di Ercolano ricomposta su documenti superstiti, Napoli 1885, reprint 1984. The results of earlier and later excavations are summarized in **A. Maiuri – H.J. Beyen,** Ercolano, Pompei e stili pompeiani, Roma 1965, being reprints of articles published in the Enciclopedia dell'Arte Antica Classica e Orientale, vols. III and IV, with splendid illustrations and extensive bibliographies. For the Villa of the Papyri see **M.R. Wojcik,** La Villa dei Papiri, Studia Archaeologica, 37, 1985.

P. 30   Chatsworth Head: **E. Gjerstad,** The story of the Chatsworth Head, in Eranos Löfstedtianus, Lund 1945; **Caroline Houser,** Greek Monumental Bronze Sculpture, with photographs by **David Finn,** London 1983, pp. 70–75; **Claude Rolley,** Les bronzes grecs, 1983; Die griechischen Bronzen, 1984, p. 40, fig. 208.

P. 30   Acropolis Youth: **C. Houser,** op.cit., pp. 38–42.

P. 30   Bronze heads from Olympia: **C. Houser,** op.cit., pp. 32–37; **C. Rolley,** op. cit., p. 33, fig. 15.

P. 30   Hellenistic Ruler: **H. von Heintze,** in **Helbig,** III, No. 2275; **Lullies,** figs. 274–275.

P. 30   Seated Boxer: **W. Fuchs,** in **Helbig,** III, No. 2272; **Lullies,** figs. 294–295.

P. 30   Delphi Charioteer: **F. Chamoux,** L'Aurige de Delphes, Fouilles de Delphes, IV:5, 1955; **Lullies,** figs. 88–89; **C. Houser,** op.cit., pp. 18–31; **C. Rolley,** op.cit., p. 36, fig. 18.

P. 30   Poseidon from Livadhostro Bay: **C. Houser,** op.cit., pp. 44–49.

P. 30   Bronzes from Piraeus: **S. Meletzis – H. Papadakis,** National Museum of Archaeology, Athens, 1963, pp. 59–61, 76–79; **C. Houser,** op.cit., pp. 50–69; **C. Rolley,** op.cit., p. 36, fig. 17, p. 44, fig. 22, p. 227, fig. 207.

P. 30   Bronzes found off Anticythera: **P.C. Bol,** Die Skulpturen des Schiffsfundes von Antikythera, in Mitteilungen des Deutschen Archäologischen Instituts, Athenische Abteilung, Beiheft 2, 1972; **Lullies,** figs. 216–217, 258–259; **C. Houser,** op.cit., pp. 91–101.

P. 30   Bronzes found off Mahdia: **W. Fuchs,** Der Schiffsfund von Mahdia, Tübingen 1963; **C. Rolley,** op.cit., p. 46, fig. 25.

P. 30   Ephebus from the Bay of Marathon: **Lullies,** figs. 220–221; **C. Houser,** op. cit., pp. 102–107.

P. 30   Bronze statuary found off Cape Artemision: **Lullies,** figs. 112–113; **C. Houser,** op.cit., pp. 76–90; **C. Rolley,** op.cit., p. 46, fig. 26.

P. 30 f.   Bronze Athlete found in the Adriatic: **J. Frel,** Antiquities in the J. Paul Getty Museum, Sculpture, I, Greek Originals, Malibu Ca 1979, No. 50; **P. Moreno,** Il bronzo Getty ed una statuetta di Eracle ai Musei Vaticani, in Rendiconti della Pontificia Accademia Romana di Archeologia, 51–52, 1982, pp. 69–89; **C. Houser,** op.cit., pp. 108–115; **C. Rolley,** op.cit., pp. 44 f., fig. 23.

P. 31   Philosopher of Porticello: **Claudio Sabbione,** in I bronzi di Riace, 1981, pp. 36–39; **C. Rolley,** op.cit., p. 40, fig. 21. The head belonged to a statue which was broken into pieces and loaded, together with other bronze scrap, on a ship which was wrecked in the dangerous Strait of Messina about 400 B.C. Two bronze heads from the wreck were found by clandestine divers and sold to Switzerland.

P. 31   Bronze Warriors found off Riace: **A. Busignani,** Gli eroi di Riace, Daimon e Techne, Firenze 1981; I bronzi di Riace, Novara 1981 (with text by **G. Foti**); **L. Barbera,** L'avventura dei bronzi di Riace, Messina 1981; **C. Houser,** op.cit., pp. 116–133; **C. Rolley,** op.cit., pp. 36 ff., figs 1, 19, 20; **F. Coarelli – L. Satriani,** Gli eroi venuti dal mare, 1984. The offici ! publication, by various authors, is entitled Due bronzi da Riace: rinvenimento, restauro, analisi ed ipotesi di interpretazione, Bollettino d'Arte, Serie speciale, 3, Roma, Istituto Poligrafico e Zecca dello Stato, 1984.

P. 31   Bronze Wolf at the Lateran: **F. von Duhn,** Dante e la Lupa Capitolina, in Studi Etruschi, 2, 1928, pp. 9 ff. and pl. I:2, reproducing a fifteenth-century drawing of the place of executions at the Lateran, showing the bronze she-wolf, without twins, on a ledge projecting from the wall of a tower.

P. 31   Equestrian statue of Marcus Aurelius: **H. von Heintze,** in **Helbig,** II, No. 1161; **Margaret H. Scherer,** op. cit., pp. 133 ff., pls. 211–214.

P. 32   Publications of the Society of Dilettanti: Antiquities of Athens, measured and delineated by **J. Stuart** and **N. Revett,** I, 1762, II, 1787–90, III, 1794–97, IV, 1814–16, 2nd ed. 1825–30; Antiquities of Athens and Other Places in Greece, Sicily, etc., delineated and illustrated by **C.R. Cockerell, W. Kinnard, T.L. Donaldson, W. Jenkins** and **W. Railton,** 1830; Ionian Antiquities, by **R. Chandler, N. Revett** and **W. Pars,** I, 1769, II, 1797, III, 1840, IV, 1881, V, 1915.

P. 33 ff.   Travelling and antique hunting in Greece and the Levant: **Comte de Choiseul-Gouffier,** Voyage pittoresque de la Grèce, 1782–1809; **E. Dodwell,** A Classical and Topographical Tour through Greece, during the years 1801, 1805, and 1806, I–II, 1819; **C. Fellows,** Journal written during an Excursion in Asia Minor, 1839; **C.T. Newton,** Travels and Discoveries in the Levant, 1865; **C.R. Cockerell,** Travels in Southern Europe and the Levant 1810–1817, edited by S.P. Cockerell, 1903; **W. St.**

Clair, Lord Elgin and the Marbles, 1967; **C.P. Bracken,** Antiquities Acquired: The Spoliation of Greece, 1975; **Chr. Callmer,** Georg Christian Gropius als Agent, Konsul and Archäologe in Griechenland 1803–1850, Scripta Minora, Studier utgivna av Kungl. Humanistiska Vetenskapssamfundet i Lund, 1982–1983:1, Lund 1982; **H. Haller von Hallerstein,** . . . und die Erde gebar ein Lächeln: Der erste deutsche Archäologe in Griechenland, Carl Haller v. Hallerstein, 1774–1817, 1983.

P. 33   Lord Elgin's firman: The Turkish original of the document was lost, and its wording is only known through a copy in faulty Italian, saying that the ambassador's team was permitted to take away *qualche pezzi di pietra con iscrizioni e figure,* which means "some pieces of stone with inscriptions and figures" (not "any pieces . . .", as in a British Museum booklet about the Elgin Marbles).

P. 34   Debate on Elgin Marbles: Memorandum on the Subject of the Earl of Elgin's Pursuits in Greece, London 1810, reedited 1811 and 1815; Elgin Marbles: Letter from the Chevalier Antonio Canova on the Sculptures in the British Museum and Two Memoirs read to the Royal Institute of France by the Chevalier Visconti . . . with the Report from the Select Committee of the House of Commons, London 1816.

P. 34   Parthenon: **Overbeck,** Nos. 624–626; **A.H. Smith,** The Sculptures of the Parthenon, 1910; **F. Brommer,** Die Parthenon-Skulpturen: Die Metopen, der Fries, die Giebel, das Kultbild, 1979; **Lullies,** figs. 134–157; **M. Pavan,** L'avventura del Partenone: Un monumento nella storia, 1983; Parthenon-Kongress Basel, Referate und Berichte 4. bis 8. April 1982, Band I und II, herausgegeben von **Ernst Berger,** 1984.

P. 34 f.   Aegina and Bassae: **O.M. von Stackelberg,** Der Apollotempel zu Bassae, 1826; **C.R. Cockerell,** The Temples . . . at Aegina and . . . Bassae, 1860; **A. Furtwängler** and others, Ägina, Heiligtum der Aphaia, Text und Tafeln, 1906; **H. Kenner,** Der Fries des Tempels von Bassae-Phigalia, 1946, Neudruck 1970; **W.B. Dinsmoor,** The Sculptured Frieze from Bassae, in American Journal of Archaeology, 60, 1956; **Lullies,** figs. 62–73; **B.C. Madigan,** The Sculptured Metopes from the Temple of Apollo at Bassai, 1983.

P. 35   Strangford Shield and other copies of the shield reliefs of Athena Parthenos: see note to p. 46.

P. 35   Aphrodite of Melos: **J. Aichard,** Recherches sur l'histoire de la découverte de la Vénus de Milo, 1874; **O. Voutier,** Découverte et acquisition de la Vénus de Milo, 1874; **J. Charbonneaux,** La Vénus de Milo, 1958.

P. 36   Lycian monuments: **C. Fellows,** An Account of Discoveries in Lycia, 1841; **C. Niemann,** Das Nereiden-Monument in Xanthos, 1922.

P. 36   Mausoleum at Halicarnassus: **Overbeck,** Nos. 1177–1178; **C.T. Newton – R.P. Pullan,** A History of Discoveries at Halicarnassus, Cnidus and Branchidae, I–II, 1862–1863; **Lullies,** figs. 198–203.

P. 36   Cnidian Demeter: **B. Ashmole,** 'Demeter of Cnidus', in Journal of Hellenic Studies, 71, 1951, pp. 13–28, pls. 1–7.

P. 36   Altar frieze fom Pergamon: **H. Kähler,** Der grosse Fries von Pergamon, 1948; **Lullies,** figs. 263–270.

P. 36   Archaeological discoveries: **A. Michaelis,** Ein Jahrhundert kunstarchäologischer Entdeckungen, 2nd ed. 1908; **W. Schierung,** Geschichte der Archäologie, Ausgrabungen, Museen, in Handbuch der Archäologie, Neuausgabe 1969; **S. Moscati,** Italia sconosciuta, 1971; **G. Daniel,** A Hundred and Fifty Years of Archaeology, 1976; **G. Hafner,** Sternstunden der Archäologen: Wissenschaftler auf den Spuren alter Kulturen, 1978; **Id.,** Tatort Antike: Archäologen auf den Spuren verschollener Kunstwerke, 1979; **R. Battaglia,** Archeologia: mito, avventura, scienza, 1979; **P.L. MacKendrick,** The Mute Stones Speak: The Story of Archaeology in Italy, 2nd ed. 1983; **Id.,** The Mute Stones Speak: The Story of Archaeology in Greek Lands, 2nd ed. 1983; **S. Moscati,** Italia ricomparsa: preistorica, greca, fenicia, 1983; **Id.,** Italia ricomparsa: etrusca-italica, 1984.

P. 36   Cesnola: **J.L. Myres,** Handbook to the Cesnola Collection, 1914.

P. 37   Excavations in the sanctuary of Diana Nemorensis: **A. Andrén,** Architectural Terracottas from Etrusco-Italic Temples, 1940, pp. 381 ff., with bibliography referring to the excavations of 1885–89 and the antiquities at Nottingham.

P. 37   Cypriote antiquities in Stockholm: **Vassos Karageorghis, Carl-Gustaf Styrenius, Marie-Louise Winblad,** Cypriote Antiquities in the Medelhavsmuseet, Stockholm, Memoir 2, 1977.

P. 38 f.   Athens during the Turkish domination: see note to p. 20.

P. 39   Temple at Ilissus: **A. Krug – S. von Boeckelberg,** Der Fries des Tempels am Ilissos, Die Friese des Hephasteion, Antike Plastik, Lief. XVII: 1–2, 1979.

P. 40   Populonia: **A. De Agostino,** Populonia, la città e la necropoli, Itinerari dei Musei, Gallerie e Monumenti d'Italia, 109, 1965; **F. Fedeli,** Populonia, storia e territorio, I–II, 1983.

P. 41   Early discoveries of Orvietan antiquities: The record of tombs and tomb gifts found in the Pozzo di San Patrizio in 1532, first referred to by **L.**

Fiumi, Orvieto, 1891, p. 191, note 1, is quoted in full by **Pericle Perali,** "Vulsinii" e "Fanum Voltumnae", in Orvieto Etrusca, Roma 1928, p. 48, note 1.

P. 42   Father Labat visiting Etruscan tombs at Tarquinia: Voyages du P. **Labat** de l'ordre des F.F. Prescheurs, en Espagne et en Italie, Tome Cinquième, Amsterdam 1731, pp. 38–41.

P. 42 f.   Sir William Hamilton's collections: **d'Hancarville,** Antiquités étrusques, grecques et romaines tirées du cabinet de M. Hamilton Envoyé extraordinaire de S.M. Britannique à la cour de Naples, I–IV, Florence 1766, nouv. éd. 1801–1808; **W. Tischbein,** Collection of engravings from ancient vases mostly of pure Greek workmanship discovered in sepulchres in the Kingdom of the Two Sicilies but chiefly in the neighbourhood of Naples, during the course of the years 1789 and 1790, now in the possession of Sir W. Hamilton, with remarks on each vase by the collector, I–IV, Naples 1791–1795.

P. 43   George Dennis: **D.E. Rhodes,** Dennis of Etruria, London 1973.

P. 43   Tomb robbing and research at Vulci: **G. Dennis,** The Cities and Cemeteries of Etruria, 3rd ed. 1883, I, pp. 447 ff.; **S. Gsell,** Fouilles dans la nécropole de Vulci, 1891; **F. Messerschmidt,** Nekropolen von Vulci, Ergängzungshefte zum Jahrbuch des Deutschen Archäologischen Instituts, 12, 1930; **A. Hus,** Vulci étrusque et étrusco-romaine, 1971; **M.T. Falconi Amorelli,** Vulci, Scavi Bendinelli (1919–23), 1983.

P. 43   'Etruscan' vases: **L. Lanzi,** De' vasi antichi dipinti volgarmente chiamati etruschi, 1806.

P. 43   Brothers Campanari: **G. Dennis,** op.cit., I, pp. 464 f., 474; **G. Colonna,** Archeologia dell'età romantica in Etruria: I Campanari di Toscanella e la Tomba dei Vipiana, in Studi Etruschi, 46, 1978.

P. 43 f.   Tomba François: **T. Dohrn,** in **Helbig,** IV, No. 3239.

P. 43 f.   Torlonia collection: **P.E. Visconti,** Catalogo del Museo Torlonia di sculture antiche, 1876; **C.L. Visconti,** I monumenti del Museo Torlonia riprodotti con la fototipia, 1884–1885; **Carlo Gasparri,** Materiali per servire allo studio del Museo Torlonia di scultura antica, con la collaborazione di **Ida Caruso,** Memorie della Classe di scienze morali, storiche e filologiche dell'Accademia Nazionale dei Lincei, Serie VIII, Vol. XXIV, Fasc. 2, 1980.

P. 44   Campana collection: **G.P. Campana,** Antiche opere in plastica, discoperte, raccolte e dichiarate, 1842; Cataloghi del Museo Campana, I–XII, 1858; **H. d'Escamps,** Galerie des marbres antiques du Musée Campana à Rome, sculptures grecques et romaines avec une introduction et une texte déscriptif, 2. éd. Berlin 1868; **S. Reinach,** Esquisse d'une histoire de la collection Campana, in Revue Archéologique, 4, 1904, and 5, 1905; **G.Q. Giglioli,** in Studi Romani, 3, 1955.

P. 44   Tomba Campana: **L. Banti,** Le pitture della tomba Campana a Veii, in Studi Etruschi, 38, 1970, pp. 27–43, pls. III–IV; **Filippo Del Pino,** Sulla scoperta della tomba Campana a Veio: un falso dell'archeologia romantica?, lecture delivered in the Pontificia Accademia Romana di Archeologia on June 27th, 1985, to be published in the Rendiconti of the Academy.

P. 44   Archaic painted terracotta slabs from Caere: **F. Roncalli,** Le lastre dipinte da Cerveteri, Studi e Materiali dell'Istituto di Etruscologia e Antichità Italiche dell'Università di Roma, IV, 1965.

P. 44   Campana reliefs: **H. von Rhoden – H. Winnefeld,** Architektonische römische Tonreliefs der Kaiserzeit, I–II, 1911; **A.H. Borbein,** Campanareliefs, typologische und stilkritische Untersuchungen, Mitteilungen des Deutschen Archäologischen Instituts, Römische Abteilung, Ergänzungsheft 14, 1968.

P. 44   Augusto Castellani and his collections: **R. Bartoccini – A. De Agostini,** Museo di Villa Giulia, Antiquarium e Collezione dei Vasi Castellani, 1961; **T. Dohrn, E. Simon, H. Sichtermann,** in **Helbig,** II, Nos, 1541–1577; **T. Dohrn, P. Zanker,** in **Helbig,** III, Nos. 2712–2751; **P. Mingazzini,** Catalogo dei vasi della collezione Augusto Castellani, I–II, 1971–1972; **I. Caruso,** Museo Nazionale Etrusco di Villa Giulia, Collezione Castellani: Le Ceramiche, 1985.

P. 45   Tomba Regolini-Galassi: **T. Dohrn,** in **Helbig,** I, pp. 479 ff., Nos. 622–672.

P. 45   Tomba Barberini and Tomba Bernardini: **T. Dohrn,** in **Helbig,** III, pp. 752 ff., Nos. 2857–2941; **F. Canciani,** Tomba Bernardini, in Civiltà del Lazio primitivo, exhibition catalogue, Rome 1976, pp. 221–246, pls. XLV–LV; **F. Canciani – F.W. von Hase,** La Tomba Bernardini di Palestrina, Latium Vetus, II, 1979.

P. 45   Thracian tomb treasures: **I. Venedikov – T. Gerassimov,** Thrakische Kunst 1973; **I. Venedikov,** The Archaeological Wealth of Ancient Thrace, in the exhibition catalogue Thracian Treasures from Bulgaria, The Metropolitan Museum of Art, New York, 1977; **G. von Bülow,** Treasures of Thrace, 1985.

P. 45   Scythian tomb treasures: **Tamara Talbot Rice,** The Scythians, 1957; **M.I. Artamov – W. Forman,** Goldschatz der Skythen in der Eremitage, 1970.

P. 45   Vergina tombs: **M. Andronikos,** Les tombes royales de Vergina, in Archeologia, 125, 1978; **Id.,** The Tombs and the Great Tumulus of

Vergina, in Acta of the XI International Congress of Classical Archaeology, London 1979; **Id.**, Vergina: The Royal Tombs, Athens 1984. The excavator's arguments for his having discovered the tombs of Philip II of Macedon and his consort have been discussed, among others, by **Anna Maria Prestiani Giallombardo** and **Bruno Tripodi**, Le tombe regali di Vergina: quale Filippo?, in Annali della Scuola Normale Superiore di Pisa, Cl. di lett. e fil., Ser. 3, 10, 1980; **Phyllis William Lehmann**, The so-called Tomb of Philip II: A different interpretation, in American Journal of Archaeology, 84, 1980; **E.A. Fredricksmeyer**, Again the so-called Tomb of Philip II, ibid., 85, 1981; **Ph.W. Lehmann**, The so-called Tomb of Philip II: An addendum, ibid., 86, 1982. The fact, however, that among the skeletal remains found in the gold box of Tomb II was part of a skull showing a healed injury to the right ocular region seems to prove that this tomb was really that of Philip II, who had lost his right eye in war; see **J.M. Musgrave, R.A.H. Neave, A.J.N.W. Prag**, The Skull from Tomb II at Vergina: King Philip II of Macedon, in Journal of Hellenic Studies, 104, 1984, pp. 60–78.

P. 45 Aerial photography for archaeological research: **J. Bradford**, Etruria from the air, in Antiquity, 21, 1947; **Raymond Chevallier**, L'avion à la découverte du passé, 1964; **René Goguey**, De l'aviation à l'archéologie: recherches sur les méthodes et les techniques de l'archéologie aérienne, 1968; **A. Rieche**, Das antike Italien aus der Luft, 1978; **B. Jones**, Aerial Photography for the Archaeologist, 1980; **D.R. Wilson**, Air Photo Interpretation for Archaeologists, 1982.

P. 45 Spina: **S. Aurigemma**, Il R. Museo di Spina, 1935; **P.E. Arias – N. Alfieri**, Spina, 1958; **Id.**, Spina, Il Museo Archeologico di Ferrara, 1960.

P. 45 f. Technical devices for archaeological field prospecting: **R. Bartoccini, C.M. Lerici, M. Moretti**, La tomba delle Olimpiadi, 1959; **C.M. Lerici**, Alla scoperta delle civiltà sepolte, 1960; Scritti di archeologia ed arte in onore di Carlo Maurilio Lerici, Stoccolma 1970 (with numerous contributions about geophysical prospecting); **A.H.A. Hogg**, Surveying for Archaeologists and other Field Workers, 1980; **P.M. Fischer**, Applications of Technical Devices in Archaeology: the use of X-rays, microscope, electrical and electro-magnetic devices and subsurface interface radar, Studies in Mediterranean Archaeology, 63, Göteborg 1980; **Ph. Berker**, Techniques of Archaeological Excavation, 2nd ed. 1983.

P. 45 Location of Sybaris: **F.G. Rainey, C.M. Lerici** and others, The Search for Sybaris 1960–1965, 1967.

P. 46 Submarine archaeology: **H. Frost**, Under the Mediterranean, 1963; **M.L. Katzew**, Resurrecting the oldest known Greek Ship, in National Geographic Magazine, 137:6, 1970; **David I. Owen**, Excavating a classical shipwreck, in Archaeology, April 1971; **P.E. Cleator,** Underwater Archaeology, London 1973; **M.L. Katzew,** Cyprus Ship Discovery, in Illustrated London News, June 1974; **L. Bivona,** Rinvenimenti sottomarini nelle acque di Terrasini (Palermo), in Kokalos, 19, 1973; **V. Giustolisi,** Le navi romane di Terrasini e l'avventura di Amilcare sul Monte Heirkte, Note epigrafiche di **Livia Bivona,** 1975; **R. Battaglia,** Archeologia subacquea, 1975; **O.T. Engvig, P. Åström,** Hala Sultan Tekke, II, The Cape Kiti Survey, Studies in Mediterranean Archaeology, 45:1, 1975; **K. Muckelroy,** Maritime Archaeology, 1978; **H. Blanck,** Der Schiffsfund von der Secca di Capistello bei Lipari, in Mitteilungen des Deutschen Archäologischen Instituts, Römische Abteilung, 85, 1978; **C. Cerdá Juan,** La nave romano-republicana de la colonia de Sant Jordi (Ses Salines, Mallorca), 1980; **V. Santa Maria Scrinari,** Le navi del Porto di Claudio, 1981; **H. Frost** and others, Lilybaeum (Marsala), The Punic Ship, Final Excavation Report, Notizie degli Scavi 1976, Supplemento, 1981; **P.A. Gianfrotta – P. Pomey,** Archeologia subacquea, storia, techniche, scoperte e relitti, con la collaborazione di **F. Coarelli,** 1981; **E. Ciabatti,** L'archeologo subacqueo: Manuale di ricerca e di scavo, 1984. Discoveries in Italian waters are described by various authors in two supplements to the Bollettino d'Arte 1982 and 1984, published in 1983 and 1985, with the title Archeologia subacquea, I and II. See also **Piero A. Gianfrotta, L. Fozzati, C. Micchegiani Carpano, F. Pallarés,** Archeologia subacquea, Dossier of the monthly Archeo, Attualità del Passato, 5, July 1985.

P. 46   Excavations at beachfront of Herculaneum: **J. Judge,** in National Geographic, December 1982; **Rick Gore,** with photographs by **O. Louis Mazzatenta,** ibid., May 1984.

P. 46   Eruption of Vesuvius and death of Pliny the Elder: **Antonio Scherillo,** Plinio e il Vesuvio, in Plinio il Vecchio, Giornata lincea indetta nella ricorrenza del 19° Centenario della eruzione del Vesuvio e della morte di Plinio il Vecchio (Roma, 4 dicembre 1979), Atti dei Convegni Lincei, 53, 1983.

P. 46   Copies of the shield reliefs of Pheidias' Athena Parthenos: **H. Schrader,** Zu den Kopien nach dem Schildrelief der Athena Parthenos, in Corolla L. Curtius, 1937; **Suzanne Ras,** L'Amazonomachie du bouclier de la Athéna Parthénos, in Bulletin de Correspondance Hellénique, 68–69, 1944–45; **G. Becatti,** Problemi Fidiaci, 1951, pp. 109 ff., pl. 66, figs. 195–197, pp. 244 ff., pls. 103–111, figs. 309–333.

P. 46   Marble statues from the Blue Grotto: **A. De Franciscis,** Le statue della Grotta Azzura nell'Isola di Capri, 1964; **A. Andrén,** Capri: From the Stone Age to the Tourist Age, Studies in Mediterranean Archaeology, Pocket-books, 13, 1980, pp. 82 f., figs. 21–22.

P. 46   Marble sculptures from Baiae: The excavation of a submerged Roman villa off Baiae, with a nymphaeum adorned with marble statues representing Odysseus and Polyphemus, Dionysus, and ladies of the House of the emperor Claudius, is described by various authors in Il ninfeo imperiale sommerso di Punta Epitaffio, Napoli 1983; by **Piero A. Gianfrotta,** Il ninfeo di Baia, in the dossier Archeologia subacquea, cited above; and by **B. Andreae** and **F. Zevi,** Scavi sottomarini a Baia: primi risultati, in Rendiconti della Pontificia Accademia Romana di Archeologia (forthcoming volume).

P. 47   Metal detectors: On the Swedish island of Gotland, the soil of which is extremely rich in Roman, Viking Age and Arabian coins, all private treasure hunting by means of metal detectors is prohibited by law since July 1st, 1985.

P. 48   Seated goddess in Berlin: **Lullies,** figs. 84–86.

P. 48   Standing goddess in Berlin: **Lullies,** figs. 26–27.

P. 48   Kouros in New York: **Lullies,** figs. 16–17.

P. 48 f.   Antiquities from "an old Etruscan city" in the Ny Carlsberg Glyptotek: **F. Poulsen,** Aus einer alten Etruskerstadt, Det Kgl. Danske Videnskabernes Selskab, Historisk-filologiske Meddelelser, XII:3, 1927; **P.J. Riis,** Etruscan Types of Heads, Det Kongelige Danske Videnskabernes Selskab, Historisk-filosofiske Skrifter, 9:5, 1981, pp. 83 f., Appendix on the provenience of the so-called "Orvieto Find" in Copenhagen.

P. 49 f.   Euphronios' krater in New York: **D. von Bothmer,** Greek Vase Painting, An Introduction, The Metropolitan Museum of Art Bulletin, Volume XXXI, Number 1, Fall 1972, No. 15; **K.E. Meyer,** The Plundered Past, 1973, pp. 86 f., revised edition, 1977, pp. 94 ff.

P. 50   Ephebus of Selinunte: **P. Marconi,** L'efebo di Selinunte, in Monumenti dell'Istituto di Archeologia e Storia dell'Arte, Roma 1929; **B. Pace,** Arte e Civiltà della Sicilia Antica, II, 1928, pp. 56 ff., figs 59–61.

P. 52   Ancient copies, adaptions and eclectic creations: **A. Furtwängler,** Über Statuenkopieen im Altertum, in Abhandlungen der K. Bayerischen Akademie der Wissenschaften, I. Classe, XX. Band, III. Abteilung, 1897; **G. Lippold,** Kopien und Umbildungen griechischer Statuen, 1923; **M. Borda,** La scuola di Pasitele, 1953; **Gisela M.A. Richter,** Ancient Italy, Jerome Lectures, Fourth Series, 1955, Chapter III: Graeco-Roman Art, Copies and Adaptions of Greek Sculptures; Appendix I: The Pointing Process; Appendix II: The Pasiteleans; **M. Bieber,** Ancient Copies, 1977; **Brunilde Sismondo Ridgway,** Roman Copies of Greek Sculpture: The Problem of the Originals, Jerome Lectures, Fifteenth Series, 1984.

P. 52   Sculptors' signatures: **E. Loewy,** Inschriften griechischer Bildhauer, 1885; **J. Marcadé,** Recueil des signatures de sculpteurs grecs, 1–2,
Paris 1953 and 1957.

P. 53   Architectural terracottas: **A. Andrén,** articles Acroterio, Antefis-
sa, Antepagmenta and Terracotta, in Enciclopedia dell'Arte Antica Classica e Orientale, with extensive bibliographies. Valuable insight into the
production and technique of hand- and mould-made architectural terracottas has been obtained through the excavations at Acquarossa, Poggio
Civitate, San Giovenale and Selvasecca; see **A. Andrén,** Osservazioni
sulle terrecotte architettoniche etrusco-italiche, Lectiones Boëthianae, I,
in Skrifter utgivna av Svenska Institutet i Rom, 4°, XXXI:1, Opuscula
Romana, VIII:1, 1971; **J.P. Small,** The Banquet Frieze from Poggio
Civitate, in Studi Etruschi, 39, 1971; **Ingrid E.M. Edlund,** The Seated
Statue Akroteria from Poggio Civitate (Murlo), in Dialoghi di Archeolo-
gia, 6, 1972; **T.N. Gantz,** The Procession Frieze from the Etruscan Sanctuary at Poggio Civitate, in Mitteilungen des Deutschen Archäologischen
Instituts, Römische Abteilung, 81, 1974; **J. Niels,** The Terracotta Gor-
goneia of Poggio Civitate (Murlo), ibid., 83, 1976; **N.A. Winter,**
Architectural Terracottas with Human Heads from Poggio Civitate (Murlo), in Archeologia Classica, 29, 1977; **Charlotte Wikander,** Painted
Architectural Terracottas from Acquarossa, in Skrifter utgivna av Svens-
ka Institutet i Rom, 4°, XXXV, Opuscula Romana, XI, 1976; **Ead.,** The
Painted Architectural Terracottas: Catalogue and Architectural Context,
ibid., XXXVIII:I, 1, Acquarossa, Vol. I, 1981; **Örjan Wikander,**
Architectural Terracottas from San Giovenale, ibid., XXXVII, Opuscula
Romana, XIII, 1981; **Eva Rystedt,** Early Etruscan Akroteria from Ac-
quarossa and Poggio Civitate (Murlo), ibid., XXXVIII:IV, Acquarossa,
Vol. IV, 1983.

P. 53   Lysistratos: Presuming that Pliny's notes on modellers in clay,
wax and plaster had been confused, **E. Sellers,** The Elder Pliny's Chapters
on the History of Art, maintained that his statement about clay casts
taken from statues (*idem et de signis effigies exprimere invenit,* etc.) refers
back to Butades; whereas **Gisela M.A. Richter,** Ancient Italy, p. 113,
preferred to move the sentence down to N.H. XXXV, 156, making *idem*
refer to Pasiteles, active in the first century B.C. See my objections in
Gnomon, 29, 1957, pp. 602 ff.

P. 53   Plaster moulds and casts from Baiae: **B.S. Ridgway,** op.cit., pp.
32 f., and note 7; **C. von Hees-Landwehr,** Die antiken Gipsabgüsse aus
Baiae: Griechische Bronzestatuen in Abgüssen römischer Zeit,
Archäologische Forschungen, 14, 1985.

P. 53   Amazons of Ephesus: **Overbeck,** Nos. 768, 946; **H. von Steuben,**
in **Helbig,** I, Nos. 126, 423, 433, II, Nos. 1422, 1643, 1875, 1890; **M.**

Weber, Die Amazonen von Ephesos, in Jahrbuch des Deutschen Archäologischen Instituts, 91, 1976.

P. 53   Sculptors' workshops: **D. Mustilli,** Botteghe di scultori, marmorarii, bronzieri e caelatores in Pompei, in Pompeiana, Raccolta di studi per il secondo centenario degli scavi di Pompei, Napoli 1950, pp. 206 ff., with references to discoveries and inscriptions indicating the existence of such workshops in Rome, Puteoli, Delos, etc. For an attempt to locate sculptors' workshops in different Mediterranean countries, see **B.S. Ridgway,** op.cit., pp. 86 ff.

P. 53   Crouching Aphrodite: **Gisela M.A. Richter,** op.cit., pp. 47 f., figs 150–157; **H. von Steuben,** in **Helbig,** I, No. 205, II, No. 2292; **Lullies,** fig. 252; **B.S. Ridgway,** op.cit., pl. 34.

P. 54   Ephebus signed by Stephanus: **P. Zanker,** in **Helbig,** IV, No. 3236; **B.S. Ridgway,** op.cit., pl. 35.

P. 54   Pheidias' Athena Parthenos: **Overbeck,** Nos. 645–690.

P. 59   Pheidias' Zeus in Olympia: **Overbeck,** Nos. 692–754.

P. 54   Niobids on armrests of Zeus' throne in Olympia: **C. Vogelpohl,** Die Niobiden vom Thron des Zeus in Olympia, Zur Arbeitsweise römischer Kopisten, in Jahrbuch ds Deutschen Archäologischen Instituts, 95, 1980.

P. 54   Apollo of Piombino: **Brunilde Sismondo Ridgway,** The Bronze Apollo from Piombino in the Louvre, in Antike Plastik, Lieferung VII:1–6, 1967, pp. 43–75, figs. 1–33, pls. 24–34b.

P. 55   Hermes in Olympia: **Lullies,** figs. 226–227; **B.S. Ridgway,** Roman Copies, pp. 85 f.

P. 55 f.   Moulds and casts of Greek metalware: **Gisela M.A. Richter,** Ancient plaster casts of Greek metalware, in American Journal of Archaeology, 62, 1958; **E. Reeder Williams,** Ancient clay impressions from Greek metalwork, in Hesperia, 45, 1976.

P. 58   Antiques acquired by Louis XIV of France: **Ch. Pinatel,** Les statues antiques des jardins de Versailles, 1963.

P. 58   Marble copy of Aristogeiton in Rome: **W. Fuchs,** in **Helbig,** II, No. 1646 (cf. No. 1768); **Lullies,** fig. 81.

P. 59   'Restorations' of marble copies of Myron's Discobolus: **W. Fuchs,** in **Helbig,** II, No. 1232; **G. Hafner,** Sternstunden der Archäologen, pp. 132 ff., with bibliography pp. 361 f.

P. 59   Lansdowne collection: **A.H. Smith,** A Catalogue of the Ancient Marbles at Lansdowne House, London 1889; Catalogue of the Celebrated Collection of Ancient Marbles the Property of The Most Honourable The Marquess of Lansdowne, Cristie's 5.3.1930.

P. 59 Cavaceppi: **Seymour Howard,** Bartolomeo Cavaceppi, Eighteenth-century Restorer, New York & London 1982.

P. 59 Lancelotti and Castelporziano copies of Myron's Discobolus: **E. Paribeni,** Museo Nazionale Romano, Sculture greche del V secolo, originali e repliche, 1953, Nos. 20–21; **W. Fuchs,** in **Helbig,** III, No. 2269; **Lullies,** fig. 127.

P. 59 Piranesi pastiche: **H. von Steuben,** in **Helbig,** IV, No. 3266.

P. 59 f. Antiques collected by Gustaf III of Sweden: **E. Kjellberg,** Piranesis antiksamling i Nationalmuseum, in Nationalmusei Årsbok, 2, 1929; **L. Kjellberg, E. Kjellberg,** Stockholm, Nationalmuseum, in Photographische Einzelaufnahmen antiker Skulpturen, Ser. XVII B, Nos. 4951–4985, Text pp. 1–31, 1947; **Boo von Malmborg,** Gustaf III:s antikmuseum, Katalog, 1966.

P. 60 Thorvaldsen's restoration of the Aegina pediments: **R. Wünsche,** Thorvaldsen e la ricostruzione dei frontoni di Egina, in Rendiconti della Pontificia Accademia Romana di Archeologia (forthcoming volume).

P. 60 f. Belvedere Torso: **A. Andrén,** Il Torso del Belvedere, in Skrifter utgivna av Svenska Institutet i Rom, 4°, XVI, Opuscula Archaeologica, VII, 1952; **W. Fuchs,** in **Helbig,** I, No. 265; **G. Säflund,** The Belvedere Torso, in Skrifter utgivna av Svenska Institutet i Rom, 4°, XXXV, Opuscula Romana, XI, 1976; **L. Eckhart,** Der Torso vom Belvedere, Wiederherstellung, Deutung, Arbeitstechnik, in Römische Historische Mitteilungen herausgegeben vom Österreichischen Kulturinstitut in Rom und der Österreichischen Akademie der Wissenschaften, 19. Heft, 1977.

P. 61 f. New antiques: **Eberhard Paul,** Gefälschte Antike von der Renaissance bis zur Gegenwart, Leipzig 1981; **Karina Türr,** Fälschungen antiker Plastik seit 1800, Berlin 1984, with extensive bibliographies.

P. 61 f. Clythia: **J. Jucker,** Das Bildnis im Blätterkelch, 1961; **E. Paul,** op.cit., pp. 76 ff., fig. 63.

P. 62 Vatican portrait of Octavian: **H. von Heintze,** in **Helbig,** I, No. 157; **E. Paul,** op.cit., pp. 115 ff., figs. 90–92.

P. 62 Technique of Campanian wall paintings: **Selim Augusti,** La tecnica dell'antica pittura parietale pompeiana, in Pompeiana, 1950, pp. 313–354.

P. 62 Forged 'Herculanean' wall paintings: **M. Cagiano de Azevedo,** in Bollettino dell'Istituto Centrale del Restauro, 1, 1950, pp. 41 ff.; **E. Paul,** op.cit., p. 114.

P. 62   Jupiter and Ganymede, by Raphael Mengs: **E. Paul,** op.cit., pp. 111 ff., fig. 88.

P. 62   Forged mosaics: **E. Paul,** op.cit., pp. 206 ff., figs 162–170.

P. 63   Ancient gems: **P.** and **H. Zazoff,** Gemmensammler und Gemmenforscher: Von einer noblen Passion zur Wissenschaft, 1983.

P. 63 f.   Early coin forgers: **R.H. Lawrence,** The Paduans, Medals by Giovanni Cavino, 1883; **H. Dressel,** Pirro Ligorio als Münzfälscher, in Zeitschrift für Numismatik, 22, 1900.

P. 64 f.   Bronze patina: **B. Bearzi,** Considerazioni sulla formazione delle patine e delle corrosioni sui bronzi antichi, in Studi Etruschi, 21, 1950–1951; **Patrik Reuterswärd,** Studien zur Polychromie der Plastik, Griechenland und Rom, Stockholm 1960, discussing, *inter alia,* the much-debated question of whether Greek artists used to give an artificial patina to new bronzes, on the basis of the ambiguous statement of **Pliny,** N.H. XXXIV, 15: *bitumine antiqui tinguebant eas (sc. statuas), quo magis mirum est placuisse auro integere.*

P. 65   Reconstruction of the Laokoon group: **F. Magi,** Il ripristino del Laocoonte, Memorie della Pontificia Accademia Romana di Archeologia, Serie III, Vol. IX:1, 1960; **P. Åström,** Arkeologiskt detektivarbete (with English summaries), Studies in Mediterranean Archaeology, Pocket-books, 11, 1980, pp. 97 ff. The integrated cast of the group is reproduced in **F. Magi,** op.cit., pl. 44, and in **B.S.Ridgway,** Roman Copies, pl. 30.

P. 65 f.   Restorations of the Apollo Belvedere: **W. Fuchs,** in **Helbig,** I, No. 226; **G. Daltrop,** Zur Überlieferung und Restaurierung des Apollo vom Belvedere, in Rendiconti della Pontificia Accademia Romana di Archeologia, 48, 1975–76, publ. 1977; **Lullies,** fig. 231.

P. 66   Barberini Faun: **Lullies,** fig. 254/255.

P. 67   Plastic works in terracotta: **A. Andrén,** article Terracotta, in the Enciclopedia dell'Arte Antica Classica e Orientale, with extensive bibliographical references.

P. 67   Tanagra and Myrina figurines: **D. Burr-Thompson,** articles Myrina and Tanagra, in the Enciclopedia dell'Arte Antica Classica e Orientale; **G. Kleiner,** Tanagrafiguren: Untersuchungen zur hellenistischen Kunst und Geschichte. Neu herausgegeben von **K. Parlasca** unter Mitwirkung von **Andreas Linfert,** 1983.

P. 67   Forged Tanagra and Myrina figurines: **E. Paul,** op.cit., pp. 174 ff., figs. 147–152.

P. 67   Caeretan terracotta sarcophagus in the Musée du Louvre: **G.M.A.**

Hanfmann, Etruskische Plastik, 1956, pl. 13; **M.F. Brighet,** Le sarcophage des époux de Cerveteri, in La revue du Louvre et des Musées de France, Février 1981, No. 1.

P. 67 f.   Forged terracotta sarcophagus in the British Museum: **C.T. Newton,** The Castellani Collection, 1874, pp. 5 ff., pls. 18–20; **A.S. Murray,** Terracotta Sarcophagi Greek and Etruscan in the British Museum, 1898, pp. 21–25, pls. 9–11; **Herta Sauer,** Die archaischen etruskischen Terracottasarkophage aus Caere, Diss. Leipzig 1930; **E. Paul,** op.cit., pp. 256 f., fig. 208; **K. Türr,** op.cit., E 8, with bibliography.

P. 68   Caeretan terracotta sarcophagus in the Museo di Villa Giulia: **L. Goldscheider,** op.cit., pls. 10–13; **T. Dohrn,** in **Helbig,** III, No. 2582; **F. Magi,** Sui volti degli "Sposi" di Villa Giulia e del Louvre, in Rendiconti della Pontificia Accademia Romana di Archeologia, 43, 1970–1971.

P. 68   Forgeries in the British Museum: An Exhibition of Forgeries and deceptive Copies held in the Department of Prints and Drawings, British Museum, 1961; **S. Cole,** in Antiquity, 35, 1961.

P. 69 ff.   Forged terracotta statues in New York: **Gisela M.A. Richter,** Etruscan Terracotta Warriors in the Metropolitan Museum of Art, with a Report on Structure and Technique by C.F. Binns, Papers No. 6, 1937; **D. von Bothmer, J.V. Noble,** An Inquiry into the Forgery of the Etruscan Terracotta Warriors in the Metropolitan Museum of Art, Papers No. 11, 1961; **E. Paul,** op.cit., pp. 259 ff., figs. 218–221; **K. Türr,** op.cit., E 4, E 6, E 7, E 14, with bibliography.

P. 69 f.   Etruscan terracotta statues from Veii: **T. Dohrn,** in **Helbig,** III, Nos. 2553–2558; **G. Colonna,** Il maestro dell'Ercole e della Minerva: Nuova luce sull'attività dell'officina veiente, Lectio Boëthiana 1986, to be published in the Opuscula Romana of the Swedish Institute in Rome.

P. 71   Terracotta relief slabs from Orvieto and "from Bolsena": **A. Andrén,** Architectural Terracottas from Etrusco-Italic Temples, 1940, p. 201, III:3, pl. 74: 252, 253, pp. 205 ff., I:1–I:5, pl. 77: 260–264; **D. von Bothmer, J.V. Noble,** op.cit., pp. 14 f., pls. XXII: A–E, XXIII: A–D. There is some uncertainty as regards the slabs said to come from Bolsena. **P.J. Riis,** Etruscan or Modern?, in Acta Archaeologica, 35, 1964, pp. 81 ff., pls. I–II, pointing out that ceramics of undisputed antiquity have been found through laboratory tests to contain small amounts of mangan, concluded that three relief slabs "from Bolsena" in the Danish National Museum could be genuine. And according to **T. Dohrn,** in **Helbig,** I, No. 811, it is not demonstrated that all specimens of these series of slabs are forged.

P. 72   Terracotta kore in the Ny Carlsberg Glyptotek: **F. Poulsen,** in Die Antike, 8, 1932, pp. 95 ff., figs 1–6, pls. 13–15; **P.J. Riis,** in From the Collections of the Ny Carlsberg Glyptothek, III, 1942, pp. 1 ff., figs. 1–5;
120

H.W. Parsons, in Art News, 60, 1962, pp. 34 ff., figs. 11–13; **E. Paul,** op.cit., pp. 262 f., figs. 225–226; **K. Türr,** op.cit., E 5, with bibliography.

P. 73   Terracotta statuette of Diana in St. Louis: **R. Herbig,** Die Terrakottagruppe einer Diana mit dem Hirschkalb, in Abhandlungen der Heidelberger Akademie der Wissenschaften, Philosophisch-historische Klasse, 1956:3; **H.W. Parsons,** op.cit., figs. 5–9; **E. Paul,** op.cit., p. 262, figs. 222–223; **K. Türr,** op.cit., E 11, with bibliography.

P. 74   Painted terracotta slabs "from Caere": **F. Roncalli,** A proposito delle lastre dipinte di Boston, in Archeologia Classica, 21, 1969, pp. 172–189; **S.J. Fleming, H. Jucker, J. Riederer,** Etruscan wall-paintings on terracotta: A study in authenticity, in Archaeometry, 13, 1971, pp. 143–167.

P. 74 f.   Forged marble sculptures in archaic, classical and Praxitelean style: **A. Furtwängler,** Neuere Faelschungen von Antiken, 1899, pp. 1–14, figs. 1–8; **E. Paul,** op.cit., pp. 160 f., fig. 124, pp. 170 ff., figs. 138–142, pp. 217 ff., figs. 179–183, pp. 220 f., fig. 191; **K. Türr,** op.cit., A 29, K 16.

P. 75   Ludovisi collection: **B. Palma,** I Marmi Ludovisi: Storia della collezione, Museo Nazionale Romano, Catalogo Generale, I:4, 1983.

P. 75 ff.   Ludovisi Throne: **H. von Steuben,** in Helbig, III, No. 2340; **Lullies,** figs. 114–117.

P. 75 ff.   Boston Throne: **F. Studniczka,** Das Gegenstück der Ludovisischen Thronlehne, in Jahrbuch des Deutschen Archäologischen Instituts, 26, 1911; **A. von Gerkan,** Untersuchungen am Ludovisischen und Bostoner Relief, in Jahreshefte des Österreichischen Archäologischen Institutes, 25, 1929; **E. Nash,** Über die Auffindung und den Erwerb des 'Bostoner Thrones', in Mitteilungen des Deutschen Archäologischen Instituts, Römische Abteilung, 66, 1959; **F. Baroni,** Osservazioni sul "Trono di Boston", Studia Archaeologica, 2, 1961; **H. Jucker,** Archäologische Berichte, Sachliches zur Echtheitsfrage des Bostoner 'Throns' oder Kassation des Urteils gegen die Götter, in Museum Helveticum, 22, fasc. 2, 1965; **B. Ashmole,** The Three-sided Relief in Boston, in Boston Museum Bulletin, No. 332, 1965; **G. Becatti,** s.v. Trono di Boston, in the Enciclopedia dell'Arte Antica Classica e Orientale, VII, 1966; **W.J. Young – B. Ashmole,** The Boston Relief and the Ludovisi Throne, in Boston Museum Bulletin, No. 346, 1968; **Licia Vlad Borrelli,** Ambiguità del falso, in Archeologia Classica, 23, 1971, pp. 99 f.

P. 77   Forged fragments of the Parthenon frieze and other forgeries in marble: **B. Ashmole,** Forgeries of Ancient Sculpture, Creation and Detection, The First J.L. Myres Memorial Lecture, Oxford 1961; **E. Paul,** op.cit., pp. 130 ff., figs. 113–115; **K. Türr,** op.cit., K 1, K 3, K 4, RR 10.

P. 79   Grueneisen collection: Art Classique, sculpture grecque – romaine – étrusque, Exposition de la Collection W. de Grueneisen, Paris 1925; **E. Paul,** op.cit., pp. 172 f., figs. 192–193, 201–204; **K. Türr,** op.cit., A 13.

P. 79   'Archaic' marble sculptures by Alceo Dossena and other forgers: **F. Studniczka,** Neue archaische Marmorskulpturen, Falsches und Echtes, in Jahrbuch des Deutschen Archäologischen Instituts, 43, 1928, pp. 140 ff., pls. 1–3; **B. Ashmole,** Forgeries of Ancient Sculpture, pp. 10 ff., figs. 20–31; **E. Paul,** op.cit, pp. 211 ff., 219 f., figs. 171–178, 189, 199–200, 203–204; **K. Türr,** op.cit., A 12, A 14, A 15, A 16.

P. 80 f.   Marble relief from Nemus Aricinum: **A. Furtwängler,** Die antiken Gemmen, 1900, III, pp. 231, 266 ff., fig. 140; **F. Altheim,** Griechische Götter im alten Rom, 1930, pp. 104 ff.; **G.Q. Giglioli,** L'arte etrusca, 1935, pl. CXXV:1; **F. Poulsen,** Katalog over antike Skulpturer, Ny Carlsberg Glyptotek, 1940, No. 30; **M. Borda,** L'Egistofonia di Ariccia ed il suo significato stilistico, in Latomus, 10, 1951; **Gisela M.A. Richter,** Ancient Italy, pp. 31 f., fig. 121; **E. Gummey Pemberton,** A note on the Death of Aigisthos, in American Journal of Archaeology, 70, 1966, pp. 377 ff.; **G. Hafner,** Das Relief vom Nemisee in Kopenhagen, in Jarhrbuch des Deutschen Archäologischen Instituts, 82, 1967, pp. 246 ff.

P. 81   Marble sculpture from Etruria: **A. Andrén,** Marmora Etruriae, in Antike Plastik, Lieferung VII:1–6, 1967, pp. 7 ff., pls. 1–25.

P. 81   Greek artists in Etruria: The fascinating art of the Etruscans, developed under strong influence of Greek artistic conceptions, but retaining a dynamic expressiveness of its own, cannot be understood merely as the result of imitation of art objects imported from the Greek world, but postulates instruction of Etruscan apprentices in workshops established in Etruria by immigrant Greek artists, especially in the case of such difficult processes as the manufacture of fine painted pottery, polychrome statues and architectural ornaments of terracotta, and bronze statuary modelled in wax and cast à cire perdue. It is therefore reasonable to accept as essentially true the tradition retold by **Pliny** N.H. XXXV, 16 and 152, of how a Corinthian nobleman named Damaratos fled from his native city to escape the violence of the tyrant Cypselus (c. 655–625 B.C.) and settled at Tarquinii together with his fellow countrymen, the painter Ekphantos and three modellers called Eucheir, Diopos and Eugrammos, who were said to have introduced the technique of terracotta statuary to Etruria. The presence of Greek artists and merchants in Etruria, moreover, is amply confirmed by archaeological discoveries, such as clay vases with Greek votive inscriptions to Hera found at Caere (**R. Mengarelli,** Il luogo e i materiali del Tempio di Hera a Caere, in Studi Etruschi, 10, 1936, pp. 67 ff.), the homogeneous group of painted hydriae made in a Greek pottery in the same city (**J.M. Hemelrijk,** Caeretan Hydriae, Kerameus, Band 5, 1984), and the remains of an archaic Greek cult place excavated at Graviscae, with small temples and clay vases bearing inscribed dedications in Greek or Etruscan to the goddesses Aphrodite/Turan, Hera/Uni, and Demeter/Vei (**M. Torelli,** Il santuario greco di Gravisca, in Lazio arcaico e mondo greco, La Parola del Passato, 32, 1977, pp. 398–458). From the same sanctuary comes the curved marble arm of a big anchor with a late-sixth-century Greek inscription in the dialect and alphabet of Aegina, saying that the piece was dedicated to the Aeginetan Apollo by Sostratos (**M. Pallottino,** The Etruscans, London 1974, p. 112, with note 12 and plate 11). The seafaring trader who dedicated part of his anchor to his god at Graviscae was probably the one recorded by Herodotus (IV, 152) as Sostratos, son of Laodamas, of Aegina, the most successful of all Greek merchants of his time. For the marble cult statue of the goddess Vei found in the Cannicella necropolis at Orvieto, see **A. Andrén,** Marmora Etruriae, pp. 10–24, figs. 1–2, pls. 1–8, and Studi Etruschi, 35, 1967, pp. 41 ff., pls. XVI–XIX. See also **M. Torelli,** Terrecotte architettoniche arcaiche da Gravisca e una nota a Plinio, NH XXXV, 151–152, in Nuovi Quaderni dell' Istituto di Archeologia dell'Università di Perugia, I. Studi in onore di Filippo Magi, 1979.

P. 82   Ancient bronze casting: **E. Pernice,** Untersuchungen zur antiken Toreutik, in Jahreshefte des Österreichischen Archäologischen Institutes, 7–11, 1904–08; **K. Kluge – K. Lehmann-Hartleben,** Die antiken Grossbronzen der römischen Kaiserzeit, I–III, 1927; **K. Kluge,** Die antike Erzgestaltung und ihre technischen Grundlagen, 1927; **Id.,** Die Gestaltung des Erzes in der archaisch-griechischen Kunst, in Jahrbuch des Deutschen Archäologischen Instituts, 44, 1929; **A.J. Forbes,** Metallurgy in Antiquity, A Note-Book for Archaeologists and Technologists, Leiden 1950; **R. Raven-Hart,** The Casting-Technique of Certain Greek Bronzes, in The Journal of Hellenic Studies, 78, 1958; **C. Mattusch,** Casting Techniques of Greek Bronze Sculpture, Foundries and Foundry Remains from the Athenian Agora with Reference to other Ancient Sources, Diss. Ann Arbor 1978; **P.C. Bol,** Grossplastik aus Bronze in Olympia, Olympische Forschungen, IX, 1978; **C. Rolley,** op.cit., pp. 13 ff.

P. 82   Mars of Todi: **F. Roncalli,** Il "Marte" di Todi, Memorie della Pontificia Accademia Romana di Archeologia, XI:2, 1973. See also **T. Dohrn,** Der Arringatore, p. 6, stating that this late Etruscan statue is composed of seven parts cast hollow *à cire perdue* + the feet, which are made solid for the sake of stability.

P. 82   Apollo Stroganoff: **A. Furtwängler,** Meisterwerke der griechischen Plastik, 1893, pp. 659 ff.; **E. Paul,** op.cit., pp. 163 ff., figs. 135–137.

P. 82   Forged bronze heads of the "Sappho" type: **A. Furtwängler,** Neuere Faelschungen von Antiken, pp. 23 ff., figs. 19–20; **E. Paul,** op.cit., pp. 158 f., figs. 120–123; **K. Türr,** op cit., K 19.

P. 82 f.   Lutetia Parisiorum: **A. Furtwängler,** Neuere Faelschungen von Antiken, pp. 26 ff., fig. 21.

P. 83   Bronze horse in New York: **J.V. Noble,** The Forgery of Our Greek Bronze Horse, in The Metropolitan Museum of Art Bulletin, February 1969, pp. 253 ff.; **C. Blümel,** Zur Echtheitsfrage des antiken Bronzepferdes im Metropolitan Museum in New York, in Archäologischer Anzeiger, 84, 1969, pp. 208 ff.; **D.W. Zimmermann, M.P. Yuhas, P. Meyers,** Thermoluminescence authenticity measurements on core material from the bronze horse of the Metropolitan Museum of Art, in Archaeometry, 16:1, 1974, pp. 19 ff.; **C. Rolley,** op.cit., p. 110, fig. 91.

P. 83   Bronze horse from Olympia: **Lullies,** fig. 83; **C. Rolley,** op.cit., p. 89, fig. 65.

P. 84   Ancient jewellery: **M. Rosenberg,** Geschichte der Goldschmiedekunst auf technischer Grundlage, Abteilung Granulation, 1918; **G. Piccardi,** Sulla oreficeria granulata, in Studi Etruschi, 22, 1952–53, pp. 199 ff.; **F. Chlebecek,** Beitrag zur Technik der Granulation, ibid., pp. 203 ff.; **G. Piccardi – S. Bordi,** Sull'oreficeria granulata etrusca, ibid., 24, 1955–56, pp. 354 ff.; **G. Becatti,** Oreficerie antiche dalle minoiche alle barbariche, 1955; **E. Coche de la Ferté,** Les bijoux antiques, 1956; **R.A. Higgins,** Greek and Roman Jewellery, 1961, 2nd ed. 1980; **A. Andrén,** Opere di un orafo etrusco, in Hommages à Albert Grenier, Collection Latomus, 58, 1962, pp. 135 ff.; **H. Hoffmann – V. von Vlaer,** Museum für Kunst und Gewerbe, Hamburg: Antiker Gold- und Silberschmuck, Katalog mit Untersuchungen der Objekte auf technischer Grundlage, 1968; **G. Bordenache Battaglia,** Gioielli antichi dall'età micenea all'ellenismo, Museo Nazionale di Villa Giulia, Collezione A. Castellani, 1980; **J. Ogden,** Jewellery of the Ancient World, the Materials and Techniques, 1983; **J. Wolters,** Die Granulation, 1983; **M. Cristofano – M. Martelli,** L'Oro degli Etruschi, 1983; **M. Scarpignato,** Oreficerie etrusche arcaiche, Monumenti Musei e Gallerie Pontificie, Museo Gregoriano Etrusco, Cataloghi, I. 1985.

P. 84 f.   Forged Graeco-Scythian gold treasures: **A. Furtwängler,** Intermezzi, Kunstgeschichtliche Studien, 1896, pp. 79 ff.; **Id.,** Neuere Faelschungen von Antiken, pp. 28 ff., figs. 22–23; **E. Paul,** op.cit., pp. 180 ff., figs. 153–156.

P. 85   Schliemann: **David A. Traill,** Schliemann's 'discovery' of 'Priam's Treasure', in Antiquity, 57, 1983; **Id.,** Schliemann's discovery of 'Priam's Treasure': a re-examination of the evidence, in Journal of Hellenic Studies, 104, 1984. The evidence for 'Priam's Treasure' being a hoax has been contested by **Donald Easton,** Schliemann's mendacity – a false trail?, in Antiquity, 58, 1984; but at the same time Mr. Easton demonstrates how Schliemann repeatedly used his fairly sober diaries and notes on different excavations to build up highly romantic and sensational accounts for his printed works.

P. 86   Dawson: **Kenneth P. Oakley,** The Piltdown Problem reconsidered, in Antiquity, 50, 1976, pp. 9 ff., with bibliography p. 13.

P. 86 ff.   Glozel: **O.G.S. Crawford,** in Antiquity, 1, 1927, pp. 100 f., 181–188, 259 f., 387; ibid., 2, 1928, pp. 4 f.; **A. Vayson de Pradenne,** ibid., 4, 1930, pp. 201 ff.; **H. MacKerrell, V. Mejdahl, H. François, G. Portal,** Thermoluminescence and Glozel, in Antiquity, 48, 1974, pp. 265 ff., pls. XXIX–XXXI; see also Antiquity, 49, 1975, pp. 267 ff. (cf. Editorial, pp. 2 f., Notes and News, pp. 219 ff.); 50, 1976, p. 2; 51, 1977, pp. 7, 89 ff.

P. 88 ff.   Fibula Praenestina: **Margherita Guarducci,** La cosiddetta Fibula Praenestina: Antiquari, eruditi e falsari nella Roma dell'Ottocento, in Memorie dell' Accademia Nazionale dei Lincei, Classe di Scienze morali, storiche e filologiche, Serie VIII, Vol, XXIV, Fasc. 4, 1980, pp. 411–574, pls. I–XI; **W. Belardi,** Numerius nella latinità delle origini, in Rendiconti dell' Accademia Nazionale dei Lincei, Classe di Scienze morali, etc., vol. XXXV, Fasc. 5–6, 1980, pp. 343–351; **M. Guarducci,** La cosiddetta Fibula Praenestina; Elementi nuovi, in Memorie della Accademia Nazionale dei Lincei, Classe di Scienze morali, etc., Serie VIII, Vol. XXVIII, Fasc. 2, 1984, pp. 127–177, pls. I–VI.

P. 92   Helbig's autobiography: **W. Helbig.** Eine Skizze meines wissenschaftlichen Bildungsganges, reprinted in **F. Poulsen,** Helbig Museet, 1925, pp. III–XVI.

P. 93   Praenestine bronze cistae: **G. Foerst,** Die Gravierungen der Praenestinischen Cisten, Archaeologica, 7, 1978; **G. Bordenache Battaglia – A. Emiliozzi,** Le ciste prenestine, I–II, 1979.

P. 94 f.   Nephele dish: **A. Furtwängler,** Neuere Faelschungen von Antiken, pp. 33 ff., fig. 24.

P. 95 f.   Scientific dating and authenticity tests: **J. Thimme –J. Riederer,** Sinteruntersuchungen an Marmorobjekten, in Archäologischer Anzeiger, 1969, pp. 89–105; **D.L. Caroll,** Drawn wire and identification of forgeries in ancient jewellery, in American Journal of Archaeology, 74, 1970; **M.S. Tite,** Methods of Physical Examination in Archaeology, 1972; **M.J. Aitken,** Physics and Archaeology, 2nd ed. 1974; **Stuart J. Flemming,** Authenticity in Art: The Scientific Detection of Forgery, 1975; **J.J. Sweeny,** The Scientific Revolution in Archaeology, Diss. St. Louis Mo

1976; **Stuart J. Fleming,** Thermoluminescence Techniques in Archaeology, 1979; **R. Berger, H.E. Suess** (ed.), Radiocarbon Dating, 1979; **Z. Coffer,** Archaeological Chemistry, 1979; **P.M. Fischer,** op.cit. (above, note to p. 45).

P. 96   Technique of pottery: **J.V. Noble,** The Techniques of Painted Attic Pottery, 1965; **J. Scheibler,** Griechische Töpferkunst: Herstellung, Handel und Gebrauch antiker Tongefässe, 1983; **Ninina Cuomo di Caprio,** La ceramica in archeologia: antiche tecniche di lavorazione e moderni metodi di indagine, La Fenice, 6, 1985.

P. 96   Technique of sculpture: **S. Casson,** The Technique of Early Greek Sculpture, 1933; **C. Blümel,** Griechische Bildhauer an der Arbeit, 1940, 4. Aufl. 1953; **Id.,** Greek Sculptors at Work, 1955; **S. Adam,** The Technique of Greek Sculpture in the Archaic and Classical Periods, The British School of Archaeology at Athens, Suppl. 3, 1966; **H. Etienne,** The Chisel in Greek Sculpture: A study of the way in which material, technique, and tools determine the design of the sculpture of ancient Greece, 1968.

Some recent publications may be cited here in addition to those referred to under the following headings:

P. 34   Parthenon: **B.F. Cook,** The Elgin Marbles, 1984; **J. Boardman,** The Parthenon and its Sculptures, 1985.

P. 46   Submarine archaeology: Navigia Fundo Emergunt: Trentatré anni di ricerche e di attività in Italia e all' estero del Centro Sperimentale di Archeologia Sottomarina. Quaderni della Soprintendenza Archeologica della Liguria, Genova 1983.

P. 82   Ancient bronze casting: **P.C. Bol,** Antike Bronzetechnik, 1985.

P. 84   Ancient jewellery: **B. Deppert-Lippitz,** Griechischer Goldschmuck, 1985.

ILLUSTRATIONS

Fig. 1 – Kore. One of the many fine archaic marble sculptures of the Acropolis of Athens which were mutilated by Xerxes' soldiers in 480 B.C., buried on the citadel after the defeat of the Persians, and brought to light again in the 1980's.

Fig. 2 – Head of Odysseus. A fragment of the "Odyssey in marble" made by the masters of the Laokoon group and set up in the "Cave of Tiberius" at Sperlonga. The sculptures were reduced to pieces probably by Christians abhorring heathen images.

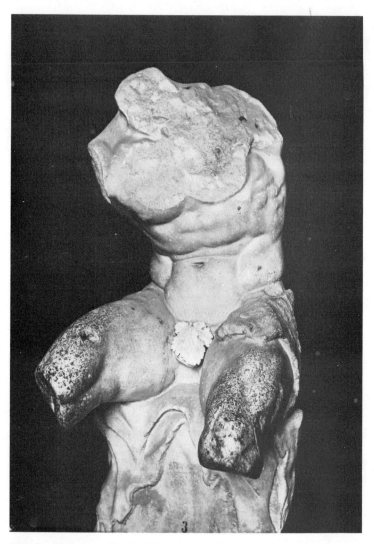

Fig. 3 – Belvedere Torso. The huge mutilated marble statue, signed by Apollonios, son of Nestor, of Athens, was discovered before the 1430's and has remained unintegrated through five centuries of restoration.

Fig. 4 – Death of Laokoon and his sons. The famous marble group, discovered in Rome in 1506, was cleared of its restorations in the 1950's and supplemented with the father's right arm, recovered in 1905.

Fig. 5 – *Apollo Belvedere. The famous marble statue, made in Roman times after a bronze original probably by Leochares, was extolled by neo-classical artists and critics, and enigmatized by modern archaeologists, through the removal of its sixteenth-century restorations.*

Fig. 6 – Discobolus. A careful marble copy of Myron's famous bronze statue of a discus-thrower in action, made in the age of Hadrian and discovered at Castelporziano, at a time when restoration of ancient marbles had become obsolete.

Fig. 7 – Hermes. One of the many fine bronze copies of Greek originals that were saved from destruction by the eruption of Vesuvius in 79 A.D. and brought to light from the Villa of the Papyri at Herculaneum in the years 1750–1765.

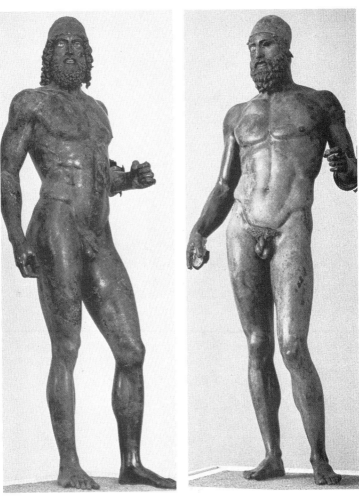

Fig. 8 – Warriors from the sea. Two impressive Greek bronze statues, made in the second half of the fifth century B.C. and saved from destruction by having formed part of a shipload wrecked off Riace in Calabria, where they were raised from the deep in 1972.

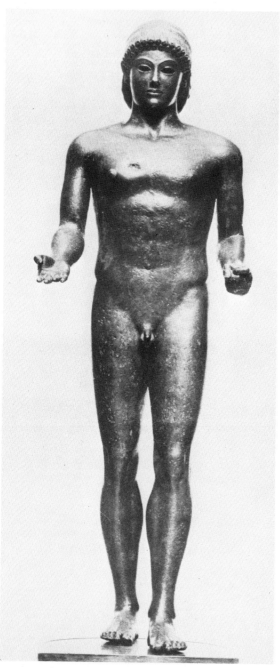

Fig. 9 – Apollo of Piombino. A bronze statue found in the sea off Populonia about 1830, acquired by the Musée du Louvre, and regarded as a Greek original of the first half of the fifth century B.C., until it was exposed in 1967 as a forgery of the first century B.C.

Fig. 10 – Bronze statuette of a horse. Acquired by the Metropolitan Museum of New York in 1923, and long admired as a Greek masterpiece of about 470 B.C., the horse was condemned as a modern forgery in 1969 but shown to be antique through a thermoluminescence test. Its over-elegant form, however, suggests a late Hellenistic forgery in imitation of Greek fifth-century models.

Fig. 11 – Terracotta sarcophagus. A grotesque piece of clay modelling, acquired by the British Museum in 1873, as a precious example of archaic Etruscan art. Its authenticity was soon called in question by many scholars, whereas many others rejected or disregarded their arguments. But the study of important works of archaic figurative art discovered in Etruria in later years eventually convinced all critics that the sarcophagus was an ugly forgery, made by a restorer in the service of the Marchese Campana. It was removed from exhibition in 1935.

Fig. 12 – Fighting warrior. One of the huge terracotta warriors which were acquired by the Metropolitan Museum of New York in the years 1915–1921, being described as materpieces of archaic Etruscan art. They were exposed in 1961 as having been made in Orvieto by the Riccardi-Fioravanti team of forgers, and a thermoluminescence test gave them an age of about 60 years.

Fig. 13 – Kore. A small terracotta statue modelled in the style of the Veientine statues and acquired by the Ny Carlsberg Glyptotek in 1930. It was exposed some thirty years later as a clever forgery made by A.A. Fioravanti. A thermoluminescence test gave the girl an age of 48 years.

Fig. 14 – Diana the Huntress. A small terracotta statue, acquired by the City Art Museum of St. Louis in 1952, and exposed in 1962 as a forgery made by Alceo Dossena in imitation of the Veientine statues. A thermoluminescence test gave the Diana an age of 40 years.

Fig. 15 – "Clythia". A marble bust of a lovely Roman girl in the British Museum, probably made in the eighteenth century by an Italian sculptor.

Fig. 16 – Studniczka's "Entführungsgruppe". One of the many marble sculptures in archaic Greek style which were made by the prolific forger Alceo Dossena, with the help of photographic reproductions of well-known originals.

Fig. 17 – Ludovisi Throne. Front relief representing the Birth of Aphrodite (?).

Fig. 18 – Boston Throne. Front relief representing Eros weighing the lives of Adonis and Tithonos between Aphrodite and Eos (?).

Fig. 19 – Saitapharnes' tiara. A magnificent gold headgear acquired by the Musée du Louvre and shown to be one of many 'Graeco-Scythian' ornaments made by a Russian goldsmith in the 1890's.

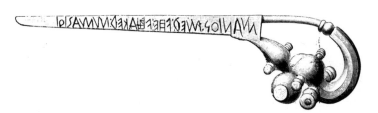

Fig.20–The so-called Fibula Praenestina. The inscribed gold fibula, said to have been found at Palestrina, ancient Praeneste, was the subject of much discussion ever since its mysterious appearance in 1887. Some scholars questioned its authenticity, others maintained that it was a genuine document of supreme historical and philological importance, giving us the earliest extant example of Latin writing. The dispute continued for close on a century, until a series of examinations, epigraphic, linguistic, and technical, combined with inquiries into the nineteenth-century antique market of Rome, definitely proved that the fibula and its inscription were made to serve a well-staged fraud.

Fig. 21 – Inscribed clay tablet from Glozel.

147

Index

Acropolis of Athens, 5, 12, 19, 20, 30, 33 f., 37, 98, 128
Acropolis Museum, Athens, 39
Actium, 9
Adamo, 63
Adaptions and variants in sculpture, 53, 115
Adriatic Sea, 31
Aegean Sea, 28
Aegina, 34, 60, 123
Aeginetan bronze, 29
Aeginetan pediments, 39, 60, 66, 74, 109, 118
Aelian, 10
Aerial photography, 45, 113
Aerugo nobilis, 64
Aetolians, 8
Africanus, P. Cornelius Scipio, 8
Agora of Athens, 5, 53, 54
Agrigento/Agrigentum, 32, 50
Agrippa's baths in Rome, 12
Agropolis, 18
Air pollution, 31, 39
Alaric the Visigoth, 16
Albani, Alessandro, 24, 25
Albani, Giuseppe, 27
Aldrovandi, Ulisse, 24
Alexander the Great, 5, 6
Alexander, bronze statue by Lysippos, in Rome, 14
Alexander and his bodyguard, bronze group by Lysippos, in Rome, 12, 102
Alexander on Bucephalus, bronze statue by Lysippos, 14
Alexander on paintings by Apelles, in Rome, 14
Alexander I of Russia, 27
Alexander VII, Pope, 20
Alexandria, 9, 14, 18
Algardi, Alessandro, 61
Alkamenes, 83
Altheim, F., 81
Altoviti, Bindo, 23
Amazon, bronze figure owned by Nero, 10
Amazonomachy, on shield of Athena Parthenos, 46, 54, 114
Amazons, bronze statues at Ephesus, 53, 116 f.
Amphion and Zethos punishing Dirke, bronze group in Rome, 13
148

Amsterdam, 26

Anaphe, 35

Andronikos, Manolis, 45

Antenor, 5, 53, 98

Anticythera, bronzes found off, 30, 107

Antiochus III of Syria, 8, 9

Antique hunting in Greece and the Levant, 39 ff., 108 f.

Antique market of ancient Rome, 9, 41, 55 f.

Antonia, consort of Drusus, 62

Antoninus Pius, 5

Antoninus and Faustina, temple of, in Rome, 20

Apelles, 12, 13, 14

Aphaea, temple of, in Aegina, 34, 60, 66, 109

Aphrodite, birth of, on Ludovisi Throne (?), 76, 144

Aphrodite, bronze statue by Praxiteles, in Rome, 12, 15

Aphrodite, marble statue by Doidalsas (?), in Rome, 53, 117

Aphrodite, marble statue by Pheidias, in Rome, 12

Aphrodite, marble statue by Praxiteles, in Cnidos, 12, 15, 19

Aphrodite, marble statue by Skopas, in Rome, 12

Aphrodite, marble statue from Melos, in Paris, 35, 109

Aphrodite Anadyomene, painting by Apelles, in Rome, 13, 102

Aphrodite Anadyomene, painting by Dorotheos, in Rome, 13

Apollo, 5, 11, 19

Apollo, bronze statue by Myron, restored from Rome to Ephesus, 10

Apollo, bronze statue from Piraeus, 30, 107

Apollo, bronze statue from Tamassus, 30, 107

Apollo, marble statue from Anaphe, 35

Apollo, terracotta statue from Veii, 69, 74

Apollo Belvedere, marble copy in the Vatican, 22 f., 27, 65 f., 82, 119, 132

Apollo Citharoedus, bronze statue from Pompeii, 29

Apollo Philesios, bronze statue by Kanachos, 5, 98

Apollo of Piombino, bronze statue found off Populonia, 54 f., 83, 117, 136

Apollo Stroganoff, forged bronze statuette, 82, 123

Apollo Temenites/Tuscanicus, colossal bronze statue, removed from Syracuse to Rome, 10, 100

Apollo, temple of, in Bassae, 35, 36, 109

Apollo, temple of, in Pyrgi, 10

Apollo, temple of, on the Palatine, Rome, 14

Apollonios, son of Nestor, of Athens, 22, 30, 130

Apollonios of Tralles, 13

Apoxyomenos, bronze statue by Lysippos, in Rome, 12, 102

Apuan Alps, 28

Apulian tomb paintings, 28
Aquileia, 23
Arcadia, 35
Arch of Titus, in Rome, 11, 101
Archaeological discoveries, 36, 110
Archaeological field prospecting, 45 f., 113
Archaeological underwater exploration, 45 f., 113 f.
Architectural terracottas, 8, 28, 48, 53, 67, 69, 71, 116
Arezzo/Arretium, 23
Aristeides, 12, 15
Aristogeiton, 5, 53, 58, 65, 117
Artemis, bronze statues from Piraeus, 30, 107
Artemis, marble statue by Timotheos, in Rome, 14
Artemisia, Queen of Caria, 36
Arundel, 24
Ashmole, Bernard, 77 f.
Ashmolean Museum, Oxford, 95
Asia Minor, 23, 35
Asinius Pollio's gallery in Rome, 13, 102
Åström, Paul, 46
Athanadoros, 13
Athena, bronze statue from Piraeus, 30, 107
Athena, marble statue from Velletri, 53
Athena, temple of, at Paestum, 20
Athena, temple of, in Syracuse, 20
Athena Nike, temple of, in Athens, 20, 34, 39
Athena Parthenos, chryselephantine statue by Pheidias, 35, 36, 46, 54,
    117
Ahena Promachos, bronze colossus by Pheidias, 19, 103
Athens, 5, 8, 14, 20, 22, 23, 32, 33, 34, 38 f., 53, 54, 103
Athlete, bronze statue found off Numana, 30 f., 108
Athlete, 'restored' marble statue "from Formia", 75, 78, 93
Atomic absorption spectometry, 96
Attalus III of Pergamum, 9, 55
Attica, 48
Attila the Hun, 16
Attus Navius, bronze statue in Rome, 28, 106
Augsburg, 26, 58
Augustus, 10, 13, 21, 40, 62, 83
Augustus, colossal portrait head from Veii, 21, 104
Augustus, temple of, in Rome, 10
Aurelian Wall, in Rome, 20
Aventine, Rome, 6, 7

Azzolino, Decio, 26
Azzolino, Pompeo, 26

Babin, Jesuit, 38
Baiae, marble sculptures from, 46, 115
Baiae, moulds and casts from, 53, 116
Bandinelli, Baccio, 57, 65
Banditaccia necropolis, Cerveteri, 74
Barberini collection, 24, 105
Barberini Faun, 66, 119
Baroni, Fiorenza, 77 f.
Barracco, Giovanni, 92
Bassae, 35, 39, 109
Becatti, Giovanni, 78
Becker, Carl Wilhelm, 63 f.
Belardi, Walter, 91
Belisarius, 16, 17
Belvedere collection, 22 f., 25
Belvedere temple, Orvieto, 67
Belvedere Torso, 23, 30, 60 f., 118, 130
Berlin, Berlin museums, 36, 37, 48, 84
Bernini, Gian Lorenzo, 66
Bianco, Simone, 61
Bibliothèque Nationale, Paris, 27, 63, 83
Blue Grotto, Capri, marble statues from, 46, 114
Blümel, Carl, 83
Boccanera, L., 37
Boccanera slabs, from Caere, 74
Boccaporco, 70
Bologna, 73
Bolsena, 70, 71, 99, 120
Bonaparte, Lucien, 43
Boncompagni-Ludovisi, Don Rudolfo, 76
Borda, Maurizio, 81
Borghese collection, 24, 105
Boston Throne, 75–78, 96, 121, 144
Bothmer, Dietrich von, 49, 71
Boxer, bronze statue found in Rome, 22, 30, 107
Boxer, head of bronze statue found at Olympia, 30, 107
Boy Jockey, bronze figure found off Cape Artemision, 30, 107
Bramante, Donato, 57
Brettingham, Matthew, 25
British Museum, 33, 34, 35, 36, 43, 54, 59, 62, 67, 68, 69, 74, 75, 78, 93, 97,
    120, 138, 142

Brocklesby Park, 25
Brøndsted, P.O., 34
Bronze alloys, 29
Bronze casting, 15, 53, 82, 123
Bronze patina, 64 f., 82, 119
Bronze statues of early Romans, 28, 106
Bronzes from the sea, 30 f., 107 f.
Brunn, Heinrich, 93
Brutus Callaecus' temple of Mars, in Rome, 12
Bryaxis, 36
Bucchero, 42
Bucephalus, 14
Butades of Sicyon, 53, 116
Byron, Lord, 38
Byzantium, 16

Caelian hill, Rome, 24
Caere/Cerveteri, 43, 44, 45, 46, 49 f., 67, 68, 74, 122 f.
Caeretan hydriae, 122 f.
Caeretan painted terracotta slabs, 44, 74, 112, 121
Caeretan terracotta sarcophagi, 67 f., 119 f.
Caesar, Gaius Julius, 9, 13
Caesar, forged marble bust in the British Museum, 77
Caesar, temple of, in Rome, 13
Caesar's horse, bronze statue in Rome, 14
Caligula, Emperor, 10, 15
Callmer, Christian, 4
Camillus, Marcus Furius, 6, 7
Camillus, Marcus Furius, bronze statue in Rome, 28, 106
Campana, Gian Pietro, 43, 44, 67, 68, 74, 138
Campana collection, 44, 67, 111 f.
Campana reliefs, 44, 112
Campana slabs, 44, 74, 112
Campanari, brothers, 43, 111
Campo Santo, Pisa, 22
Campus Martius, Rome, 20
Canino, 43
Cannicella necropolis, Orvieto, 81, 123
Canova, Antonio, 27, 60, 62
Cape Artemision, bronzes found off, 30, 107
Capitol, Capitoline hill, 8, 19, 24, 28, 31, 106
Capitoline collections, 27
Capitoline Temple, 15, 16, 28, 70

Capitoline Museum, 24, 59, 66
Capitoline Wolf, bronze statue in Rome, 7, 22, 31, 100, 108
Capodiferro, Girolamo, 23
Capodimonte, Naples, 25
Capri, 21, 43, 46, 104, 114
Capua, 9, 41
Caracalla, 13, 22, 23
Caracalla, marble statue in Stockholm, 27, 105
Caracalla, thermae of, in Rome, 13, 23
Carcopino, J., 8
Caria, 36
Carrara, 28
Carthage/Carthaginians, 6, 8, 16, 17
Caryatids of the Erechteum, Athens, 34, 39
Caserta, 21
Casino Berghese, Rome, 61
Cassiodorus, 17, 41
Castel Sant' Angelo, Rome, 20
Castellani, Alessandro, 67, 68, 75
Castellani, Augusto, 44, 67, 84, 93, 112
Castellani, Fortunato, 84
Castelporziano, 59, 133
Castelvetrano, 50
Castle Howard, 25
Casts of metalware, 56 f., 117
Casts of statues, 53, 116
Cato, M. Porcius, 8
Cavaceppi, Bartolomeo, 25, 59, 61, 118
Cavino, Giovanni dal, 63, 119
Cellini, Benvenuto, 58, 63
Celtic-Roman period, 88
Ceres, temple of, in Rome, 15, 28
Cerigo, 34
Cerveteri, see Caere
Cesnola, Luigi Palma di, 36, 110
Cesi, Federico, 23
Cestius, Gaius, 10
Charioteer, bronze statue from Delphi, 30, 107
Charles of Bourbon, 25, 26
Charles I of England, 24
Charles V, Holy Roman Emperor, 23
Chatsworth Head, bronze head from Tamassus, Cyprus, 30, 107
Chigi, Agostino, 25

Chigi, Cardinal, 20
Chigi collection, 24, 25
Chigi Zondadari, Marchese, 92
Chimaera, bronze statue from Arezzo, in Florence, 23, 105
Chios, 19
Chiusi/Clusium, 68, 92
Choiseul-Gouffier, Comte de, 33, 35, 38
Christina, Queen of Sweden, 26 f., 58, 105
Chryselephantine statues, 11, 19, 54, 101
Ciampolini collection, Rome, 23
Cicero, M. Tullius, 7, 9, 10, 15, 89, 100
Cilicia, 9
Circus Flaminius, Rome, 12
Cire-perdue casting, 53, 82
City Art Museum, St. Louis, 73, 141
Civita/Pompeii, 26
Civita Castellana, 73
Civitavecchia, 18, 24
Clandestine excavations and wreck-plunders, 47–50, 108
Claudius, Emperor, 12, 14, 15, 46
Claudius' harbour at Ostia, 46
Clement VII, Pope, 23, 63
Clement IX, Pope, 26
Clement XII, Pope, 24
Clement XIV, Pope, 25
Cleopatra, 9
Cleveland Museum, 79
Clodius, Publius, 106
Clusium, see Chiusi
Clythia, marble bust in the British Museum, 61 f., 118, 142
Cnidos, 12, 15, 19, 36, 39, 110
Cock, Hieronymus, 24
Cockerell, C.R., 34, 38
Collections and collectors, 5, 13, 19, 22–27, 29, 33–37, 42–44, 48, 56, 57 f.,
    59 f., 63 f., 67, 80, 94, 102, 104 f., 111 f., 117 f.
Colonna collection, 22
Colonna, Giovanni, 90
Colonna, Prospero, 22
Colosseum, 16, 20
Colossus Neronis, 15 f., 56, 102 f.
Comacchio, 45
Comitium, Rome, 106
Commodus, Emperor, 16, 17

Concord, temple of, at Agrigento, 20
Constans II, Emperor, 18
Constantine the Great, 16, 18, 31
Constantinople, 18 f., 27, 30, 31, 32, 36, 103
Conze, Alexander, 36
Copies and copying, 52–54, 55 f., 57–59, 115
Corinth, 8, 9, 15, 33, 40, 53, 56
Corinthian bronze/bronzes, 9 f., 29, 55, 56 f., 65
Corinthian vases, 43, 44
Cornelia, bronze statue in Rome, 106
Corradini, Antonio, 62
Crassus, Lucius, 55
Crawford, O.G.S., 87
Crawford, T.D., 88
Croesus, King of Lydia, 5, 98
Crusaders plundering Constantinople, 19, 103
Curia, Senatus, Rome, 20
Curiosum, 15
Curtis, Charles Densmore, 89
Curtius Rufus, 6
Cyprus, 30, 36, 46
Cypselus, 122
Cyriac of Ancona, 22
Czartorywski Museum, Cracow, 93

Damaratos, 122
Damasippus, 56
Damophilos, 15, 28
Dandolo, Enrico, 19
Dante, 63
Darius, 5
Dawson, Charles, 86, 125
Delian bronze, 29
Della Rovere, Giuliano/Julius II, Pope, 22
Della Valle, Andrea, 23
Delphi, 5, 11, 19, 30, 98, 101
Demeter of Cnidos, marble statue in the British Museum, 36, 110
Dendrochronology, 95
Dennis, George, 43, 74, 111
Despuig y Dameto, Antonio, 25, 80
Diadoumenos, bronze statue by Polykleitos, 53, 54
Diadoumenos, forged marble copy in Copenhagen, 75, 78, 93
Diana, marble statue in Stockholm, 60

Diana the Huntress, forged terracotta statue in St. Louis, 73, 74, 95, 121, 141

Diana Nemorensis, 25, 37, 80, 110

Didyma, 5

Dio Cassius, 16

Dio Chrysostomus, 65

Diomedes 'restored' from Discobolus torso, 59

Dionysius of Halicarnassus, 106

Dionysius, tyrant of Syracuse, 10, 101

Dionysus and Ariadne, painting by Aristeides, in Rome, 15

Diopos, 122

Dioscuri, marble statues in Rome, 22

Discobolus, bronze statue by Myron, 53, 54, 59, 66, 117, 133

Dodona, bronze statuette from, 70

Dodwell, E.A., 33, 38

Doidalsas of Bithynia, 53

Dolabella, Gnaeus Cornelius, 9

Donatello, 23

Domitius, Gnaeus, 12

Domus Aurea Neronis, 11, 16

Dorotheos, 13

Doryphoros, bronze statue by Polykleitos, 53

Dosio, Giovanni Antonio, 21

Dossena, Alceo, 73 f., 77, 78–80, 95, 122, 141, 143

Douglas, J.A., 86

Dresden, 25

Drottningholm, 27

Dümmler, Ferdinand, 89

Dupérac, Étienne, 21

Dussaud, René, 87

Dying Gaul, marble statue in Rome, 27

Ecbatana, 5

Eclectic sculptures, 53 f., 115

Ectypa, 53

Egypt, 33

Ekphantos, 122

Elba, 40

Eleusis, 33

Elgin, Lord, 33 f., 35, 37–39

Elgin Marbles, 34, 37–39, 60, 109

Endymion, marble statue in Stockholm, 60

Endymion 'restored' from Discobolus torso, 59

Ephebus, bronze statue from Bay of Marathon, 30, 107
Ephebus, bronze statue from Pompeii, 29
Ephebus, bronze statue from Selinunte, 50, 115
Ephebus, marble statue by Stephanus, in Rome, 54, 117
Ephesus/Ephesians, 10, 36, 39, 53
Erechtheum, 34, 39
Eros Enagonios, bronze statue found off Mahdia, 30, 107
Eros of Thespiae, marble statue by Praxiteles, 15, 102
Eros (?) on Boston Throne, 76, 144
Esquiline, 59
Este, Ippolito d', 23, 63
Etruria/Etruscans, 6, 7, 10, 40, 79, 81, 84, 97, 122
Etruscan art in ancient Rome, 6–8, 10, 28
Etruscan tomb paintings, 28, 42, 45, 46
Eucheir, 122
Eugrammos, 122
Euphranor, 12
Euphronios, 49, 115
Euxitheos, 49
Evander, C. Avianius, 14, 56
Evander's dish, 56
Evocatio, 8, 99

Fabius Maximus, Quintus, 8
Fabretti, Ariodante, 68
Falconieri, Cardinal, 20
Falerii/Faliscans, 44, 73
Falling Warrior 'restored' from Discobolus torso, 59, 66, 117
Farnese, Alessandro/Paul III, Pope, 23
Farnese, Elisabetta, 25
Farnese collection, 5, 13, 25
Fasti triumphales, 7
Fauvel, L-F-S., 33, 34, 35
Favisae, 8, 31
Fea, Carlo, 59
Felicitas, temple of, in Rome, 12, 15
Fellows, C., 35, 38
Ferdinand, King of Naples, 21
Festus, 7
Fibula Praenestina, 88–94, 125, 146
Fichard, Johann, 24
Ficoroni, Francesco de', 25
Filigree, 84

Fioravanti, Alfredo Adolfo, 71, 72, 73, 80, 95, 140
Firman, Lord Elgin's, 33, 109
First Punic War, 7
First World War, 40, 49
Flamininus, T. Quinctius, 8
Flavian amphitheatre, see Colosseum
Florence, 23, 32, 59, 70
Fontainebleau, 24, 58
Fontana, Pietro, 80
Forged bronzes, 54 f., 81 ff., 124
Forged coins, 63 f., 119
Forged engravings on Praenestine cistae, 93
Forged gems, 63
Forged gold ornaments and jewellery, 84 f., 88 ff., 124
Forged marble sculptures, 74–79, 121, 122
Forged metal vessels, 55 f.
Forged mosaics, 62, 119
Forged patina, 91
Forged terracottas, 67–74, 95 f., 119, 120
Forged vase paintings, 94 f., 125
Forged wall paintings, 62, 118
Forma Urbis, 21, 104
Fortuna, temple of, in Rome, 7
Forum Augusti, Rome, 14
Forum Boarium, Rome, 7, 20
Forum Holitorium, Rome, 20
Forum Pacis, Rome, 17
Forum Romanum, 7, 18, 20
Fourth Crusade, 19, 103
Fradin, Émile, 86 f.
Francis I, King of France, 23, 24, 58
François, Alessandro, 43, 111
Friedrich August I of Saxony, 25
Friederichs, Carl, 5
Fufetia, see Tarracia Gaia
Fulvius Flaccus, Marcus, 7, 100
Fulvius Nobilior, Marcus, 8
Furtwängler, Adolf, 52, 63, 74, 78, 80, 82, 84 f., 93, 94
Fuschini, Domenico, 69

Gaeseric the Vandal, 16, 17, 47
Galleria degli Uffizi, Florence, 59, 105
Galli collection, Rome, 23

Gamma-ray shadowgraphy, 83, 96

Gauls, 11, 97, 101

Gellius, Aulus, 8

Gems, 63, 119

German Archaeological Institute, 73, 92, 93, 94

Getty Victor, bronze statue found in the Adriatic Sea, 31, 108

Giglio, island of, ship found off, 46

Giulio Romano, 23, 59, 92

Gjerstad, Einar, 30

Glozel, 86–88, 125, 147

Glykon of Athens, 23

Goddess from Keratea, in Berlin, 48, 80, 115

Goddess from Tarentum, in Berlin, 48, 115

Goethe, J.W. von, 32, 64

Gonzaga, Federico, 23

Gonzaga Cameo, 27

Gordon, A.E., 89

Gorgasos, 15, 28

Gothic war, 17

Gragnano/Stabiae, 26

Grand Tour, 25

Granulation, 84, 124

Graviscae, 41, 123

Greece, *passim*

Greek art in ancient Rome, 11–18, 102

Greek art in ancient Constantinople, 18 f., 103

Greek artists in ancient Rome, 13 f., 15, 81

Greek artists in Etruria, 6, 81, 122 f.

Greek marble, 74, 77

Greek metal ware, 55

Greek War of Independence, 35, 37, 39

Gregory, Master, 22

Greppe di Sant' Angelo, Cerveteri, 49 f.

Grimani collection, 23

Grimani, Domenico, 23

Grimani, Giovanni, 23

Gropius, G., 34

Grotta Campana, Cerveteri, 44

Grueneisen collection, 79, 122

Guarducci, Margherita, 30, 90 f.

Guerra, Giuseppe, 62

Gustaf III, King of Sweden, 25, 59–60, 118

Gustavus II Adolphus, King of Sweden, 26

Haag, The, 26

Hadrawa, Norbert, 21, 43, 104

Hadrian, Emperor, 5, 16, 62

Hadrian's Mausoleum in Rome, 17, 20

Hadrian's Villa at Tivoli, 5, 23, 24, 25, 28, 59, 60, 62, 106

Haeberlin, C.H., 64

Hafner, German, 81

Hagesander, 13

Hala Sultan Tekke, Cyprus, 46

Halicarnassus, 36, 39, 110

Haller von Hallerstein, Carl, 34

Hamilton, Gavin, 25

Hamilton, Lady Emma, 42

Hamilton, Sir William, 42 f., 111

Hannibal, 8

Harbour of Claudius, Ostia, 46

Harmodios, 5, 58

Harpy Tomb, Xanthus, 36

Hartwig, Paul 76 f., 94 f.

Hecht, Robert E., 49

Heemskerck, Marten van, 21, 24, 104

Hegesias, 100

Heifer, bronze statue by Myron, in Rome (?), 17, 103

Helbig, Wolfgang, 75, 76 f., 89, 91–94, 125

Helbig Museum, Copenhagen, 92

Hellenistic Ruler, bronze statue found in Rome, 22, 30, 107

Hera, temple of, at Olympia, 55

Hera, votive offerings to, at Caere, 122

Hera of Girgenti, forged marble head, 75, 121

Herbig, Reinard, 73

Herculaneum, 26, 29, 46, 62, 105, 107, 114, 134

Hercules, bronze statue by Lysippos removed from Tarentum to Rome,
    19

Hercules, marble statue from the Farnese collection, in Naples, 23, 105

Hercules, marble statue from Queen Christina's collection, in Stockholm,
    27, 105

Hercules, statue removed from Syracuse to Tyre, 6

Hercules, terracotta statue by Vulca of Veii, in Rome, 70

Hercules, terracotta statue from Veii, in Rome, 69, 120

Hermes, bronze statue in the Agora of Athens, 53

Hermes, bronze statue from Herculaneum, 134

Hermes, head of terracotta statue from Veii, in Rome, 69, 120

Hermes and infant Dionysus, marble group at Olympia, 55, 117

Hermitage, Leningrad, 27, 36
Herodotus, 5, 19, 98, 123
Hill, Sir George F., 64
Hipparchus, 5
Hippodrome of Constantinople, 19
Holkham Hall, 25
Honorius, Emperor, 86
Hope, Thomas, 43
Horace, 14, 56
Horatius Cocles, bronze statue in Rome, 28, 106
Horse, bronze statuette from Olympia, 83, 124
Horse, bronze statuette in New York, 83, 96, 124, 137
Horses of San Marco, bronze statues in Venice, 19, 27, 31, 103
Hortensius, Q., 9, 10
Horti Sallustiani, Rome, 75
Hoving, M., 49
Howard, Thomas, Earl of Arundel, 24
Hunt, Rev. Philip, 33

Iberians, 97
Idolino, bronze statue from Pesaro, in Florence, 23
Iliad, 56, 85
Ilissus, temple at, in Athens, 39, 110
Influence of classical sculptures, 23, 32, 105
Italy, *passim*
Italian marble, 80 f.
Italic tribes, 97

Jacobsen, Carl, 75, 77, 78, 91, 92, 93
Jahn, Otto, 92
Jandolo, Antonio and Alessandro, 75
Jandolo, Elio and Ugo, 71
Jeffery, L.H., 55
Jenkins, Thomas, 25
Jerusalem, temple treasures from, 11, 16 f., 101
Jewellery, 44, 84, 89, 124
Josephine, Empress of France, 27
Josephus, 10, 11, 16
Julius II, Pope, 22
Jullian, C., 88
Juno, statue removed from Veii to Rome, 6
Juno, temple of, in Roman Veii, 21, 103 f.
Jupiter, statue presented to Francis I of France, 23

Jupiter Capitolinus, temple of, in Rome, 8, 70
Jupiter Capitolinus, terracotta statue by Vulca of Veii, 70
Jupiter and Ganymede, 'Herculanean' painting by Rapael Mengs, 62, 119
Justinian, Emperor, 16, 17

Kairos, bronze statue by Lysippos, 19
Kalamis, 56
Kallon, 100
Kanachos, 5
Kansas City, 73
Karo, Georg, 89
Kedrenos, Giorgios, 19
Keratea, 48
Kings of Rome, bronze statues in Rome, 28
Kondakoff, N., 85
Kore, forged marble statue in New York, 79
Kore, forged marble statue in Stockholm, 79
Kore, forged terracotta statue in Copenhagen, 72, 95, 120 f., 140
Kouros, marble statue in New York, 48, 80, 115
Kresilas, 53
Kritios, 5, 54
Kyrenia, ship found off, 46

Labat, Père, 42, 111
Lacus Volsiniensis, 99
Lafréry, Antoine, 21
Lago di Trasimeno, 23
Lake of Nemi, 25
Lancelotti Discobolus, 59, 118
Lansdowne collection, 59, 117 f.
Lanuvio, 25
Lanzi, Luigi, 43, 111
Laokoon, marble group in the Vatican, 13, 18, 22 f., 24, 27, 57 f., 65, 102,
    119, 131
L'Arringatore, bronze statue in Florence, 23, 123
La Tène, 88
Lateran, 8, 22, 31
Latium, 25, 32, 84
Lausos collection, in Constantinople, 19
Leo X, Pope, 23
Leochares, 12, 36, 132
Lerici, Carlo Maurilio, 45
Leucothea, temple of, at Pyrgi, 10

Levant, 32, 37
Ligorio, Pirro, 63, 119
Livadhostro Bay, bronze statue from, 30, 107
Livia Augusta, 10
Livius Andronicus, 14
Livy, 6, 8, 40
Lombardo, Tullio, 61
Lost-wax casting, 82, 123
Louis XIV, King of France, 24, 58, 117
Louvre, see Musée du Louvre
Lucania, 32
Lucanian tomb paintings, 28
Lucian, 11, 53, 54, 59, 101
Lucullus, Lucius Licinius, 8
Lucullus, Marcus Licinius, 8
Ludovisi collection, 24, 75, 76 f., 78, 121
Ludovisi Throne, 75–78, 121, 144
Ludwig, Crown Prince of Bavaria, 27, 33, 34
Luna marble, 28, 74
Lupa Capitolina, see Capitoline Wolf
Lusetti, Walter, 74
Lusieri, G.B., 33 f.
Lutetia Parisiorum, bronze head in Paris, 83, 124
Lycia, 35, 110
Lysippos, 12, 14, 17, 19, 53
Lysistratos, 53, 116

Macedonia, 6, 12, 45, 84
Maenius, Gaius, bronze statue in Rome, 28
Maffei collection, in Rome, 23
Magna Graecia, 10, 32, 55, 84
Magnesia ad Maeandrum, 36
Mahdia, bronzes found off, 30, 107
Mainz, 62
Malta, 34
Mantua, 23
Marathon, Bay of, bronze statue found in, 30, 107
Marble, 18, 28 f., 74, 77
Marcellus, M. Cladius, 8
Marcus Aurelius, equestrian bronze statue in Rome, 24, 31, 108
Mark Antony, 9, 10, 14
Mars of Todi, bronze statue in the Vatican, 82, 123
Marsala, ship found off, 46, 114

Marshall, John, 69, 70, 76, 79
Martial, 56
Martin V, Pope, 22
Martinetti, Francesco, 69, 75, 76, 89, 91, 92, 93, 94, 95
Massilia, 9
Mater Matuta, temple of, in Rome, 7
Mausoleum at Halicarnassus, 36, 110
Mausoleum of Hadrian, in Rome, 20
Mausolus of Caria, 36
Mazarin, Cardinal, 24
Medici collection, in Florence, 23
Medici, Cosimo de', 58
Medici, Giovanni de'/Pope Leo X, 23
Medici, Giulio de', Cardinal, 23
Medici, Pierfrancesco de', 61
Mediterranean Sea, 18, 30, 32, 46
Melos, 35, 109
Mengs, Anton Raphael, 42, 62, 119
Meniskos, 83
Menodotos of Tyre, 55
Mentor, 55
Mercouri, Melina, 38
Metal detectors, 47, 115
Metalware, 55
Metellus, Q. Caecilius, 12
Metrodorus of Scepsis, 6, 7
Metropolitan Museum of Art, New York, 36, 49 f., 69, 70, 71, 79, 83, 95,
    137, 139
Meyer, K.E., 95
Michelangelo, 13, 23, 31, 61, 65
Microchemical tests, 96
Miletus, 5, 36
Minerva, bronze statue from Arezzo, in Florence, 23
Minerva, marble statue in Stockholm, 60
Mingazzini, Paolino, 62
Mithridates of Pontus, 8
Mommsen, Theodor, 92
Monaldeschi, Monaldo, 41 f.
Monnot, Pierre Étienne, 59
Montagu, Lady Mary W., 26
Monte Mario, Rome, 23
Monte Pincio, Rome, 75
Monterozzi necropolis, Tarquinia, 42

Montorsoli, G., 65
Morlet, Antoine, 86 f.
Morosini, Francesco, 33
Mosaics, 62
Mummius, L., 8, 15
Munich, 63, 79, 93
Munich Glyptothek, 27, 34, 35, 59, 60, 66
Musée du Louvre, 27, 33, 35, 36, 42, 44, 54, 67, 68, 74, 85, 136, 145
Musée Napoléon, 27
Musei Vaticani/Vatican, Vatican Museums, 21, 22, 24, 26 f., 42, 43, 58, 59, 62, 65, 102
Museo Archeologico, Naples, 13, 25, 29
Museo Barracco, Rome, 15
Museo Capitolino, Rome 24, 59, 66
Museo Civico, Orvieto, 71
Museo delle, Terme, Rome, 22, 59, 77
Museo di Villa Giulia, Rome, 44, 68, 71, 72, 89, 90
Museo Faina, Orvieto, 71
Museo Gregoriano Etrusco, 71, 82
Museo Pio-Clementino, 25
Museo Preistorico, Rome, 89
Muses, marble statues in Stockholm, 60
Museum and Art Gallery, Nottingham, 37, 110
Museum of Fine Arts, Boston, 37, 69, 76
Museum of Mediterranean and Near Eastern Antiquities, Stockholm, 37, 110
Museum thefts, 50
Mussolini, bust of, by Alceo Dossena, 74
Mycenae, 33, 85
Myrina figurines, 67, 119
Myron, 10, 12, 17, 54, 59
Mys, 56

Naples, 21, 25, 26, 29, 42, 58, 62, 65
Napoleon Bonaparte, 27, 33, 35, 62
Napoleon, portrait of, by Canova, 62
Napoleon's art robbery, 27, 106
Narses, 17
Nash, Ernest, 76
National Museum, Copenhagen, 71
National Museum, Stockholm, 79, 118
Naxos, marble of, 77
Necrocorinthia, 9, 56, 100

Nelson, Lord, 34, 35
Nelson Art Gallery, Kansas City, 73
Nemi, marble relief from, in Copenhagen, 26, 80 f., 122
Nemus Aricinum, 25, 37, 80, 122
Neo-Attic reliefs, 54
Nephele Dish, 94 f., 125
Neptune, temple of, in Paestum, 32
Nereid Monument, Xanthus, 36, 110
Nero, Emperor, 10, 11, 14, 15, 16, 46
Nero, bronze colossus by Zenodoros, 15 f., 102 f.
Nero's Domus Aurea, 11, 16
Nesiotes, 5, 54
Nestor's goblet, 56
New antiques, 61 f., 118
Newby Hall, 25
Newton, C.T., 36, 68
Niketas Choniates, 19, 103
Nikias, 12
Niobids, on Zeus' throne in Olympia, 54, 117
Noble, J.V., 71, 72, 83
Nola, 42
Normans sacking Rome, 18
Notitia, 15
Numana, bronze statue found off, 31, 108
Numerius Suffustius, 89
Nuremberg, 26
Ny Carlsberg Glyptotek, Copenhagen, 26, 48, 70, 72, 75, 76, 80, 92, 115, 140

Octavian, 9
Octavian, marble portrait in the Vatican, 62, 118
Odescalchi, Livio, 27
Odysseus and Diomedes, on silver bowl by Pytheas, 55
Odyssey in marble, at Sperlonga, 18, 129
Olympia, 11, 19, 30, 35, 54, 55, 107, 117, 124
Olympieum, Athens, 39
Orestes before the Areopagus, on silver cups by Zopyros, 55
Orestes slaying Aegisthus (?), on marble relief from Nemi, 80, 122
Orvieto, 41 f., 48 f., 67, 68, 70, 71, 81, 92, 99, 110 f., 115, 120, 123, 139
Ostia, 25, 46, 62
Ostrogoths, 16, 17
Otricoli, 24
Ottoman Empire, 36, 38

Padua, 63
Paestum, 32, 79
Painting/Paintings, 12, 13, 27, 42, 46, 62
Palatine, 20, 56
Palazzo Barberini, Rome, 20
Palazzo Colonna, Rome, 22, 30
Palazzo dei Conservatori, Rome, 7, 22, 44, 71
Palazzo della Cancelleria, Rome, 20
Palazzo Farnese, Rome, 23
Palazzo Massimi-Lancelotti, Rome, 59
Palazzo Nuovo, Rome, 24
Palazzo Odescalchi, Rome, 27
Palazzo Riario, Rome, 26
Palazzo Valle-Capranica, Rome, 23
Palazzo Venezia, Rome, 20
Palazzo Wedekind, Rome, 21,
Palestrina/Praeneste, 24, 25, 45, 89
Pallottino, Massimo, 70, 71, 90
Pamphili collection, 24
Pantheon, Rome, 18, 20
Papal State, 25
Paros, marble of, 28, 77
Parrhasios, 12
Parsons, H.W., 72
Parthenon, 20, 33 f., 35, 38 f., 109
Pasinati cista, 93
Pasiteles, 53 f.
Patina, 64 f., 82, 84, 91, 119
Paul III, Pope, 23
Paullus, L. Aemilius, 8
Paulus Diaconus, 18
Pausanias, 5, 11, 15, 54, 55, 99
Pausias, 13
Peleponnesus, 35
Pennelli, Enrico and Pietro, 68, 97
Pentelikon, marble of, 77
Pergamon Museum, Berlin, 36
Pergamum, 9, 36
Perseus, King of Macedonia, 8
Persia/Persians, 5, 11, 19
Peruzzi, Baldassare, 21
Pesaro, 23
Petronius, 56 f.

Pheidias, 11, 12, 17, 19, 35, 46, 53, 54
Phigaleia, 35, 109
Philip V of Macedonia, 8
Philip IV of Spain, 24
Philip V of Spain, 27
Philippe, Duc d'Orléans, 27
Philosopher, head of bronze statue found off Anticythera, 30, 107
Philosopher, head of bronze statue found off Porticello, 31, 108
Phocis, 5
Piazza d'Armi, Veii, 20, 103 f.
Piazza Colonna, Rome, 21
Piazza del Campidoglio, Rome, 31
Piazza del Quirinale, Rome, 22
Piazza Santi Apostoli, Rome, 27
Pigorini, Luigi, 89
Piltdown, 86, 125
Pinza, Giovanni, 89, 93
Pio di Capri, Rodolfo, 23
Piombino, 54
Piraeus, bronze statues from, 30, 107
Piraeus, marble lion from, 33
Piraeus, marble reliefs from, 46, 54, 114
Piranesi, Francesco, 60
Piranesi, Giambattista, 32, 60
Piranesi pastiche, 59, 60, 118
Piroli, Pacifico, 75
Pisa/Pisans, 22
Pisano, Andrea, 22
Pisano, Nicola, 22
Pisano, Vittore, 89
Pius VI, Pope, 25
Pius VII, Pope, 21
Plataea, memorial to battle of, 19
Pliny the Elder, 6, 8, 9, 10, 11–13, 14, 15, 22, 28, 29, 36, 46, 53, 54, 55, 56,
    65, 69, 101 f., 114
Pliny the Younger, 46, 102
Pointing system, 53, 115
Pollak, Ludwig, 65, 91, 93
Polydoros, 13
Polykleitos, 12, 53, 54, 75
Polykleitos the Younger, 12, 102
Pompeii, 26, 29, 62, 107, 117
Populonia, 40, 41, 54, 110, 136

Porcari collection, Rome, 23
Porphyrio, 14, 56
Porsenna of Clusium, 23
Porta, Giovan Battista della, 61
Porta Salaria, Rome, 25
Porticello, bronze head found off, 31, 108
Portici, 21, 26
Porticus Octaviae, Rome, 12
Porticus Pompei, Rome, 13
Poseidon, bronze statue from Livadhostro Bay, 30, 107
Poseidon, Thetis, Nereids and Tritons, marble group by Skopas, in Rome, 12
Poulsen, Frederik, 48, 72
Pozzo di San Patrizio, Orvieto, 41, 67, 110
Prado Museum, Madrid, 27
Praeneste, see Palestrina
Praenestine cistae, 93, 125
Prague, 26
Praxiteles, 12, 15, 55
Priam's Treasure, 85, 124 f.
Priene, 36
Primaticcio, Francesco, 24
Procopius, 16
Prodo, 69
Propertius, 7
Propylaea, Athens, 20, 39
Prostypa, 53
Pyrgi, 10, 101
Pytheas, 55, 56

Quintilian, 100
Quirinal, 22

Radiocarbon dating, 95, 126
Randall-MacIver, David, 89
Raphael, 57
Ravenna, 17
Reinach, Salomon, 79, 85, 87 f.
Peiñach, Theodore, 85
Reisch, Emil, 89
Rembrandt, 24
Removal of restored parts from ancient sculptures, 65 f.
Renaissance, 20, 24, 57, 61, 63

Resina/Herculaneum, 26
Restoration of ancient sculptures, 57–60, 64, 117
Revett, N., 32
Rex Nemorensis, 80
Rhodes, 13, 36, 55, 84
Riace, bronze warriors found off, 31, 108, 135
Riccardi brothers, 48, 70
Riccardi, Pio, 69, 71, 80
Riccardi, Riccardo, 71, 72, 95
Richelieu, Cardinal, 24
Richter, Gisela M.A., 69, 70, 71, 81
Ricimer the Goth, 16
Ridgway, Brunilde Sismondo, 52, 55
Riom, 87
Robert, Carl, 93
Robert Guiscard, 18
Roman copies, 52, 115
Romano, Gian Cristoforo, 61
Rome, *passim*
Rome-Berlin Axis, 37
Romulus, bronze statue in Rome, 106
Romulus and Remus, bronze figures added to Capitoline Wolf, 8
Roncalli, F., 82
Root-marks, 77, 81
Royal Geological Society, London, 86
Rubens, Peter Paul, 24
Ruchomovsky, Israel, 85, 97
Rudolph II, Emperor, 26
Running drill, 79

Sacco di Roma, 24
Saint-Non, Abbé J.C. de, 32
Saitapharnes' tiara, forged gold headgear, 85, 97, 145
San Clemente, Rome, 18
San Giovanni de' Fiorentini, Rome, 20
San Ildefonso, Palace of, 27
San Lorenzo in Lucina, Rome, 18
San Marco, Venice, 19, 103
San Pietro in Vincoli, Rome, 22
Sancta Maria ad Maryres, Rome, 18
Sangallo the Younger, Antonio, 23
Sansovino, Jacopo, 57
Sant' Omobono, Rome, 7, 58

Sappho, type of female head, 82, 124
Saracens, 18
Sardinia, 41
Sassi collection, Rome, 23
Savile Lumley, Sir John, 37
Schakowskoy, Nadejda, 92
Schliemann, Heinrich, 36, 85, 124 f.
Scholae Octaviae, Rome, 15
Scientific dating and authenticity tests, 95 f., 125 f.
Scipio, L. Cornelius, 8, 9
Scipio, P. Cornelius, 40
Sculptors' signatures, 52, 116
Scultors' workshops, 53 f., 117
Scythian tomb treasures, 45, 112
Scythians, 97
Second Punic War, 8, 19
Second World War, 37, 48, 66
Segesta, 32
Selinunte, 50, 115
Septizodium, Rome, 20
Serapis, temple of, in Rome, 22
Sergel, Johan Tobias, 59, 60
Severus, Septimius, 20
Sicilia/Sicily, 6, 9, 32, 50, 55
Sicyon, 19
Siena, 70
Silver chasers and silver ware, 55 f.
Siphnos, marble of, 77
Sisyphus' bronze basin, 56
Siviero, Rodolfo, 37, 50
Sixtus IV, Pope, 22
Sixtus V, Pope, 20, 22
Skopas, 12, 36
Sleeping Cupid, by Michelangelo, 61
Sleeping Satyr, see Barberini Faun
Smith-Woodward, A., 86
Society of Antiquaries, London, 86
Society of Dilettanti, London, 32, 108
Söderman, Harry, 87
Solimena, Francesco, 62
Sollas, W.J., 86
Sostratos, 123
Southern Rusia, 84

Spectographic analysis, 72, 77, 96
Spelunca/Sperlonga, 18, 103, 129
Sphinx, bronze figure given to Hortensius by Verres, 10
Spina, 45, 113
Spinario, bronze statue in Rome, 22, 27, 105
Staatliche Museen, Berlin, 76
Stabiae, 26, 46
Stackelberg, O.M. von, 34
St. Peter's basilica in Rome, 18, 20
St. Paul's basilica in Rome, 18
Statius, 14
Stephanus, 54, 117
Stettiner, Pietro, 69
Stilicho, 86
Stockholm, old castle of, 26, 27, 58
Stockholm, Royal Palace of, 60
Strabo, 9, 15, 40
Strangford, Lord, 35
Strangford Shield, 35, 54, 109
Stratford Canning, 36
Stroganoff, Grégoire, 92
Strongylion, 10
Stuart, J., 32, 38
Studniczka, F., 79, 143
Sublime Porte, 33, 35
Submarine archaeology, see Archaeological underwater exploration
Suetonius, 9, 10, 14, 16, 61
Susa, 5
Sussex, 86
Swedish Cyprus Expedition, 37
Switzerland, 49
Sybaris, 45, 113
Syracuse, 6, 8, 10, 18, 20

Tacitus, 11
Tamassus, 30
Tanagra figurines, 67, 119
Taracia Gaia, or Fufetia, bronze statue in Rome, 28
Tarentum, 8, 14, 19, 48
Tarquinia/Tarquinii, 42, 45, 46, 92, 111, 122
Tarquinius Priscus, 28, 69
Tatius, bronze statue in Rome, 106
Tauriskos of Tralles, 13

Technique of pottery, 126
Technique of sculpture, 13, 79, 126
Technique of wall painting, 62, 118
Temple at Ilissus, Athens, 31, 110
Temple of Antoninus and Faustina, Rome, 20
Temple of Aphaea, Aegina, 34, 66, 109
Temple of Apollo at Bassae, 35, 109
Temple of Apollo at Pyrgi, 10
Temple of Apollo Palatinus, Rome, 14
Temple of Athena, Paestum, 20
Temple of Athena, Syracuse, 20
Temple of Athena Nike, Athens, 20, 34, 39
Temple of Augustus, Rome, 10
Temple of Caesar, Rome, 13
Temple of Ceres, Rome, 15, 28
Temple of Concord, Agrigento, 20
Temple of Felicitas, Rome, 12, 15
Temple of Fortuna, Rome, 7
Temple of Hera, Olympia, 55
Temple of Jerusalem, 11, 16
Temple of Juno, Veii, 21
Temple of Jupiter Capitolinus, Rome, 8, 15, 16, 28
Temple of Leucothea, Pyrgi, 10
Temple of Mater Matuta, Rome, 7
Temple of Neptune, Paestum, 32
Temple of Peace, Rome, 11, 17
Temple of Serapis, Rome, 22
Temple of Venus Genetrix, Rome, 14
Temple of Venus and Roma, Rome, 20
Temple of Vertumnus, in Rome, 7
Terracottas, 8, 36, 37, 44, 48 f., 53, 66–74, 95 f., 97, 112, 119, 120
Terrasini, ships found off, 46
Thasos, marble of, 77
Theodoric, 17, 41
Theodosius II, 19
Thermae of Caracalla, Rome, 13, 23
Thermae of Constantine, Rome, 22
Thermoluminescence tests, 72, 73, 74, 83, 86, 88, 95 f., 126, 137, 139, 140, 141
Thermopylae, 5
Theseum, Athens, 20
Thespiae, 15
Thessaly, 45, 84

Thorvaldsen, Bertel, 60, 66, 74, 118
Thracian tomb treasures, 45, 112
Thracians, 97
Three Graces, marble group in Siena, 22
Tiber bridges, Rome, 20
Tiberius, Emperor, 9, 10, 12, 18, 21
Tiberius, colossal marble portrait from Veii, 21
Timoleon, 6
Timotheos, 36
Titus, Emperor, 12, 13, 15, 16
Todi, 69
Tolstoy, J., 85
Tomba Barberini, Palestrina, 45, 112
Tomba Bernardini, Palestrina, 45, 89 f., 91, 112
Tomba Campana, Veii, 44, 112
Tomba François, Vulci, 43 f., 111
Tomba della Nave, Tarquinia, 46
Tomba delle Olimpiadi, Tarquinia, 46, 113
Tomba Regolini-Galassi, Cerveteri, 45, 112
Tombaroli, 49
Tombs and tomb gifts, 9, 40–46
Torlonia, Alessandro, 43 f., 60
Torlonia collection, 44, 60, 111
Toro Farnese, 13, 23
Totila, 17
Townley, Charles, 62
Tree-ring dating, 95
Trimalchio, 56 f.
Troy, 36, 85
Turkey/Turks, 20, 33, 35, 36, 37, 38, 39
Tuscany, 32
Tyrannicides, bronze statues by Antenor, 5, 98 f.
Tyrannicides, bronze statues by Kritios and Nesiotes, 5, 23, 54, 98 f.
Tyrannicides, marble copies from the Farnese collection, in Naples, 5, 23, 58
Tyre, 6, 55
Tyszkiewicz, Michel, 92, 94

Uffizi, see Galleria degli Uffizi
Ultra-violet rays, 77, 91, 96
Undersea archaeology, see Archaeological underwater exploration
Undset, Ingvald, 60
Urban VIII, Pope,
Urbs vetus, 99

Vandals, 16, 17
Varro, M. Terentius, 7, 69
Vasari, Giorgio, 22, 23, 24, 57, 58, 61
Vatican, Vatican museums, see Musei Vaticani
Vayson de Pradenne, A., 87
Vei, marble cult statue at Orvieto, 81, 123
Veii, 6, 20 f., 44, 45, 67, 69 f., 72, 103 f., 120
Velazquez, 24
Veila, forged marbles said to come from, 79
Venice/Venetia/Venetians, 19, 23, 32 f., 42
Venus Capitolina, marble statue in Rome, 27
Venus Genetrix, temple of, in Rome, 14
Vénus de Milo, 35, 39, 109
Vergina, royal tombs at, 45, 112 f.
Verres, Gaius, 9, 10, 100
Verrius Flaccus, 7
Versailles, 58
Vertumnus, statue in Vicus Tuscus, Rome, 7
Vertumnus, temple of, in Rome, 7
Vespasian, Emperor, 11, 16
Vestal, bronze statue from Herculaneum, 26
Vesuvius, 26, 29, 32, 46, 114, 134
Vetulonia, 41, 89
Vichy, 86
Vicus Tuscus, Rome, 7
Vienna Congress, 37
Villa Albani, Rome, 25, 27, 44, 54, 59
Villa Lante, Rome, 92, 94
Villa Ludovisi, Rome, 75, 77
Villa Madama, Rome, 23
Villa Mattei, Rome, 24
Villa of M. Brutus, Tivoli, 24
Villa of the Papyri, Herculaneum, 29, 54, 107, 134
Vitellius, Emperor, 15
Vitruvius, 20
Vittiges, 17
Vlad Borelli, Licia, 78
Volpato, G., 59
Volsinii, 6 f., 99 f.
Vulca of Veii, 28, 69 f., 106
Vulci, 43, 45, 48 f., 90, 111

Warren, Edward P., 69, 76 f.
Warriors, bronze statues found off Riace, 31, 108, 135

Warriors, forged terracotta statues in New York, 69–72, 73, 95 f., 97, 120, 139

Whitney, Brian, 4

Wickert, Lothar, 92

Wilamowitz-Moellendorff, Ulrich von, 92

Wilson, Harold, 38

Winckelmann, Johann Joachim, 25, 32, 62

Winter, F., 79

Wounded Bitch, bronze figure in Rome, 15, 102

Xanthus, 36, 39, 110

Xerxes, 5, 12

X-ray crystallographic analyses, 96

X-ray flourescence test, 91, 96

Young, W.J., 77

Youth's head, part of bronze statue from the Acropolis, Athens, 30, 107

Zante, 34, 35

Zenodorus, 15, 56

Zeus, altar of, in Pergamum, 36, 110

Zeus, bronze statue found off Cape Artemision, 30, 107

Zeus, chryselephantine statue by Pheidias at Olympia, 11, 19, 54, 117

Zeus, head of bronze statue found at Olympia, 30, 107

Zeus, temple of, in Athens, 39

Zeus, temple of, at Olympia, 35

Zeuxis, 12

Zonaras, 6

Zopyros, 55

Zurich, 49